INTRODUCTORY

ILLUSTRATED SERIES™

MICROSOFT® OFFICE 365™

ACCESS® 2016

ILLUSTRATED SERIES™

MICROSOFT® OFFICE 365™

ACCESS® 2016

FRIEDRICHSEN

Australia • Brazil • Mexico • Singapore • United Kingdom • United States

CENGAGE
Learning®

**Illustrated Microsoft® Office 365™ &
Access® 2016—Introductory**
Lisa Friedrichsen

SVP, GM Skills & Global Product Management:
  Dawn Gerrain

Product Director: Kathleen McMahon

Senior Product Team Manager: Lauren Murphy

Product Team Manager: Andrea Topping

Associate Product Manager: William Guiliani

Senior Director, Development: Marah Bellegarde

Product Development Manager: Leigh Hefferon

Senior Content Developer: Christina Kling-Garrett

Developmental Editor: Lisa Ruffolo

Product Assistant: Erica Chapman

Marketing Director: Michele McTighe

Marketing Manager: Stephanie Albracht

Senior Production Director: Wendy Troeger

Production Director: Patty Stephan

Senior Content Project Manager: Stacey Lamodi

Designer: Diana Graham

Composition: GEX Publishing Services

For product information and technology assistance, contact us at
Cengage Learning Customer & Sales Support, 1-800-354-9706

For permission to use material from this text or product, submit all
requests online at **www.cengage.com/permissions**
Further permissions questions can be emailed to
permissionrequest@cengage.com

Mac users: If you're working through this product using a Mac, some of the
steps may vary. Additional information for Mac users is included with the
Data Files for this product.

Some of the product names and company names used in this book have
been used for identification purposes only and may be trademarks or
registered trademarks of their respective manufacturers and sellers.

Windows® is a registered trademark of Microsoft Corporation. © 2012
Microsoft. Microsoft and the Office logo are either registered trademarks
or trademarks of Microsoft Corporation in the United States and/or other
countries. Cengage Learning is an independent entity from Microsoft
Corporation and not affiliated with Microsoft in any manner.

Disclaimer: Any fictional data related to persons or companies or URLs used
throughout this text is intended for instructional purposes only. At the time
this text was published, any such data was fictional and not belonging to
any real persons or companies.

Disclaimer: The material in this text was written using Microsoft Windows 10
Professional and Office 365 Professional Plus and was Quality Assurance tested
before the publication date. As Microsoft continually updates the Windows 10
operating system and Office 365, your software experience may vary slightly
from what is presented in the printed text.

Library of Congress Control Number: 2015955695
ISBN: 978-1-305-87798-6

Cengage Learning
20 Channel Center Street
Boston, MA 02210
USA

Cengage Learning is a leading provider of customized learning solutions
with employees residing in nearly 40 different countries and sales in more
than 125 countries around the world. Find your local representative at
www.cengage.com

Cengage Learning products are represented in Canada by
Nelson Education, Ltd.

For your course and learning solutions, visit **www.cengage.com**

Purchase any of our products at your local college store or at our
preferred online store **www.cengagebrain.com**

Printed in the United States of America
Print Number: 03   Print Year: 2017

Brief Contents

Contents

Productivity Apps for School and Work

Corinne Hoisington

OneNote
Sway
Office Mix
Edge

Lochlan keeps track of his class notes, football plays, and internship meetings with OneNote.

Zoe is using the annotation features of Microsoft Edge to take and save web notes for her research paper.

Nori is creating a Sway site to highlight this year's activities for the Student Government Association.

Hunter is adding interactive videos and screen recordings to his PowerPoint resume.

© Rawpixel/Shutterstock.com

Being computer literate no longer means mastery of only Word, Excel, PowerPoint, Outlook, and Access. To become technology power users, Hunter, Nori, Zoe, and Lochlan are exploring Microsoft OneNote, Sway, Mix, and Edge in Office 2016 and Windows 10.

Learn to use productivity apps!
Links to companion **Sways**, featuring **videos** with hands-on instructions, are located on www.cengagebrain.com.

Introduction to OneNote 2016

notebook | section tab | To Do tag | screen clipping | note | template | Microsoft OneNote Mobile app | sync | drawing canvas | inked handwriting | Ink to Text

As you glance around any classroom, you invariably see paper notebooks and notepads on each desk. Because deciphering and sharing handwritten notes can be a challenge, Microsoft OneNote 2016 replaces physical notebooks, binders, and paper notes with a searchable, digital notebook. OneNote captures your ideas and schoolwork on any device so you can stay organized, share notes, and work with others on projects. Whether you are a student taking class notes as shown in **Figure 1** or an employee taking notes in company meetings, OneNote is the one place to keep notes for all of your projects.

Figure 1: OneNote 2016 notebook

Each **notebook** is divided into sections, also called **section tabs**, by subject or topic.

Use **To Do tags**, icons that help you keep track of your assignments and other tasks.

Type on a page to add a **note**, a small window that contains text or other types of information.

Personalize a page with a **template**, or stationery.

Write or draw directly on the page using drawing tools.

Pages can include pictures such as **screen clippings**, images from any part of a computer screen.

Attach files and enter equations so you have everything you need in one place.

Creating a OneNote Notebook

OneNote is divided into sections similar to those in a spiral-bound notebook. Each OneNote notebook contains sections, pages, and other notebooks. You can use One-Note for school, business, and personal projects. Store information for each type of project in different notebooks to keep your tasks separate, or use any other organization that suits you. OneNote is flexible enough to adapt to the way you want to work.

When you create a notebook, it contains a blank page with a plain white background by default, though you can use templates, or stationery, to apply designs in categories such as Academic, Business, Decorative, and Planners. Start typing or use the buttons on the Insert tab to insert notes, which are small resizable windows that can contain text, equations, tables, on-screen writing, images, audio and video recordings, to-do lists, file attachments, and file printouts. Add as many notes as you need to each page.

Syncing a Notebook to the Cloud

OneNote saves your notes every time you make a change in a notebook. To make sure you can access your notebooks with a laptop, tablet, or smartphone wherever you are, OneNote uses cloud-based storage, such as OneDrive or SharePoint. **Microsoft OneNote Mobile app**, a lightweight version of OneNote 2016 shown in **Figure 2**, is available for free in the Windows Store, Google Play for Android devices, and the AppStore for iOS devices.

If you have a Microsoft account, OneNote saves your notes on OneDrive automatically for all your mobile devices and computers, which is called **syncing**. For example, you can use OneNote to take notes on your laptop during class, and then open OneNote on your phone to study later. To use a notebook stored on your computer with your OneNote Mobile app, move the notebook to OneDrive. You can quickly share notebook content with other people using OneDrive.

Figure 2: Microsoft OneNote Mobile app

Taking Notes

Use OneNote pages to organize your notes by class and topic or lecture. Beyond simple typed notes, OneNote stores drawings, converts handwriting to searchable text and mathematical sketches to equations, and records audio and video.

OneNote includes drawing tools that let you sketch freehand drawings such as biological cell diagrams and financial supply-and-demand charts. As shown in Figure 3, the Draw tab on the ribbon provides these drawing tools along with shapes so you can insert diagrams and other illustrations to represent your ideas. When you draw on a page, OneNote creates a **drawing canvas**, which is a container for shapes and lines.

Figure 3: Tools on the Draw tab

Converting Handwriting to Text

When you use a pen tool to write on a notebook page, the text you enter is called **inked handwriting**. OneNote can convert inked handwriting to typed text when you use the **Ink to Text** button in the Convert group on the Draw tab, as shown in Figure 4. After OneNote converts the handwriting to text, you can use the Search box to find terms in the converted text or any other note in your notebooks.

Figure 4: Converting handwriting to text

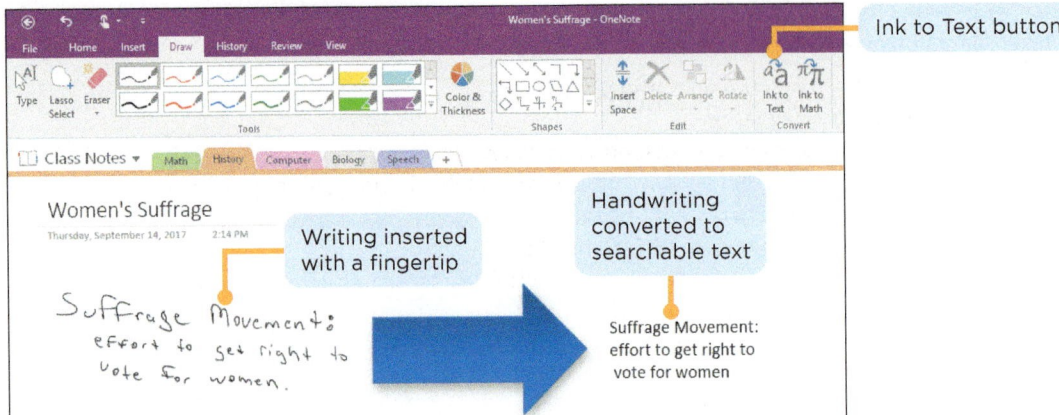

Ink to Text button

Women's Suffrage

Thursday, September 14, 2017   2:14 PM

Writing inserted with a fingertip

Handwriting converted to searchable text

Suffrage Movements: effort to get right to vote for women.

Suffrage Movement: effort to get right to vote for women

Recording a Lecture

If your computer or mobile device has a microphone or camera, OneNote can record the audio or video from a lecture or business meeting as shown in **Figure 5**. When you record a lecture (with your instructor's permission), you can follow along, take regular notes at your own pace, and review the video recording later. You can control the start, pause, and stop motions of the recording when you play back the recording of your notes.

Figure 5: Video inserted in a notebook

Record Video button

Audio & Video Recording tab

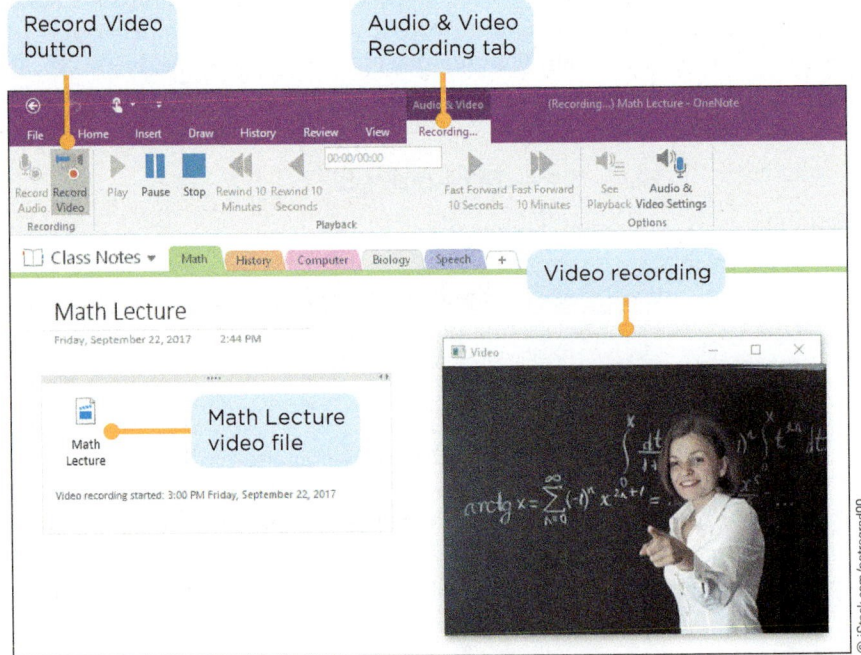

Video recording

Math Lecture

Friday, September 22, 2017   2:44 PM

Math Lecture video file

Video recording started: 3:00 PM Friday, September 22, 2017

© iStock.com/petrograd99

Try This Now

Learn to use OneNote!
Links to companion **Sways**, featuring **videos** with hands-on instructions, are located on www.cengagebrain.com.

1: Taking Notes for a Week

As a student, you can get organized by using OneNote to take detailed notes in your classes. Perform the following tasks:

a. Create a new OneNote notebook on your Microsoft OneDrive account (the default location for new notebooks). Name the notebook with your first name followed by "Notes," as in **Caleb Notes**.

b. Create four section tabs, each with a different class name.

c. Take detailed notes in those classes for one week. Be sure to include notes, drawings, and other types of content.

d. Sync your notes with your OneDrive. Submit your assignment in the format specified by your instructor.

2: Using OneNote to Organize a Research Paper

You have a research paper due on the topic of three habits of successful students. Use OneNote to organize your research. Perform the following tasks:

a. Create a new OneNote notebook on your Microsoft OneDrive account. Name the notebook **Success Research**.

b. Create three section tabs with the following names:

- **Take Detailed Notes**
- **Be Respectful in Class**
- **Come to Class Prepared**

c. On the web, research the topics and find three sources for each section. Copy a sentence from each source and paste the sentence into the appropriate section. When you paste the sentence, OneNote inserts it in a note with a link to the source.

d. Sync your notes with your OneDrive. Submit your assignment in the format specified by your instructor.

3: Planning Your Career

Note: This activity requires a webcam or built-in video camera on any type of device.

Consider an occupation that interests you. Using OneNote, examine the responsibilities, education requirements, potential salary, and employment outlook of a specific career. Perform the following tasks:

a. Create a new OneNote notebook on your Microsoft OneDrive account. Name the notebook with your first name followed by a career title, such as **Kara - App Developer**.

b. Create four section tabs with the names **Responsibilities, Education Requirements, Median Salary**, and **Employment Outlook**.

c. Research the responsibilities of your career path. Using OneNote, record a short video (approximately 30 seconds) of yourself explaining the responsibilities of your career path. Place the video in the Responsibilities section.

d. On the web, research the educational requirements for your career path and find two appropriate sources. Copy a paragraph from each source and paste them into the appropriate section. When you paste a paragraph, OneNote inserts it in a note with a link to the source.

e. Research the median salary for a single year for this career. Create a mathematical equation in the Median Salary section that multiplies the amount of the median salary times 20 years to calculate how much you will possibly earn.

f. For the Employment Outlook section, research the outlook for your career path. Take at least four notes about what you find when researching the topic.

g. Sync your notes with your OneDrive. Submit your assignment in the format specified by your instructor.

Introduction to Sway

Sway site | responsive design | Storyline | card | Creative Commons license | animation emphasis effects | Docs.com

Expressing your ideas in a presentation typically means creating PowerPoint slides or a Word document. Microsoft Sway gives you another way to engage an audience. Sway is a free Microsoft tool available at Sway.com or as an app in Office 365. Using Sway, you can combine text, images, videos, and social media in a website called a **Sway site** that you can share and display on any device. To get started, you create a digital story on a web-based canvas without borders, slides, cells, or page breaks. A Sway site organizes the text, images, and video into a **responsive design**, which means your content adapts perfectly to any screen size as shown in **Figure 6**. You store a Sway site in the cloud on OneDrive using a free Microsoft account.

Figure 6: Sway site with responsive design

You can display a Sway presentation in a web browser.

Sway uses responsive design to make sure pages fit perfectly on any device.

© iStock.com/marinello, © iStock.com/marekuliasz

Creating a Sway Presentation

You can use Sway to build a digital flyer, a club newsletter, a vacation blog, an informational site, a digital art portfolio, or a new product rollout. After you select your topic and sign into Sway with your Microsoft account, a **Storyline** opens, providing tools and a work area for composing your digital story. See **Figure 7**. Each story can include text, images, and videos. You create a Sway by adding text and media content into a Storyline section, or **card**. To add pictures, videos, or documents, select a card in the left pane and then select the Insert Content button. The first card in a Sway presentation contains a title and background image.

Design and create Sway presentations.

Share and play published Sway sites.

Arrange content in a Storyline, which contains all the text, pictures, videos, and other media in a Sway presentation.

To add content, select a card, which is designed to hold a particular type of information.

After selecting a card, click the Insert Content button to add the content to the Sway presentation.

Adding Content to Build a Story

As you work, Sway searches the Internet to help you find relevant images, videos, tweets, and other content from online sources such as Bing, YouTube, Twitter, and Facebook. You can drag content from the search results right into the Storyline. In addition, you can upload your own images and videos directly in the presentation. For example, if you are creating a Sway presentation about the market for commercial drones, Sway suggests content to incorporate into the presentation by displaying it in the left pane as search results. The search results include drone images tagged with a **Creative Commons license** at online sources as shown in **Figure 8**. A Creative Commons license is a public copyright license that allows the free distribution of an otherwise copyrighted work. In addition, you can specify the source of the media. For example, you can add your own Facebook or OneNote pictures and videos in Sway without leaving the app.

On the Job Now

If you have a Microsoft Word document containing an outline of your business content, drag the outline into Sway to create a card for each topic.

Figure 8: Images in Sway search results

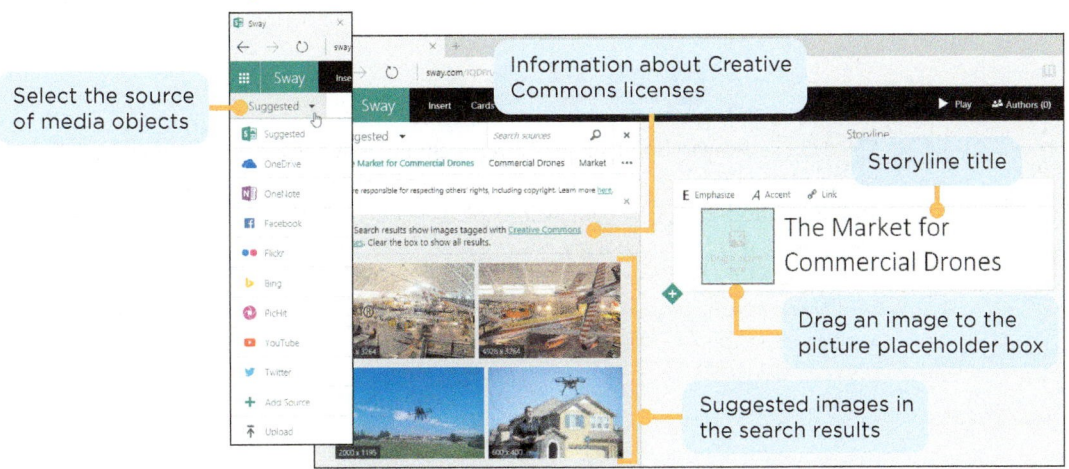

Select the source of media objects

Information about Creative Commons licenses

Storyline title

The Market for Commercial Drones

Drag an image to the picture placeholder box

Suggested images in the search results

On the Job Now

If your project team wants to collaborate on a Sway presentation, click the Authors button on the navigation bar to invite others to edit the presentation.

Designing a Sway

Sway professionally designs your Storyline content by resizing background images and fonts to fit your display, and by floating text, animating media, embedding video, and removing images as a page scrolls out of view. Sway also evaluates the images in your Storyline and suggests a color palette based on colors that appear in your photos. Use the Design button to display tools including color palettes, font choices, **animation emphasis effects**, and style templates to provide a personality for a Sway presentation. Instead of creating your own design, you can click the Remix button, which randomly selects unique designs for your Sway site.

Publishing a Sway

Use the Play button to display your finished Sway presentation as a website. The Address bar includes a unique web address where others can view your Sway site. As the author, you can edit a published Sway site by clicking the Edit button (pencil icon) on the Sway toolbar.

Sharing a Sway

When you are ready to share your Sway website, you have several options as shown in **Figure 9**. Use the Share slider button to share the Sway site publically or keep it private. If you add the Sway site to the Microsoft **Docs.com** public gallery, anyone worldwide can use Bing, Google, or other search engines to find, view, and share your Sway site. You can also share your Sway site using Facebook, Twitter, Google+, Yammer, and other social media sites. Link your presentation to any webpage or email the link to your audience. Sway can also generate a code for embedding the link within another webpage.

Figure 9: Sharing a Sway site

Try This Now

1: Creating a Sway Resume

Sway is a digital storytelling app. Create a Sway resume to share the skills, job experiences, and achievements you have that match the requirements of a future job interest. Perform the following tasks:

a. Create a new presentation in Sway to use as a digital resume. Title the Sway Storyline with your full name and then select a background image.
b. Create three separate sections titled **Academic Background, Work Experience**, and **Skills**, and insert text, a picture, and a paragraph or bulleted points in each section. Be sure to include your own picture.
c. Add a fourth section that includes a video about your school that you find online.
d. Customize the design of your presentation.
e. Submit your assignment link in the format specified by your instructor.

2: Creating an Online Sway Newsletter

Newsletters are designed to capture the attention of their target audience. Using Sway, create a newsletter for a club, organization, or your favorite music group. Perform the following tasks:

a. Create a new presentation in Sway to use as a digital newsletter for a club, organization, or your favorite music group. Provide a title for the Sway Storyline and select an appropriate background image.
b. Select three separate sections with appropriate titles, such as Upcoming Events. In each section, insert text, a picture, and a paragraph or bulleted points.
c. Add a fourth section that includes a video about your selected topic.
d. Customize the design of your presentation.
e. Submit your assignment link in the format specified by your instructor.

3: Creating and Sharing a Technology Presentation

To place a Sway presentation in the hands of your entire audience, you can share a link to the Sway presentation. Create a Sway presentation on a new technology and share it with your class. Perform the following tasks:

a. Create a new presentation in Sway about a cutting-edge technology topic. Provide a title for the Sway Storyline and select a background image.
b. Create four separate sections about your topic, and include text, a picture, and a paragraph in each section.
c. Add a fifth section that includes a video about your topic.
d. Customize the design of your presentation.
e. Share the link to your Sway with your classmates and submit your assignment link in the format specified by your instructor.

> **Learn to use Sway!**
> Links to companion **Sways**, featuring **videos** with hands-on instructions, are located on www.cengagebrain.com.

Introduction to Office Mix

add-in | clip | slide recording | Slide Notes | screen recording | free-response quiz

To enliven business meetings and lectures, Microsoft adds a new dimension to presentations with a powerful toolset called Office Mix, a free add-in for PowerPoint. (An **add-in** is software that works with an installed app to extend its features.) Using Office Mix, you can record yourself on video, capture still and moving images on your desktop, and insert interactive elements such as quizzes and live webpages directly into PowerPoint slides. When you post the finished presentation to OneDrive, Office Mix provides a link you can share with friends and colleagues. Anyone with an Internet connection and a web browser can watch a published Office Mix presentation, such as the one in **Figure 10**, on a computer or mobile device.

Figure 10: Office Mix presentation

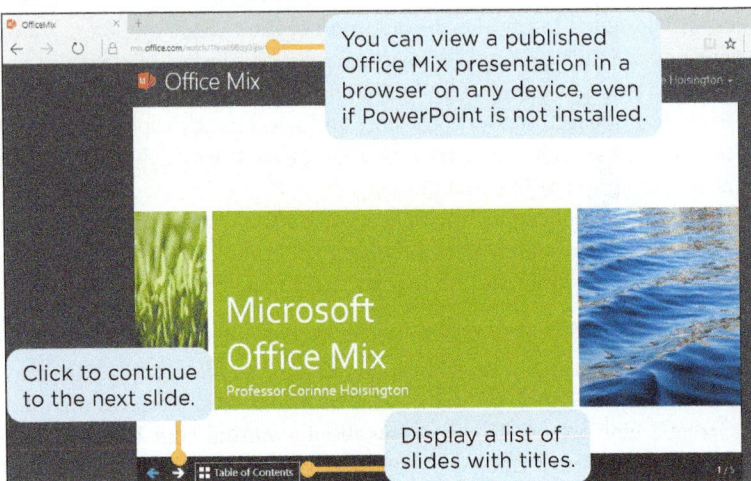

Adding Office Mix to PowerPoint

To get started, you create an Office Mix account at the website mix.office.com using an email address or a Facebook or Google account. Next, you download and install the Office Mix add-in (see **Figure 11**). Office Mix appears as a new tab named Mix on the PowerPoint ribbon in versions of Office 2013 and Office 2016 running on personal computers (PCs).

Figure 11: Getting started with Office Mix

Capturing Video Clips

A **clip** is a short segment of audio, such as music, or video. After finishing the content on a PowerPoint slide, you can use Office Mix to add a video clip to animate or illustrate the content. Office Mix creates video clips in two ways: by recording live action on a webcam and by capturing screen images and movements. If your computer has a webcam, you can record yourself and annotate the slide to create a **slide recording** as shown in **Figure 12**.

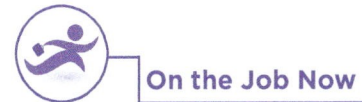

On the Job Now

Companies are using Office Mix to train employees about new products, to explain benefit packages to new workers, and to educate interns about office procedures.

Figure 12: Making a slide recording

Record your voice; also record video if your computer has a camera.

Use the Slide Notes button to display notes for your narration.

For best results, look directly at your webcam while recording video.

Use inking tools to write and draw on the slide as you record.

Choose a video and audio device to record images and sound.

When you are making a slide recording, you can record your spoken narration at the same time. The **Slide Notes** feature works like a teleprompter to help you focus on your presentation content instead of memorizing your narration. Use the Inking tools to make annotations or add highlighting using different pen types and colors. After finishing a recording, edit the video in PowerPoint to trim the length or set playback options.

The second way to create a video is to capture on-screen images and actions with or without a voiceover. This method is ideal if you want to show how to use your favorite website or demonstrate an app such as OneNote. To share your screen with an audience, select the part of the screen you want to show in the video. Office Mix captures everything that happens in that area to create a **screen recording**, as shown in **Figure 13**. Office Mix inserts the screen recording as a video in the slide.

On the Job Now

To make your video recordings accessible to people with hearing impairments, use the Office Mix closed-captioning tools. You can also use closed captions to supplement audio that is difficult to understand and to provide an aid for those learning to read.

Figure 13: Making a screen recording

Record the action on the screen within the red dashed outline.

Record audio while capturing your on-screen actions.

Select Area button

Inserting Quizzes, Live Webpages, and Apps

To enhance and assess audience understanding, make your slides interactive by adding quizzes, live webpages, and apps. Quizzes give immediate feedback to the user as shown in **Figure 14**. Office Mix supports several quiz formats, including a **free-response quiz** similar to a short answer quiz, and true/false, multiple-choice, and multiple-response formats.

Figure 14: Creating an interactive quiz

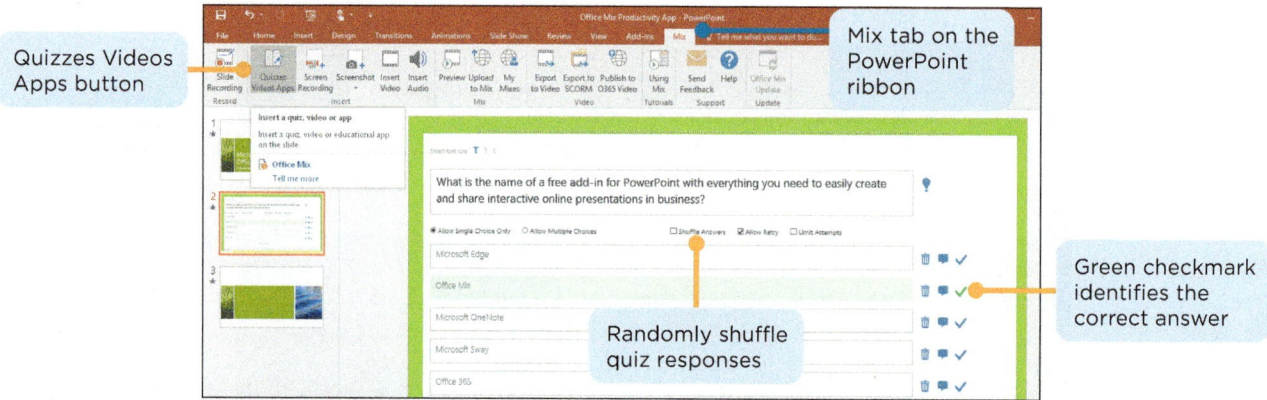

Quizzes Videos Apps button

Mix tab on the PowerPoint ribbon

Green checkmark identifies the correct answer

Randomly shuffle quiz responses

Sharing an Office Mix Presentation

When you complete your work with Office Mix, upload the presentation to your personal Office Mix dashboard as shown in **Figure 15**. Users of PCs, Macs, iOS devices, and Android devices can access and play Office Mix presentations. The Office Mix dashboard displays built-in analytics that include the quiz results and how much time viewers spent on each slide. You can play completed Office Mix presentations online or download them as movies.

Figure 15: Sharing an Office Mix presentation

Office Mix dashboard displays the quiz analytics.

Try This Now

1: Creating an Office Mix Tutorial for OneNote

Note: This activity requires a microphone on your computer.

Office Mix makes it easy to record screens and their contents. Create PowerPoint slides with an Office Mix screen recording to show OneNote 2016 features. Perform the following tasks:

    a. Create a PowerPoint presentation with the Ion Boardroom template. Create an opening slide with the title **My Favorite OneNote Features** and enter your name in the subtitle.

    b. Create three additional slides, each titled with a new feature of OneNote. Open OneNote and use the Mix tab in PowerPoint to capture three separate screen recordings that teach your favorite features.

    c. Add a fifth slide that quizzes the user with a multiple-choice question about OneNote and includes four responses. Be sure to insert a checkmark indicating the correct response.

    d. Upload the completed presentation to your Office Mix dashboard and share the link with your instructor.

    e. Submit your assignment link in the format specified by your instructor.

2: Teaching Augmented Reality with Office Mix

Note: This activity requires a webcam or built-in video camera on your computer.

A local elementary school has asked you to teach augmented reality to its students using Office Mix. Perform the following tasks:

    a. Research augmented reality using your favorite online search tools.

    b. Create a PowerPoint presentation with the Frame template. Create an opening slide with the title **Augmented Reality** and enter your name in the subtitle.

    c. Create a slide with four bullets summarizing your research of augmented reality. Create a 20-second slide recording of yourself providing a quick overview of augmented reality.

    d. Create another slide with a 30-second screen recording of a video about augmented reality from a site such as YouTube or another video-sharing site.

    e. Add a final slide that quizzes the user with a true/false question about augmented reality. Be sure to insert a checkmark indicating the correct response.

    f. Upload the completed presentation to your Office Mix dashboard and share the link with your instructor.

    g. Submit your assignment link in the format specified by your instructor.

3: Marketing a Travel Destination with Office Mix

Note: This activity requires a webcam or built-in video camera on your computer.

To convince your audience to travel to a particular city, create a slide presentation marketing any city in the world using a slide recording, screen recording, and a quiz. Perform the following tasks:

    a. Create a PowerPoint presentation with any template. Create an opening slide with the title of the city you are marketing as a travel destination and your name in the subtitle.

    b. Create a slide with four bullets about the featured city. Create a 30-second slide recording of yourself explaining why this city is the perfect vacation destination.

    c. Create another slide with a 20-second screen recording of a travel video about the city from a site such as YouTube or another video-sharing site.

    d. Add a final slide that quizzes the user with a multiple-choice question about the featured city with five responses. Be sure to include a checkmark indicating the correct response.

    e. Upload the completed presentation to your Office Mix dashboard and share your link with your instructor.

    f. Submit your assignment link in the format specified by your instructor.

Introduction to Microsoft Edge

Reading view | Hub | Cortana | Web Note | Inking | sandbox

Microsoft Edge is the default web browser developed for the Windows 10 operating system as a replacement for Internet Explorer. Unlike its predecessor, Edge lets you write on webpages, read webpages without advertisements and other distractions, and search for information using a virtual personal assistant. The Edge interface is clean and basic, as shown in **Figure 16**, meaning you can pay more attention to the webpage content.

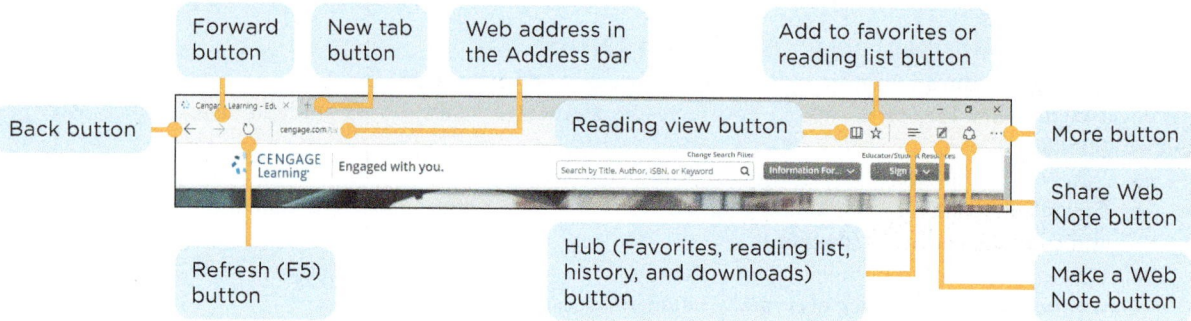

Figure 16: Microsoft Edge tools

Forward button · New tab button · Web address in the Address bar · Add to favorites or reading list button · Back button · Reading view button · More button · Refresh (F5) button · Hub (Favorites, reading list, history, and downloads) button · Share Web Note button · Make a Web Note button

Browsing the Web with Microsoft Edge

One of the fastest browsers available, Edge allows you to type search text directly in the Address bar. As you view the resulting webpage, you can switch to **Reading view**, which is available for most news and research sites, to eliminate distracting advertisements. For example, if you are catching up on technology news online, the webpage might be difficult to read due to a busy layout cluttered with ads. Switch to Reading view to refresh the page and remove the original page formatting, ads, and menu sidebars to read the article distraction-free.

Consider the **Hub** in Microsoft Edge as providing one-stop access to all the things you collect on the web, such as your favorite websites, reading list, surfing history, and downloaded files.

Locating Information with Cortana

Cortana, the Windows 10 virtual assistant, plays an important role in Microsoft Edge. After you turn on Cortana, it appears as an animated circle in the Address bar when you might need assistance, as shown in the restaurant website in **Figure 17**. When you click the Cortana icon, a pane slides in from the right of the browser window to display detailed information about the restaurant, including maps and reviews. Cortana can also assist you in defining words, finding the weather, suggesting coupons for shopping, updating stock market information, and calculating math.

Figure 17: Cortana providing restaurant information

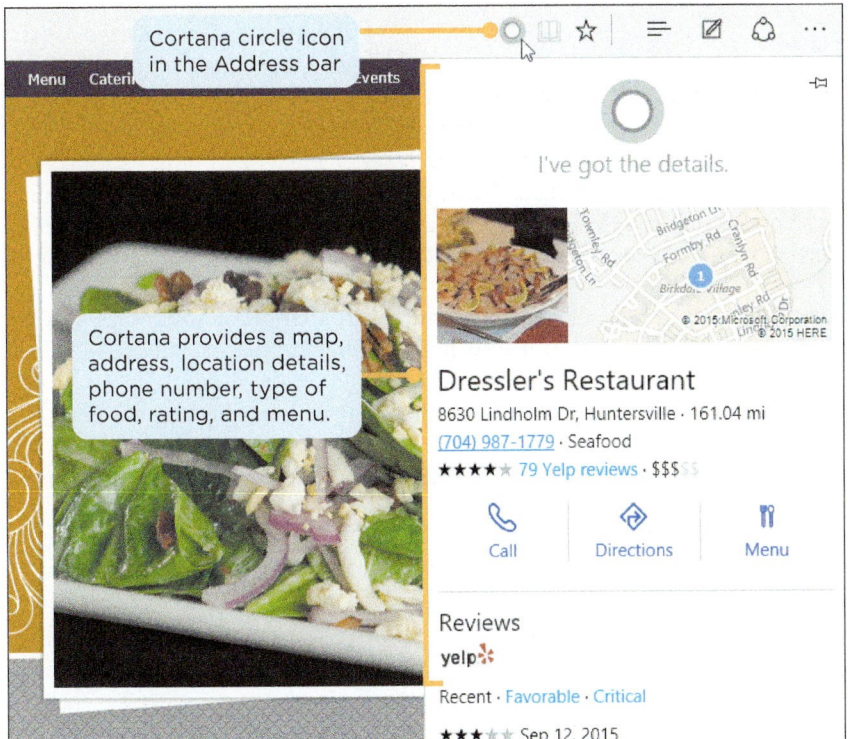

Annotating Webpages

One of the most impressive Microsoft Edge features are the **Web Note** tools, which you use to write on a webpage or to highlight text. When you click the Make a Web Note button, an **Inking** toolbar appears, as shown in **Figure 18**, that provides writing and drawing tools. These tools include an eraser, a pen, and a highlighter with different colors. You can also insert a typed note and copy a screen image (called a screen clipping). You can draw with a pointing device, fingertip, or stylus using different pen colors. Whether you add notes to a recipe, annotate sources for a research paper, or select a product while shopping online, the Web Note tools can enhance your productivity. After you complete your notes, click the Save button to save the annotations to OneNote, your Favorites list, or your Reading list. You can share the inked page with others using the Share Web Note button.

On the Job Now

To enhance security, Microsoft Edge runs in a partial sandbox, an arrangement that prevents attackers from gaining control of your computer. Browsing within the **sandbox** protects computer resources and information from hackers.

Figure 18: Web Note tools in Microsoft Edge

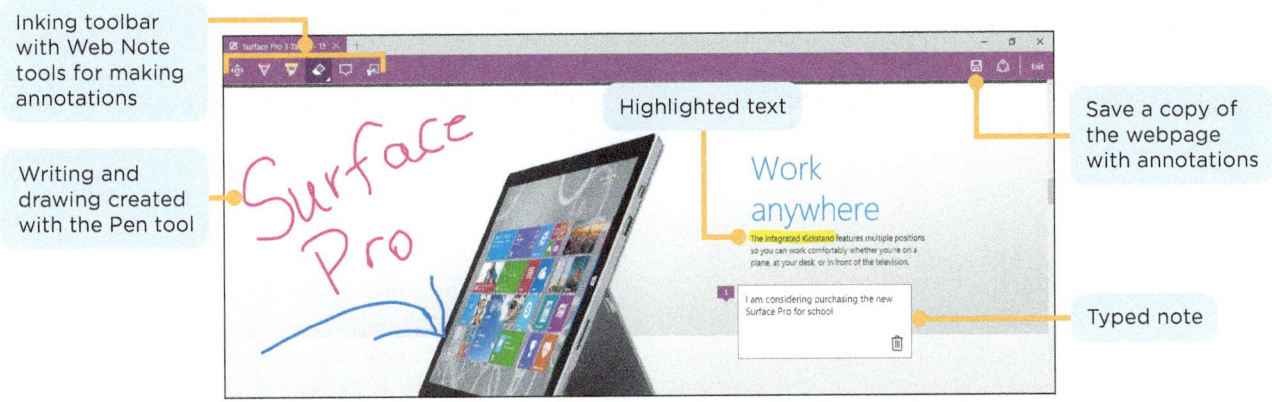

Inking toolbar with Web Note tools for making annotations

Writing and drawing created with the Pen tool

Highlighted text

Save a copy of the webpage with annotations

Typed note

Try This Now

Learn to use Edge!

Links to companion **Sways**, featuring **videos** with hands-on instructions, are located on www.cengagebrain.com.

1: Using Cortana in Microsoft Edge

Note: This activity requires using Microsoft Edge on a Windows 10 computer.

Cortana can assist you in finding information on a webpage in Microsoft Edge. Perform the following tasks:

a. Create a Word document using the Word Screen Clipping tool to capture the following screenshots.

- Screenshot A—Using Microsoft Edge, open a webpage with a technology news article. Right-click a term in the article and ask Cortana to define it.
- Screenshot B—Using Microsoft Edge, open the website of a fancy restaurant in a city near you. Make sure the Cortana circle icon is displayed in the Address bar. (If it's not displayed, find a different restaurant website.) Click the Cortana circle icon to display a pane with information about the restaurant.
- Screenshot C—Using Microsoft Edge, type **10 USD to Euros** in the Address bar without pressing the Enter key. Cortana converts the U.S. dollars to Euros.
- Screenshot D—Using Microsoft Edge, type **Apple stock** in the Address bar without pressing the Enter key. Cortana displays the current stock quote.

b. Submit your assignment in the format specified by your instructor.

2: Viewing Online News with Reading View

Note: This activity requires using Microsoft Edge on a Windows 10 computer.

Reading view in Microsoft Edge can make a webpage less cluttered with ads and other distractions. Perform the following tasks:

a. Create a Word document using the Word Screen Clipping tool to capture the following screenshots.

- Screenshot A—Using Microsoft Edge, open the website **mashable.com**. Open a technology article. Click the Reading view button to display an ad-free page that uses only basic text formatting.
- Screenshot B—Using Microsoft Edge, open the website **bbc.com**. Open any news article. Click the Reading view button to display an ad-free page that uses only basic text formatting.
- Screenshot C—Make three types of annotations (Pen, Highlighter, and Add a typed note) on the BBC article page displayed in Reading view.

b. Submit your assignment in the format specified by your instructor.

3: Inking with Microsoft Edge

Note: This activity requires using Microsoft Edge on a Windows 10 computer.

Microsoft Edge provides many annotation options to record your ideas. Perform the following tasks:

a. Open the website **wolframalpha.com** in the Microsoft Edge browser. Wolfram Alpha is a well-respected academic search engine. Type **US$100 1965 dollars in 2015** in the Wolfram Alpha search text box and press the Enter key.

b. Click the Make a Web Note button to display the Web Note tools. Using the Pen tool, draw a circle around the result on the webpage. Save the page to OneNote.

c. In the Wolfram Alpha search text box, type the name of the city closest to where you live and press the Enter key. Using the Highlighter tool, highlight at least three interesting results. Add a note and then type a sentence about what you learned about this city. Save the page to OneNote. Share your OneNote notebook with your instructor.

d. Submit your assignment link in the format specified by your instructor.

Getting Started with Microsoft Office 2016

CASE This module introduces you to the most frequently used programs in Office, as well as common features they all share.

Module Objectives

After completing this module, you will be able to:

- Understand the Office 2016 suite
- Start an Office app
- Identify Office 2016 screen elements
- Create and save a file

- Open a file and save it with a new name
- View and print your work
- Get Help, close a file, and exit an app

Files You Will Need

OF 1-1.xlsx

Understand the Office 2016 Suite

Microsoft Office 2016 is a group of programs—which are also called applications or apps—designed to help you create documents, collaborate with coworkers, and track and analyze information. You use different Office programs to accomplish specific tasks, such as writing a letter or producing a presentation, yet all the programs have a similar look and feel. Microsoft Office 2016 apps feature a common, context-sensitive user interface, so you can get up to speed faster and use advanced features with greater ease. The Office apps are bundled together in a group called a **suite**. The Office suite is available in several configurations, but all include Word, Excel, PowerPoint, and OneNote. Some configurations include Access, Outlook, Publisher, Skype, and OneDrive. **CASE** ▶ *As part of your job, you need to understand how each Office app is best used to complete specific tasks.*

DETAILS

The Office apps covered in this book include:

• ### Microsoft Word 2016

When you need to create any kind of text-based document, such as a memo, newsletter, or multipage report, Word is the program to use. You can easily make your documents look great by using formatting tools and inserting eye-catching graphics. The Word document shown in **FIGURE 1-1** contains a company logo and simple formatting.

• ### Microsoft Excel 2016

Excel is the perfect solution when you need to work with numeric values and make calculations. It puts the power of formulas, functions, charts, and other analytical tools into the hands of every user, so you can analyze sales projections, calculate loan payments, and present your findings in a professional manner. The Excel worksheet shown in **FIGURE 1-1** tracks checkbook transactions. Because Excel automatically recalculates results whenever a value changes, the information is always up to date. A chart illustrates how the monthly expenses are broken down.

• ### Microsoft PowerPoint 2016

Using PowerPoint, it's easy to create powerful presentations complete with graphics, transitions, and even a soundtrack. Using professionally designed themes and clip art, you can quickly and easily create dynamic slide shows such as the one shown in **FIGURE 1-1**.

• ### Microsoft Access 2016

Access is a relational database program that helps you keep track of large amounts of quantitative data, such as product inventories or employee records. The form shown in **FIGURE 1-1** can be used to generate reports on customer invoices and tours.

Microsoft Office has benefits beyond the power of each program, including:

• ### Note-taking made simple; available on all devices

Use OneNote to take notes (organized in tabbed pages) on information that can be accessed on your computer, tablet, or phone. Share the editable results with others. Contents can include text, web page clips (using OneNote Clipper), email contents (directly inserted into a default section), photos (using Office Lens), and web pages.

• ### Common user interface: Improving business processes

Because the Office suite apps have a similar **interface**, your experience using one app's tools makes it easy to learn those in the other apps. Office documents are **compatible** with one another, so you can easily **integrate**, or combine, elements—for example, you can add an Excel chart to a PowerPoint slide, or an Access table to a Word document.

Most Office programs include the capability to incorporate feedback—called **online collaboration**—across the Internet or a company network.

FIGURE 1-1: Microsoft Office 2016 documents

Letter created in Word

Checkbook register created in Excel

Tourism presentation created in PowerPoint

Form created in Access

Office 2016

What is Office 365?

Until recently, most consumers purchased Microsoft Office in a traditional way: by buying a retail package from a store or downloading it from Microsoft.com. You can still purchase Microsoft Office 2016 in this traditional way—but you can also now purchase it as a subscription service called Microsoft Office 365, which is available in a wide variety of configurations.

Depending on which configuration you purchase, you will always have access to the most up-to-date versions of the apps in your package and, in many cases, can install these apps on multiple computers, tablets, and phones. And if you change computers or devices, you can easily uninstall the apps from an old device and install them on a new one.

Start an Office App

Learning Outcomes
- Start an Office app
- Explain the purpose of a template
- Start a new blank document

To get started using Microsoft Office, you need to start, or **launch**, the Office app you want to use. An easy way to start the app you want is to press the Windows key, type the first few characters of the app name you want to search for, then click the app name In the Best match list. You will discover that there are many ways to accomplish just about any Windows task; for example, you can also see a list of all the apps on your computer by pressing the Windows key, then clicking All Apps. When you see the app you want, click its name. **CASE** ▶ *You decide to familiarize yourself with Office by starting Microsoft Word.*

STEPS

1. **Click the Start button ⊞ on the Windows taskbar**

   The Start menu opens, listing the most used apps on your computer. You can locate the app you want to open by clicking the app name if you see it, or you can type the app name to search for it.

2. **Type word**

   Your screen now displays "Word 2016" under "Best match", along with any other app that has "word" as part of its name (such as WordPad). See **FIGURE 1-2**.

3. **Click Word 2016**

   Word 2016 launches, and the Word **start screen** appears, as shown in **FIGURE 1-3**. The start screen is a landing page that appears when you first start an Office app. The left side of this screen displays recent files you have opened. (If you have never opened any files, then there will be no files listed under Recent.) The right side displays images depicting different templates you can use to create different types of documents. A **template** is a file containing professionally designed content and formatting that you can easily customize for your own needs. You can also start from scratch using the Blank Document template, which contains only minimal formatting settings.

Enabling touch mode

If you are using a touch screen with any of the Office 2016 apps, you can enable the touch mode to give the user interface a more spacious look, making it easier to navigate with your fingertips. Enable touch mode by clicking the Quick Access toolbar list arrow, then clicking Touch/Mouse Mode to select it. Then you'll see the Touch Mode button 👆 in the Quick Access toolbar. Click 👆, and you'll see the interface spread out.

Using shortcut keys to move between Office programs

You can switch between open apps using a keyboard shortcut. The [Alt][Tab] keyboard combination lets you either switch quickly to the next open program or file or choose one from a gallery. To switch immediately to the next open program or file, press [Alt][Tab]. To choose from all open programs and files, press and hold [Alt], then press and release [Tab] without releasing [Alt]. A gallery opens on screen, displaying the filename and a thumbnail image of each open program and file, as well as of the desktop. Each time you press [Tab] while holding [Alt], the selection cycles to the next open file or location. Release [Alt] when the program, file, or location you want to activate is selected.

FIGURE 1-2: Searching for the Word app

FIGURE 1-2: Searching for the Word app

Word 2016 app appears as a search result when you type "word"

Your list may differ

FIGURE 1-3: Word start screen

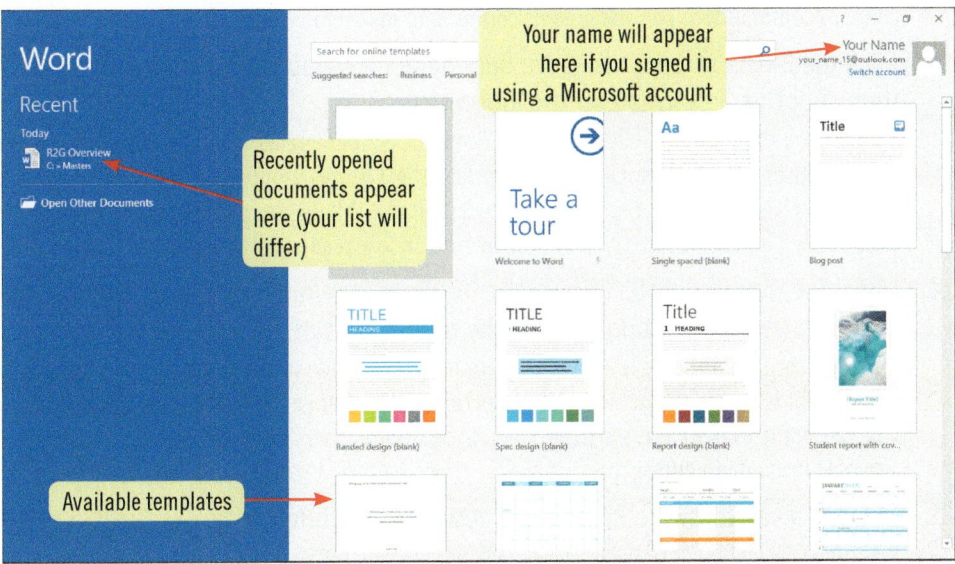

FIGURE 1-3: Word start screen

Your name will appear here if you signed in using a Microsoft account

Recently opened documents appear here (your list will differ)

Available templates

Using the Office Clipboard

You can use the Office Clipboard to cut and copy items from one Office program and paste them into others. The Office Clipboard can store a maximum of 24 items. To access it, open the Office Clipboard task pane by clicking the dialog box launcher in the Clipboard group on the Home tab. Each time you copy a selection, it is saved in the Office Clipboard. Each entry in the Office Clipboard includes an icon that tells you the program it was created in. To paste an entry, click in the document where you want it to appear, then click the item in the Office Clipboard. To delete an item from the Office Clipboard, right-click the item, then click Delete.

Identify Office 2016 Screen Elements

One of the benefits of using Office is that its apps have much in common, making them easy to learn and making it simple to move from one to another. All Office 2016 apps share a similar user interface, so you can use your knowledge of one to get up to speed in another. A **user interface** is a collective term for all the ways you interact with a software program. The user interface in Office 2016 provides intuitive ways to choose commands, work with files, and navigate in the program window. **CASE** *Familiarize yourself with some of the common interface elements in Office by examining the PowerPoint program window.*

STEPS

1. **Click the Start button ⊞ on the Windows taskbar, type pow, click PowerPoint 2016, then click Blank Presentation**

   PowerPoint starts and opens a new file, which contains a blank slide. Refer to **FIGURE 1-4** to identify common elements of the Office user interface. The **document window** occupies most of the screen. At the top of every Office program window is a **title bar** that displays the document name and program name. Below the title bar is the **Ribbon**, which displays commands you're likely to need for the current task. Commands are organized onto **tabs**. The tab names appear at the top of the Ribbon, and the active tab appears in front. The **Share button** in the upper-right corner lets you invite other users to view your cloud-stored Word, Excel, or Powerpoint file.

2. **Click the File tab**

   The File tab opens, displaying **Backstage view**. It is called Backstage view because the commands available here are for working with the files "behind the scenes." The navigation bar on the left side of Backstage view contains commands to perform actions common to most Office programs.

3. **Click the Back button ⊙ to close Backstage view and return to the document window, then click the Design tab on the Ribbon**

   To display a different tab, click its name. Each tab contains related commands arranged into **groups** to make features easy to find. On the Design tab, the Themes group displays available design themes in a **gallery**, or visual collection of choices you can browse. Many groups contain a **launcher**, which you can click to open a dialog box or pane from which to choose related commands.

4. **Move the mouse pointer ⬚ over the Ion Boardroom theme in the Themes group as shown in FIGURE 1-5, but do not click the mouse button**

   The Ion Boardroom theme is temporarily applied to the slide in the document window. However, because you did not click the theme, you did not permanently change the slide. With the **Live Preview** feature, you can point to a choice, see the results, then decide if you want to make the change. Live Preview is available throughout Office.

5. **Move ⬚ away from the Ribbon and towards the slide**

   If you had clicked the Ion theme, it would be applied to this slide. Instead, the slide remains unchanged.

6. **Point to the Zoom slider ⊟———▌———⊞ 100% on the status bar, then drag to the right until the Zoom level reads 166%**

   The slide display is enlarged. Zoom tools are located on the status bar. You can drag the slider or click the Zoom In or Zoom Out buttons to zoom in or out on an area of interest. **Zooming in** (a higher percentage), makes a document appear bigger on screen but less of it fits on the screen at once; **zooming out** (a lower percentage) lets you see more of the document at a reduced size.

7. **Click the Zoom Out button ⊟ on the status bar to the left of the Zoom slider until the Zoom level reads 120%**

FIGURE 1-4: PowerPoint program window

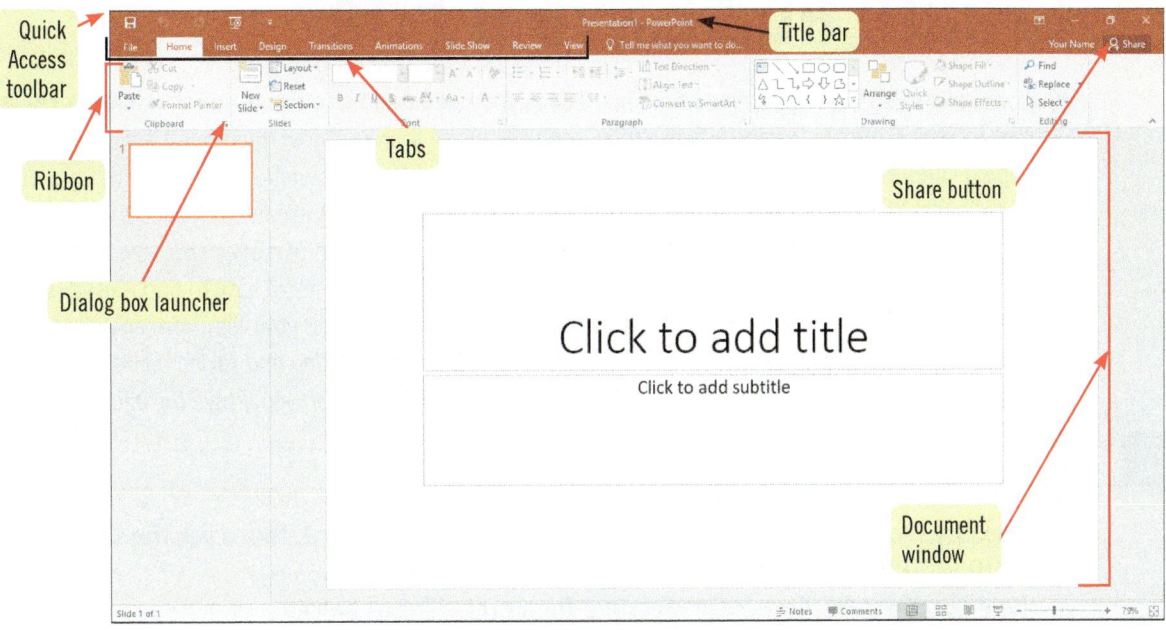

Quick Access toolbar

Ribbon

Dialog box launcher

Tabs

Title bar

Share button

Click to add title

Click to add subtitle

Document window

FIGURE 1-5: Viewing a theme with Live Preview

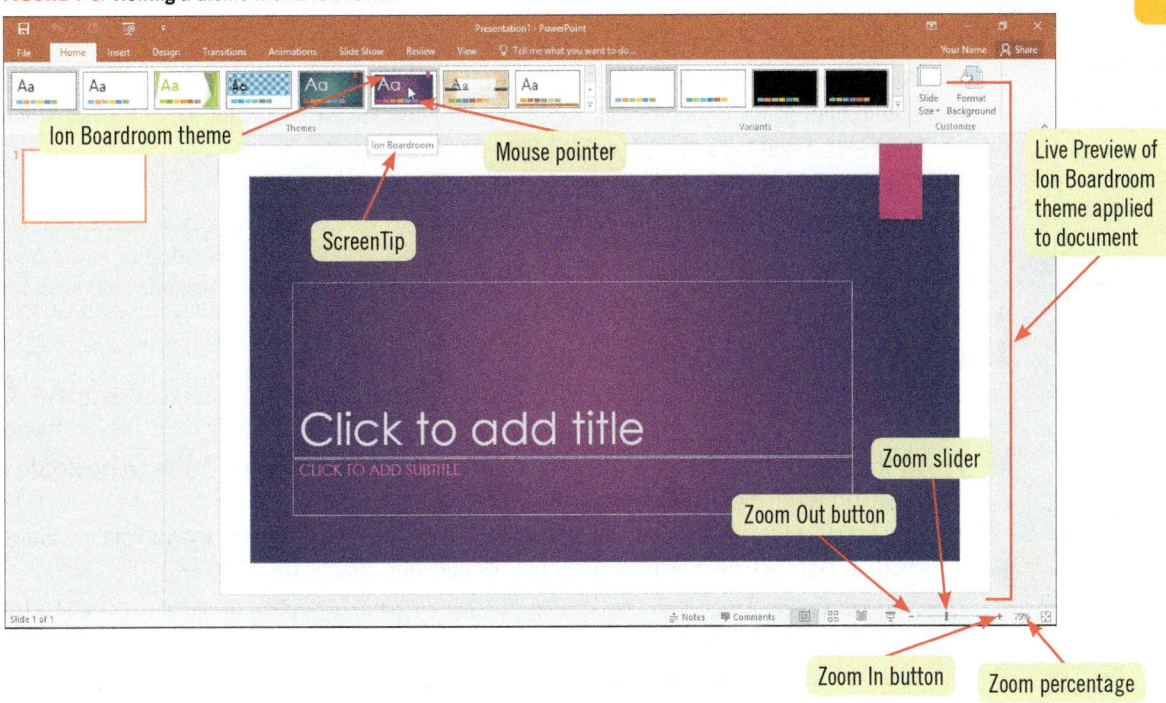

Ion Boardroom theme

Mouse pointer

ScreenTip

Live Preview of Ion Boardroom theme applied to document

Click to add title

CLICK TO ADD SUBTITLE

Zoom slider

Zoom Out button

Zoom In button

Zoom percentage

Using Backstage view

Backstage view in each Microsoft Office app offers "one stop shopping" for many commonly performed tasks, such as opening and saving a file, printing and previewing a document, defining document properties, sharing information, and exiting a program. Backstage view opens when you click the File tab in any Office app, and while features such as the Ribbon, Mini toolbar, and Live Preview all help you work *in* your documents, the File tab and Backstage view help you work *with* your documents. You can click commands in the navigation pane to open different places for working with your documents, such as the Open place, the Save place, and so on. You can return to your active document by clicking the Back button.

Create and Save a File

Learning Outcomes
- Create a file
- Save a file
- Explain OneDrive

When working in an Office app, one of the first things you need to do is to create and save a file. A **file** is a stored collection of data. Saving a file enables you to work on a project now, then put it away and work on it again later. In some Office programs, including Word, Excel, and PowerPoint, you can open a new file when you start the app, then all you have to do is enter some data and save it. In Access, you must create a file before you enter any data. You should give your files meaningful names and save them in an appropriate location, such as a folder on your hard drive or OneDrive so they're easy to find. **OneDrive** is a Microsoft cloud storage system that lets you easily save, share, and access your files from anywhere you have Internet access. **CASE** ▶ *Use Word to familiarize yourself with creating and saving a document. First you'll type some notes about a possible location for a corporate meeting, then you'll save the information for later use.*

STEPS

1. **Click the Word button** ⬛ **on the taskbar, click Blank document, then click the Zoom In button** ➕ **until the level is 120%, if necessary**

2. **Type Locations for Corporate Meeting, then press [Enter] twice**

   The text appears in the document window, and the **insertion point** blinks on a new blank line. The insertion point indicates where the next typed text will appear.

QUICK TIP

A filename can be up to 255 characters, including a file extension, and can include upper- or lowercase characters and spaces, but not ?, ", /, \, <, >, *, |, or :.

3. **Type Las Vegas, NV, press [Enter], type Chicago, IL, press [Enter], type Seattle, WA, press [Enter] twice, then type your name**

4. **Click the Save button** 💾 **on the Quick Access toolbar**

   Because this is the first time you are saving this new file, the Save place in Backstage view opens, showing various options for saving the file. See **FIGURE 1-6**. Once you save a file for the first time, clicking 💾 saves any changes to the file *without* opening the Save As dialog box.

5. **Click Browse**

   The Save As dialog box opens, as shown in **FIGURE 1-7**, where you can browse to the location where you want to save the file. The Address bar in the Save As dialog box displays the default location for saving the file, but you can change it to any location. The File name field contains a suggested name for the document based on text in the file, but you can enter a different name.

QUICK TIP

Saving a file to the Desktop creates a desktop icon that you can double-click to both launch a program and open a document.

6. **Type OF 1-Possible Corporate Meeting Locations**

   The text you type replaces the highlighted text. (The "OF 1-" in the filename indicates that the file is created in Office Module 1. You will see similar designations throughout this book when files are named.)

7. **In the Save As dialog box, use the Address bar or Navigation Pane to navigate to the location where you store your Data Files**

   You can store files on your computer, a network drive, your OneDrive, or any acceptable storage device.

QUICK TIP

To create a new blank file when a file is open, click the File tab, click New on the navigation bar, then choose a template.

8. **Click Save**

   The Save As dialog box closes, the new file is saved to the location you specified, and the name of the document appears in the title bar, as shown in **FIGURE 1-8**. (You may or may not see the file extension ".docx" after the filename.) See **TABLE 1-1** for a description of the different types of files you create in Office, and the file extensions associated with each.

TABLE 1-1: Common filenames and default file extensions

file created in	is called a	and has the default extension
Word	document	.docx
Excel	workbook	.xlsx
PowerPoint	presentation	.pptx
Access	database	.accdb

FIGURE 1-6: Save place in Backstage view

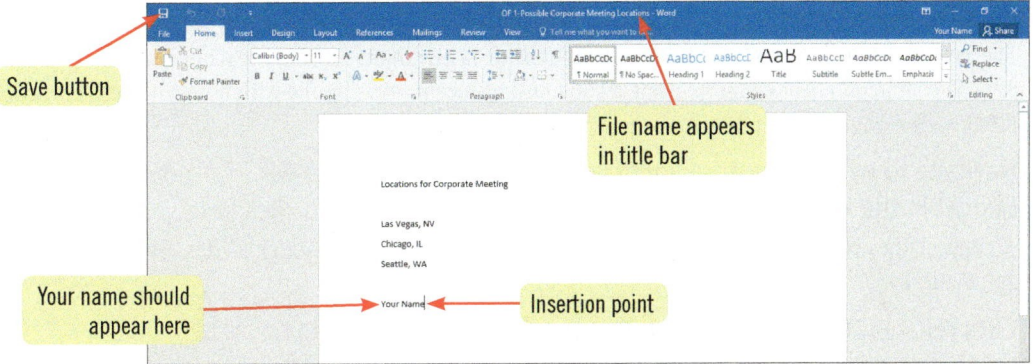

Saves to your OneDrive account

Click to display a list of recently accessed locations on this PC

Click to open the Save As dialog box

FIGURE 1-7: Save As dialog box

Navigation pane; your links and folders may differ

File name field; your computer may not display file extensions

Address bar; your location may differ

Save as type list

FIGURE 1-8: Saved and named Word document

Save button

File name appears in title bar

Your name should appear here

Insertion point

Locations for Corporate Meeting

Las Vegas, NV

Chicago, IL

Seattle, WA

Your Name

Office 2016

Saving files to OneDrive

All Office programs include the capability to incorporate feedback—called **online collaboration**—across the Internet or a company network. Using **cloud computing** (work done in a virtual environment), you can store your work in the cloud. Using OneDrive, a file storage service from Microsoft, you and your colleagues can create and store documents in the cloud and make the documents available anywhere there is Internet access to whomever you choose. To use OneDrive, you need a Microsoft Account, which you obtain at onedrive.live.com. Pricing and storage plans vary based on the type of Microsoft account you have. When you are logged into your Microsoft account and you

save a file in any of the Office apps, the first option in the Save As screen is your OneDrive. Double-click your OneDrive option, and the Save As dialog box opens displaying a location in the address bar unique to your OneDrive account. Type a name in the File name text box, then click Save and your file is saved to your OneDrive. To sync your files with OneDrive, you'll need to download and install the OneDrive for Windows app. Then, when you open Explorer, you'll notice a new folder called OneDrive has been added to your folder. In this folder is a sub-folder called Documents. This means if your Internet connection fails, you can work on your files offline.

Open a File and Save It with a New Name

Learning Outcomes
- Open an existing file
- Save a file with a new name

In many cases as you work in Office, you need to use an existing file. It might be a file you or a coworker created earlier as a work in progress, or it could be a complete document that you want to use as the basis for another. For example, you might want to create a budget for this year using the budget you created last year; instead of typing in all the categories and information from scratch, you could open last year's budget, save it with a new name, and just make changes to update it for the current year. By opening the existing file and saving it with the Save As command, you create a duplicate that you can modify to suit your needs, while the original file remains intact. **CASE** ▶ *Use Excel to open an existing workbook file, and save it with a new name so the original remains unchanged.*

STEPS

1. **Click the Start button ⊞ on the Windows taskbar, type exc, click Excel 2016, click Open Other Workbooks, This PC, then click Browse**

   The Open dialog box opens, where you can navigate to any drive or folder accessible to your computer to locate a file.

2. **In the Open dialog box, navigate to the location where you store your Data Files**

   The files available in the current folder are listed, as shown in **FIGURE 1-9**. This folder displays one file.

3. **Click OF 1-1.xlsx, then click Open**

   The dialog box closes, and the file opens in Excel. An Excel file is an electronic spreadsheet, so the new file displays a grid of rows and columns you can use to enter and organize data.

4. **Click the File tab, click Save As on the navigation bar, then click Browse**

   The Save As dialog box opens, and the current filename is highlighted in the File name text box. Using the Save As command enables you to create a copy of the current, existing file with a new name. This action preserves the original file and creates a new file that you can modify.

5. **Navigate to where you store your Data Files if necessary, type OF 1-Corporate Meeting Budget in the File name text box, as shown in FIGURE 1-10, then click Save**

   A copy of the existing workbook is created with the new name. The original file, OF 1-1.xlsx, closes automatically.

6. **Click cell A18, type your name, then press [Enter], as shown in FIGURE 1-11**

   In Excel, you enter data in cells, which are formed by the intersection of a row and a column. Cell A18 is at the intersection of column A and row 18. When you press [Enter], the cell pointer moves to cell A19.

7. **Click the Save button 🖫 on the Quick Access toolbar**

   Your name appears in the workbook, and your changes to the file are saved.

Exploring File Open options

You might have noticed that the Open button in the Open dialog box includes a list arrow to the right of the button. In a dialog box, if a button includes a list arrow you can click the button to invoke the command, or you can click the list arrow to see a list of related commands that you can apply to the currently selected file. The Open list arrow includes several related commands, including Open Read-Only and Open as Copy.

Clicking Open Read-Only opens a file that you can only save with a new name; you cannot make changes to the original file. Clicking Open as Copy creates and opens a copy of the selected file and inserts the word "Copy" in the file's title. Like the Save As command, these commands provide additional ways to use copies of existing files while ensuring that original files do not get changed by mistake.

FIGURE 1-9: Open dialog box

Available files in this folder

Your location may vary

Open button list arrow

Open button

FIGURE 1-10: Save As dialog box

Your location may vary

New filename

Save as type list arrow

FIGURE 1-11: Your name added to the workbook

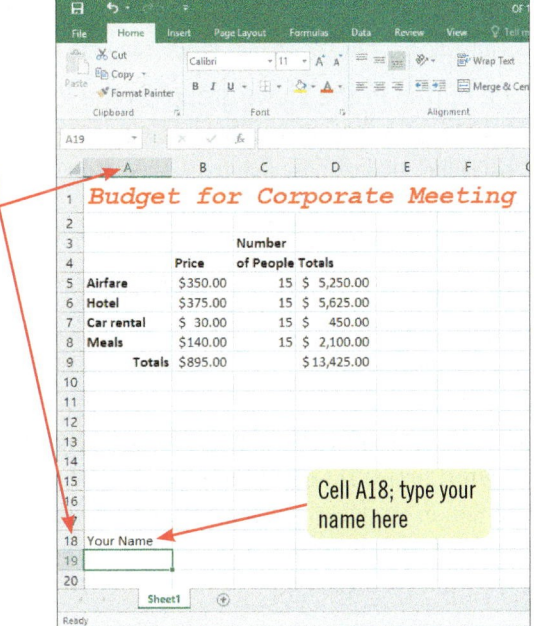

Address for cell A18 formed by column A and row 18

Cell A18; type your name here

Working in Compatibility Mode

Not everyone upgrades to the newest version of Office. As a general rule, new software versions are **backward compatible**, meaning that documents saved by an older version can be read by newer software. To open documents created in older Office versions, Office 2016 includes a feature called Compatibility Mode. When you use Office 2016 to open a file created in an earlier version of Office, "Compatibility Mode" appears in the title bar, letting you know the file was created in an earlier but usable version of the program. If you are working with someone who may not be using the newest version of the software, you can avoid possible incompatibility problems by saving your file in another, earlier format. To do this in an Office program, click the File tab, click Save As on the navigation bar, then click Browse. In the Save As dialog box, click the Save as type list arrow in the Save As dialog box, then click an option in the list. For example, if you're working in Excel, click Excel 97-2003 Workbook format in the Save as type list to save an Excel file so it can be opened in Excel 97 or Excel 2003.

View and Print Your Work

Each Microsoft Office program lets you switch among various **views** of the document window to show more or fewer details or a different combination of elements that make it easier to complete certain tasks, such as formatting or reading text. Changing your view of a document does not affect the file in any way, it affects only the way it looks on screen. If your computer is connected to a printer or a print server, you can easily print any Office document using the Print button in the Print place in Backstage view. Printing can be as simple as **previewing** the document to see exactly what the printed version will look like and then clicking the Print button. Or, you can customize the print job by printing only selected pages. You can also use the Share place in Backstage view or the Share button on the Ribbon (if available) to share a document, export to a different format, or save it to the cloud. **CASE** *Experiment with changing your view of a Word document, and then preview and print your work.*

STEPS

1. **Click the Word program button ⊞ on the taskbar**

   Word becomes active, and the program window fills the screen.

2. **Click the View tab on the Ribbon**

   In most Office programs, the View tab on the Ribbon includes groups and commands for changing your view of the current document. You can also change views using the View buttons on the status bar.

3. **Click the Read Mode button in the Views group on the View tab**

   The view changes to Read Mode view, as shown in **FIGURE 1-12**. This view shows the document in an easy-to-read, distraction-free reading mode. Notice that the Ribbon is no longer visible on screen.

4. **Click the Print Layout button ▤ on the Status bar**

   You return to Print Layout view, the default view in Word.

5. **Click the File tab, then click Print on the navigation bar**

   The Print place opens. The preview pane on the right displays a preview of how your document will look when printed. Compare your screen to **FIGURE 1-13**. Options in the Settings section enable you to change margins, orientation, and related options before printing. To change a setting, click it, and then click a new setting. For instance, to change from Letter paper size to Legal, click Letter in the Settings section, then click Legal on the menu that opens. The document preview updates as you change the settings. You also can use the Settings section to change which pages to print. If your computer is connected to multiple printers, you can click the current printer in the Printer section, then click the one you want to use. The Print section contains the Print button and also enables you to select the number of copies of the document to print.

6. **If your school allows printing, click the Print button in the Print place (otherwise, click the Back button ⊙)**

   If you chose to print, a copy of the document prints, and Backstage view closes.

Customizing the Quick Access toolbar

You can customize the Quick Access toolbar to display your favorite commands. To do so, click the Customize Quick Access Toolbar button ⯆ in the title bar, then click the command you want to add. If you don't see the command in the list, click More Commands to open the Quick Access Toolbar tab of the current program's Options dialog box. In the Options dialog box, use the Choose commands from list to choose a category, click the desired command in the list on the left, click Add to add it to the Quick Access toolbar, then click OK. To remove a button from the toolbar, click the name in the list on the right in the Options dialog box, then click Remove. To add a command to the Quick Access toolbar as you work, simply right-click the button on the Ribbon, then click Add to Quick Access Toolbar on the shortcut menu. To move the Quick Access toolbar below the Ribbon, click the Customize Quick Access Toolbar button, and then click Show Below the Ribbon.

FIGURE 1-12: Read Mode view

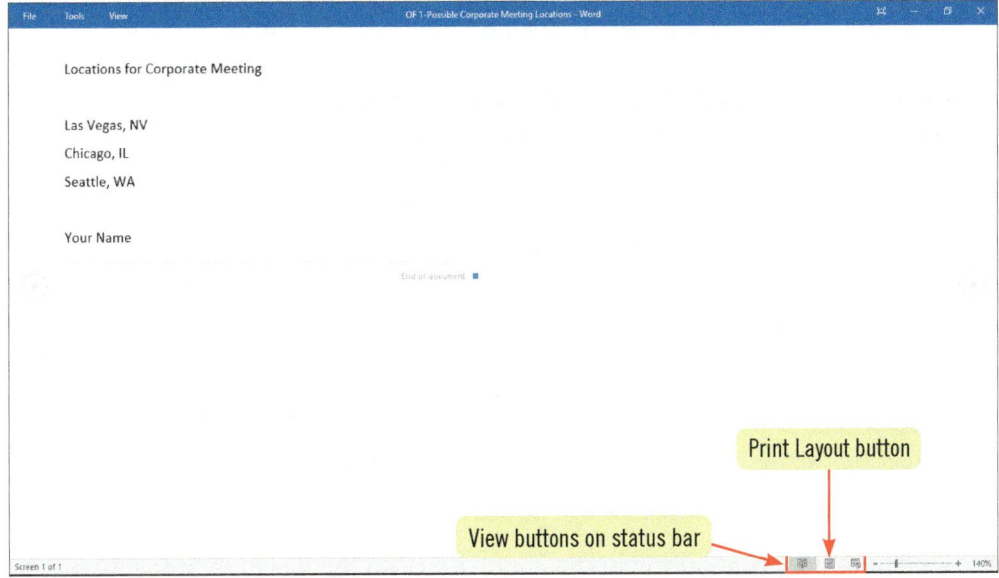

Print Layout button

View buttons on status bar

FIGURE 1-13: Print settings on the File tab

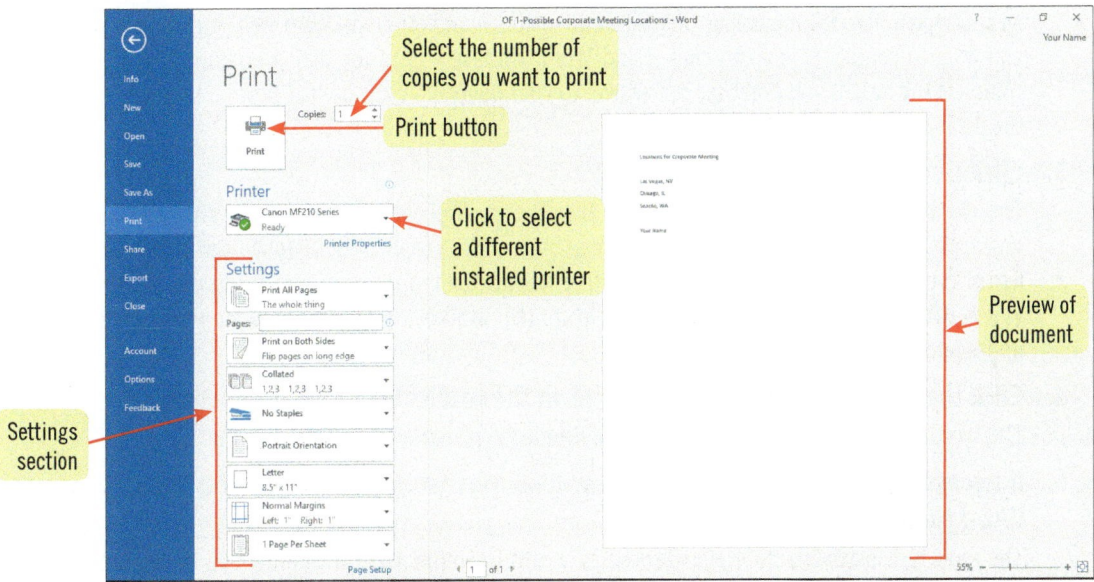

Select the number of copies you want to print

Print button

Click to select a different installed printer

Preview of document

Settings section

Office 2016

Get Help, Close a File, and Exit an App

You can get comprehensive help at any time by pressing [F1] in an Office app or clicking the Help button on the title bar. You can also get help in the form of a ScreenTip by pointing to almost any icon in the program window. When you're finished working in an Office document, you have a few choices for ending your work session. You close a file by clicking the File tab, then clicking Close; you exit a program by clicking the Close button on the title bar. Closing a file leaves a program running, while exiting a program closes all the open files in that program as well as the program itself. In all cases, Office reminds you if you try to close a file or exit a program and your document contains unsaved changes. **CASE** ▶ *Explore the Help system in Microsoft Office, and then close your documents and exit any open programs.*

STEPS

1. **Point to the Zoom button in the Zoom group on the View tab of the Ribbon**
   A ScreenTip appears that describes how the Zoom button works and explains where to find other zoom controls.

2. **Click the Tell me box above the Ribbon, then type Choose a template**
   As you type in the Tell me box, a Smart list anticipates what you might want help with. If you see the task you want to complete, you can click it and Word will take you to the dialog box or options you need to complete the task. If you don't see the answer to your query, you can use the bottom two options to search the database.

3. **Click Get Help on "choose a template"**
   The Word Help window opens, as shown in **FIGURE 1-14**, displaying help results for choosing a template in Word. Each entry is a hyperlink you can click to open a list of topics. The Help window also includes a toolbar of useful Help commands such as printing and increasing the font size for easier readability, and a Search field. Office.com supplements the help content available on your computer with a wide variety of up-to-date topics, templates, and training.

4. **Click the Where do I find templates link in the results list Word Help window**
   The Word Help window changes, and a more detailed explanation appears below the topic.

5. **If necessary, scroll down until the Download Microsoft Office templates topic fills the Word Help window**
   The topic is displayed in the Help window, as shown in **FIGURE 1-15**. The content in the window explains that you can create a wide variety of documents using a template (a pre-formatted document) and that you can get many templates free of charge.

6. **Click the Keep Help on Top button 📌 in the lower-right corner of the window**
   The Pin Help button rotates so the pin point is pointed towards the bottom of the screen: this allows you to read the Help window while you work on your document.

7. **Click the Word document window, notice the Help window remains visible**

8. **Click a blank area of the Help window, click 📌 to Unpin Help, click the Close button ✕ in the Help window, then click the Close button ✕ in the Word program window**
   Word closes, and the Excel program window is active.

9. **Click the Close button ✕ in the Excel program window, click the PowerPoint app button 📘 on the taskbar if necessary, then click the Close button ✕ to exit PowerPoint**
   Excel and PowerPoint both close.

FIGURE 1-14: Word Help window

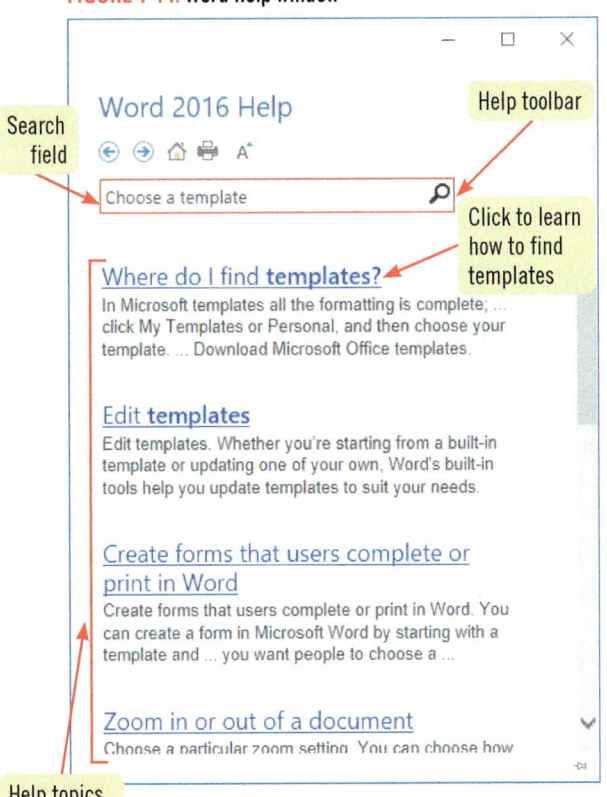

- Search field
- Help toolbar
- Click to learn how to find templates
- Help topics are updated frequently; your list may differ

FIGURE 1-15: Create a document Help topic

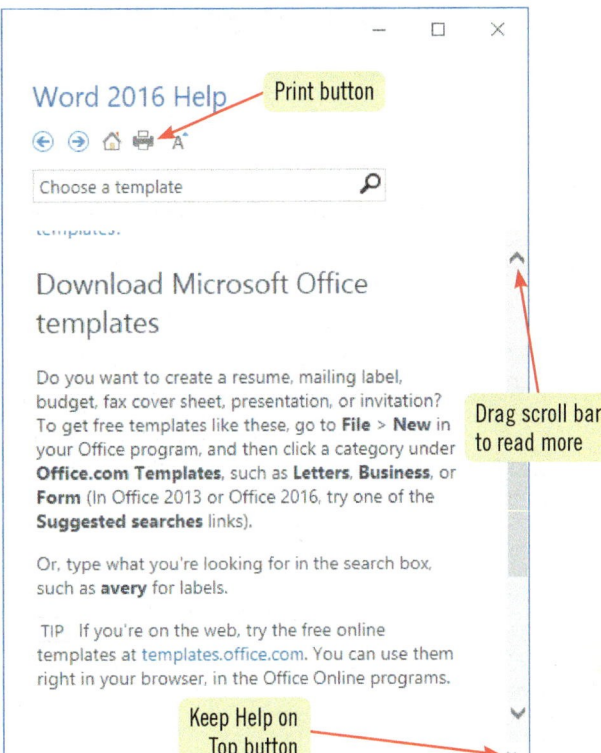

- Print button
- Drag scroll bar to read more
- Keep Help on Top button

Using sharing features and co-authoring capabilities

If you are using Word, Excel, or PowerPoint, you can take advantage of the Share feature, which makes it easy to share your files that have been saved to OneDrive. When you click the Share button, you will be asked to invite others to share the file. To do this, type in the name or email addresses in the Invite people text box. When you invite others, you have the opportunity to give them different levels of permission. You might want some people to have read-only privileges; you might want others to be able to make edits. Also available in Word, Excel, and PowerPoint is real-time co-authoring capabilities for files stored on OneDrive. Once a file on OneDrive is opened and all the users have been given editing privileges, all the users can make edits simultaneously. On first use, each user will be prompted to automatically share their changes.

Recovering a document

Each Office program has a built-in recovery feature that allows you to open and save files that were open at the time of an interruption such as a power failure. When you restart the program(s) after an interruption, the Document Recovery task pane opens on the left side of your screen displaying both original and recovered versions of the files that were open. If you're not sure which file to open (original or recovered), it's usually better to open the recovered file because it will contain the latest information. You can, however, open and review all versions of the file that were recovered and save the best one. Each file listed in the Document Recovery task pane displays a list arrow with options that allow you to open the file, save it as is, delete it, or show repairs made to it during recovery.

Practice

Concepts Review

Label the elements of the program window shown in FIGURE 1-16.

FIGURE 1-16

Match each project with the program for which it is best suited.

8. **Microsoft PowerPoint**
9. **Microsoft Word**
10. **Microsoft Excel**
11. **Microsoft Access**

a. Corporate convention budget with expense projections
b. Presentation for city council meeting
c. Business cover letter for a job application
d. Department store inventory

Independent Challenge 1

You just accepted an administrative position with a local independently owned insurance agent who has recently invested in computers and is now considering purchasing a subscription to Office 365. You have been asked to think of uses for the apps and you put your ideas in a Word document.

a. Start Word, create a new Blank document, then save the document as **OF 1-Microsoft Office Apps Uses** in the location where you store your Data Files.
b. Change the zoom factor to 120%, type **Microsoft Access**, press [Enter] twice, type **Microsoft Excel**, press [Enter] twice, type **Microsoft PowerPoint**, press [Enter] twice, type **Microsoft Word**, press [Enter] twice, then type your name.
c. Click the line beneath each program name, type at least two tasks you can perform using that program (each separated by a comma), then press [Enter].
d. Save the document, then submit your work to your instructor as directed.
e. Exit Word.

Getting Started with Access 2016

CASE Julia Rice is the developer for a new initiative at Reason 2 Go (R2G), a specialized type of travel company that combines volunteer opportunities and tourism into meaningful experiences for its customers. Julia has been asked to create products to meet a market demand for shorter experiences in the United States. Julia uses Microsoft Access 2016 to store, maintain, and analyze customer and trip information.

Module Objectives

After completing this module, you will be able to:

- Understand relational databases
- Explore a database
- Create a database
- Create a table

- Create primary keys
- Relate two tables
- Enter data
- Edit data

Files You Will Need

R2G-1.accdb	Contacts-1.accdb
LakeHomes-1.accdb	Basketball-1.accdb
Salvage-1.accdb	

Understand Relational Databases

Learning Outcomes
- Describe relational database concepts
- Explain when to use a database
- Compare a relational database to a spreadsheet

Microsoft Access 2016 is relational database software that runs on the Windows operating system. You use **relational database software** to manage data that is organized into lists, such as information about customers, products, vendors, employees, projects, or sales. Many small companies track customer, inventory, and sales information in a spreadsheet program such as Microsoft Excel. Although Excel offers some list management features, Access provides many more tools and advantages for managing data. Some advantages are due to Access using a relational database model whereas Excel manages data as a single list. **TABLE 1-1** compares the two programs. **CASE** ▶ *You and Julia review the advantages of database software over spreadsheets for managing lists of information.*

DETAILS

The advantages of using Access for database management include the following:

- **Duplicate data is minimized**

  FIGURES 1-1 and **1-2** compare how you might store sales data in a single Excel spreadsheet list versus three related Access tables. With Access, you do not have to reenter information such as a customer's name and address or trip name every time a sale is made, because lists can be linked, or "related," in relational database software.

- **Information is more accurate, reliable, and consistent because duplicate data is minimized**

  The relational nature of data stored in an Access database allows you to minimize duplicate data entry, which creates more accurate, reliable, and consistent information. For example, customer data in a Customers table is entered only once, not every time a customer makes a purchase.

- **Data entry is faster and easier using Access forms**

  Data entry forms (screen layouts) make data entry faster, easier, and more accurate than entering data in a spreadsheet.

- **Information can be viewed and sorted in many ways using Access queries, forms, and reports**

  In Access, you can save multiple queries (questions about the data), data entry forms, and reports, allowing you to use them over and over without performing extra work to re-create a particular view of the data.

- **Information is more secure using Access passwords and security features**

  Access databases can be encrypted and password protected.

- **Several users can share and edit information at the same time**

  Unlike spreadsheets or word-processing documents, more than one person can enter, update, and analyze data in an Access database at the same time.

FIGURE 1-1: Using a spreadsheet to organize sales data

Customer information is duplicated when the same customer purchases multiple trips

Trip information is duplicated when the same trip is purchased by multiple customers

FIGURE 1-2: Using a relational database to organize sales data

TABLE 1-1: Comparing Excel with Access

feature	Excel	Access
Layout	Provides only a tabular spreadsheet layout	Provides tabular layouts as well as the ability to create customized data entry screens called forms
Storage	Restricted to a file's limitations	Virtually unlimited when coupled with the ability to use Microsoft SQL Server to store data
Linked tables	Manages single lists of information—no relational database capabilities	Relates lists of information to reduce data redundancy and create a powerful relational database
Reporting	Limited	Provides the ability to create an unlimited number of reports
Security	Limited to file security options such as marking the file "read-only" or protecting a range of cells	When used with SQL Server, provides extensive security down to the user and data level
Multiuser capabilities	Not allowed	Allows multiple users to simultaneously enter and update data
Data entry	Provides only one spreadsheet layout	Provides the ability to create an unlimited number of data entry forms

Explore a Database

You can start Access in many ways. If you double-click an existing Access database icon or shortcut, that specific database opens directly within Access. This is the fastest way to open an existing Access database. If you start Access on its own, however, you see a window that requires you to make a choice between opening a database and creating a new database. **CASE** *Julia Rice has developed a database called R2G-1, which contains trip information. She asks you to start Access 2016 and review this database.*

STEPS

1. **Start Access**

   Access starts, as shown in **FIGURE 1-3**. This window allows you to open an existing database, create a new database from a template, or create a new blank database.

2. **Click the Open Other Files link, navigate to the location where you store your Data Files, click the R2G-1.accdb database, click Open, then click the Maximize button** ▣ **if the Access window is not already maximized**

   The R2G-1.accdb Access database application contains five tables of data named Categories, Customers, Sales, States, and Trips. It also includes five queries, six forms, and four reports. Each of these items (table, query, form, and report) is a different type of **object** in an Access database application and is displayed in the **Navigation Pane**. The purpose of each object is defined in **TABLE 1-2**. To learn about an Access database application, you explore its objects.

3. **In the Navigation Pane, double-click the Trips table to open it, then double-click the Customers table to open it**

   The Trips and Customers tables open in Datasheet View to display the data they store. A **table** is the fundamental building block of a relational database because it stores all of the data.

4. **In the Navigation Pane, double-click the TripSales query to open it, double-click any occurrence of Heritage in "American Heritage Tour," type Legacy, then click any other row**

   A **query** selects a subset of data from one or more tables. In this case, the TripSales query selects data from the Trips, Sales, and Customers tables. Entering or editing data in one object changes that information in every other object of the database, because all objects build on the same data stored only in the tables.

5. **Double-click the CustomerRoster form to open it, double-click Tour in "American Legacy Tour," type Project, then click any name in the middle part of the window**

   An Access **form** is a data entry screen. Users prefer forms for data entry (rather than editing and entering data in tables and queries) because forms can present information in any layout and include command buttons to make common tasks easy to perform.

6. **Double-click the TripSales report to open it**

   An Access **report** is a professional printout that can be distributed electronically or on paper. As shown in **FIGURE 1-4**, the edits made to the American Legacy Project name have carried through to the report, demonstrating the power and productivity of a relational database.

7. **Click the Close button** ✖ **in the upper-right corner of the window**

   Clicking the Close button in the upper-right corner of the window closes Access as well as the database on which you are working. Changes to data, such as the edits you made to the American Legacy Project record, are automatically saved as you work. Access will prompt you to save design changes to objects before it closes.

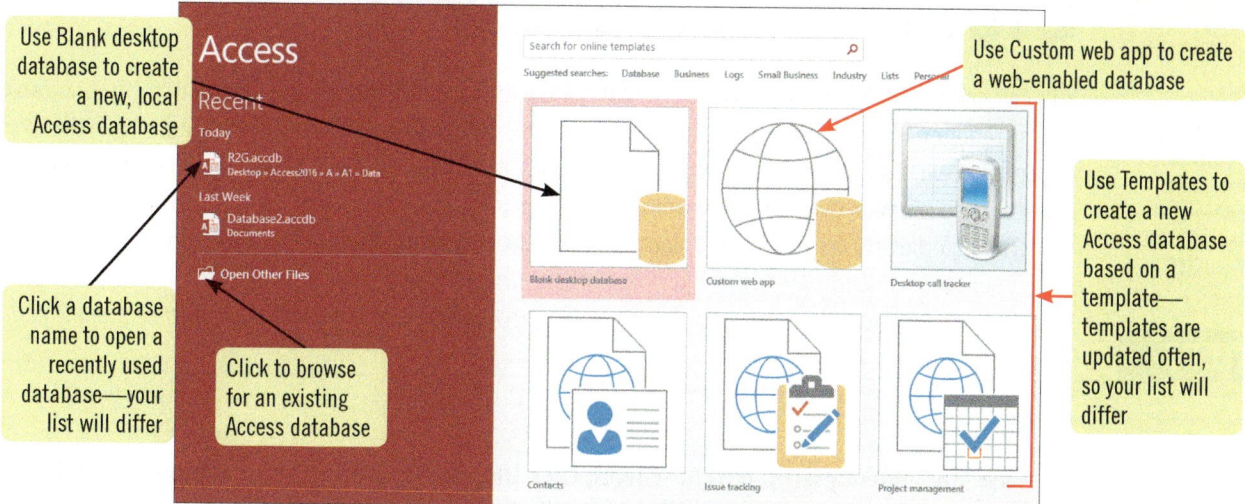

FIGURE 1-3: Opening the Microsoft Access 2016 window

Use Blank desktop database to create a new, local Access database

Use Custom web app to create a web-enabled database

Use Templates to create a new Access database based on a template—templates are updated often, so your list will differ

Click a database name to open a recently used database—your list will differ

Click to browse for an existing Access database

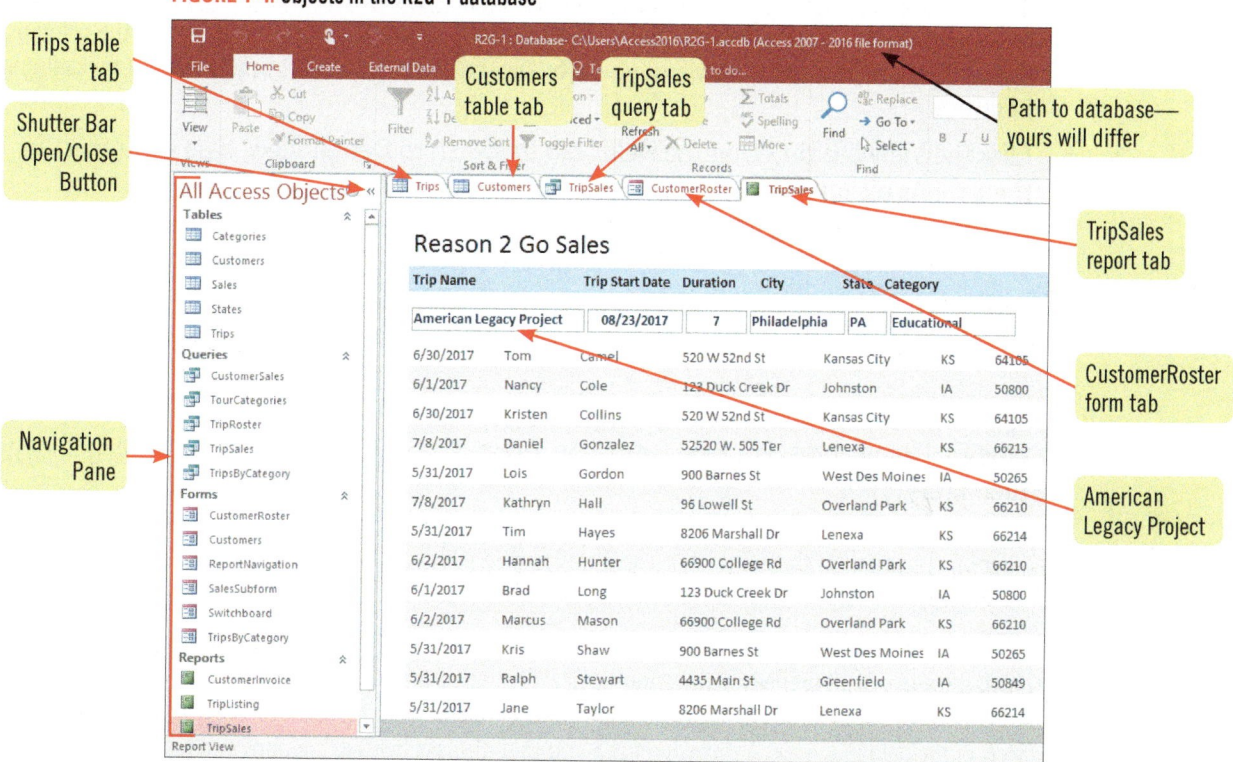

FIGURE 1-4: Objects in the R2G-1 database

Trips table tab

Shutter Bar Open/Close Button

Customers table tab

TripSales query tab

Path to database—yours will differ

TripSales report tab

CustomerRoster form tab

Navigation Pane

American Legacy Project

TABLE 1-2: Access objects and their purpose

object	icon	purpose
Table		Contains all of the data within the database in a spreadsheet-like view called Datasheet View; tables are linked with a common field to create a relational database, which minimizes redundant data
Query		Allows you to select a subset of fields or records from one or more tables; create a query when you have a question about the data
Form		Provides an easy-to-use data entry screen
Report		Provides a professional presentation of data with headers, footers, graphics, and calculations on groups of records

Access 2016

Learning Outcomes
- Create a database
- Create a table
- Define key database terms

Create a Database

You can create a database using an Access **template**, a sample database provided within the Microsoft Access program, or you can start with a blank database to create a database from scratch. Your decision depends on whether Access has a template that closely resembles the type of data you plan to manage. If it does, building your own database from a template might be faster than creating the database from scratch. Regardless of which method you use, you can always modify the database later, tailoring it to meet your specific needs. **CASE** ▶ *Julia Rice reasons that the best way for you to learn Access is to start a new database from scratch, so she asks you to create a new database that will track customer communication.*

STEPS

1. **Start Access**

2. **Click the Blank desktop database icon, click the Browse button 📁, navigate to the location where you store your Data Files, type R2G in the File name box, click OK, then click the Create button**

   A new database file with a single table named Table1 is created, as shown in **FIGURE 1-5**. Although you might be tempted to start entering data into the table, a better way to build a table is to first define the columns, or **fields**, of data that the table will store. **Table Design View** provides the most options for defining fields.

3. **Click the View button ☑ on the Fields tab to switch to Design View, type Customers in the Save As dialog box as the new table name, then click OK**

   The table name changes from Table1 to Customers, and you are positioned in Table Design View, a window you use to name and define the fields of a table. Access automatically created a field named ID with an AutoNumber data type. The **data type** is a significant characteristic of a field because it determines what type of data the field can store such as text, dates, or numbers. See **TABLE 1-3** for more information about data types.

4. **Type CustID to rename ID to CustID, press [▼] to move to the first blank Field Name cell, type FirstName, press [▼], type LastName, press [▼], type Phone, press [▼], type Birthday, then press [▼]**

   Be sure to always separate a person's first and last names into two fields so that you can easily sort, find, and filter on either part of the name later. The Birthday field will only contain dates, so you should change its data type from Short Text (the default data type) to Date/Time.

5. **Click Short Text in the Birthday row, click the list arrow, then click Date/Time**

   With these five fields properly defined for the new Customers table, as shown in **FIGURE 1-6**, you're ready to enter data. You switch back to Datasheet View to enter or edit data. **Datasheet View** is a spreadsheet-like view of the data in a table. A **datasheet** is a grid that displays fields as columns and records as rows. The new **field names** you just defined are listed at the top of each column.

6. **Click the View button 🔲 to switch to Datasheet View, click Yes when prompted to save the table, press [Tab] to move to the FirstName field, type *your* first name, press [Tab] to move to the LastName field, type *your* last name, press [Tab] to move to the Phone field, type 555-666-7777, press [Tab], type 1/32/1990, then press [Tab]**

   Because 1/32/1990 is not a valid date, Access does not allow you to make that entry and displays an error message, as shown in **FIGURE 1-7**. This shows that selecting the best data type for each field in Table Design View before entering data in Datasheet View helps prevent data entry errors.

TROUBLE
Tab through the CustID field rather than typing a value. The CustID value automatically increments to the next number.

7. **Press [Esc], edit the Birthday entry for the first record to 1/31/1990, press [Tab], enter two more sample records using realistic data, right-click the Customers table tab, then click Close to close the Customers table**

FIGURE 1-5: Creating a database with a new table

FIGURE 1-6: Defining field names and data types for the Customers table in Table Design View

FIGURE 1-7: Entering your first record in the Customers table

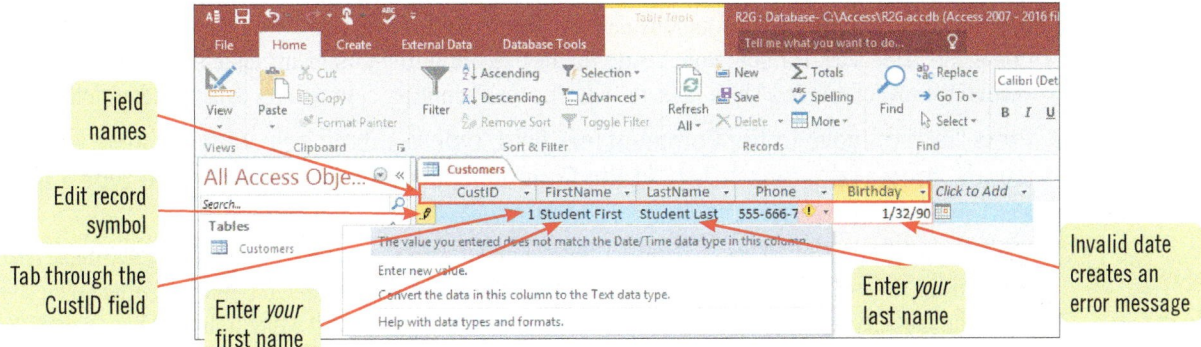

TABLE 1-3: Data types

data type	description of data
Short Text	Text or numbers not used in calculations such as a name, zip code, or phone number less than 255 characters
Long Text	Lengthy text greater than 255 characters, such as comments or notes
Number	Numeric data that can be used in calculations, such as quantities
Date/Time	Dates and times
Currency	Monetary values
AutoNumber	Sequential integers controlled by Access
Yes/No	Only two values: Yes or No
OLE Object	OLE (Object Linking and Embedding) objects such as an Excel spreadsheet or Word document
Hyperlink	Web and email addresses or links to local files
Attachment	Files such as .jpg images, spreadsheets, and documents
Calculated	Result of a calculation based on other fields in the table
Lookup Wizard	The Lookup Wizard helps you set Lookup properties, which display a drop-down list of values for the field; after using the Lookup Wizard, the final data type for the field is either Short Text or Number depending on the values in the drop-down list

Create a Table

Learning Outcomes
- Create a table in Table Design View
- Set appropriate data types for fields

After creating your database and first table, you need to create new, related tables to build a relational database. Creating a table consists of these essential tasks: defining the fields in the table, selecting an appropriate data type for each field, naming the table, and determining how the table will participate in the relational database. **CASE** *Julia Rice asks you to create another table to store customer comments. The new table will eventually be connected to the Customers table so each customer record in the Customers table may be related to many records in the Comments table.*

STEPS

1. **Click the Create tab on the Ribbon, then click the Table Design button in the Tables group**

   You create and manipulate the structure of an object in **Design View**.

2. **Enter the field names and data types, as shown in FIGURE 1-8**

   The Comments table will contain four fields. CommentID is set with an AutoNumber data type so each record is automatically numbered by Access. The CommentText field has a Long Text data type so a long comment can be recorded. CommentDate is a Date/Time field to identify the date of the comment. CustID has a Number data type and will be used to link the Comments table to the Customers table later.

   > **TROUBLE**
   > To rename an object, close it, right-click it in the Navigation Pane, and then click Rename.

3. **Click the View button ▦ to switch to Datasheet View, click Yes when prompted to save the table, type Comments as the table name, click OK, then click No when prompted to create a primary key**

   A **primary key field** contains unique data for each record. You'll identify a primary key field for the Comments table later. For now, you'll enter the first record in the Comments table in Datasheet View. A **record** is a row of data in a table. Refer to **TABLE 1-4** for a summary of important database terminology.

4. **Press [Tab] to move to the CommentText field, type Wants to help with the Rose Bowl Parade, press [Tab], type 1/7/17 in the CommentDate field, press [Tab], then type 1 in the CustID field**

   You entered 1 in the CustID field to connect this comment with the customer in the Customers table that has a CustID value of 1. Knowing which CustID value to enter for each comment is difficult. After you relate the tables properly (a task you have not yet performed), Access can make it easier to link each comment to the correct customer.

   > **TROUBLE**
   > The CommentID field is an AutoNumber field, which will automatically increment to provide a unique value. If the number has already incremented beyond 1 for the first record, AutoNumber still works as intended.

5. **Point to the divider line between the CommentText and CommentDate field names, and then double-click the ↔ pointer to widen the CommentText field to read the entire comment, as shown in FIGURE 1-9**

6. **Right-click the Comments table tab, click Close, then click Yes if prompted to save the table**

Creating a table in Datasheet View

You can also create a new table in Datasheet View using the commands on the Fields tab of the Ribbon. However, if you use Design View to design your table before entering data, you will probably avoid some common data entry errors. Design View helps you focus on the appropriate data type for each field.

Selecting the best data type for each field before entering any data into that field helps prevent incorrect data and unintended typos. For example, if a field has a Number, Currency, or Date/Time data type, you will not be able to enter text into that field by mistake.

FIGURE 1-8: Creating the Comments table

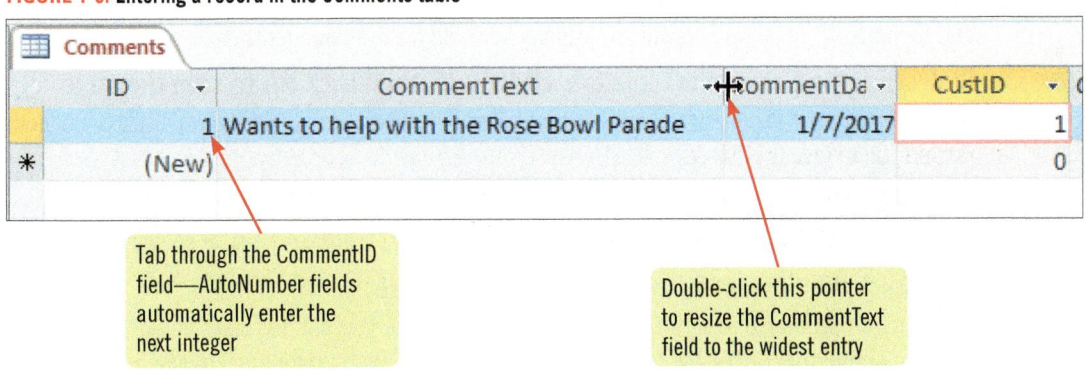

Enter these Field Names →

Enter these Data Types ←

FIGURE 1-9: Entering a record in the Comments table

Tab through the CommentID field—AutoNumber fields automatically enter the next integer

Double-click this pointer to resize the CommentText field to the widest entry

TABLE 1-4: Important database terminology

term	description
Field	A specific piece or category of data such as a first name, last name, city, state, or phone number
Record	A group of related fields that describes a person, place, thing, or transaction such as a customer, location, product, or sale
Key field	A field that contains unique information for each record, such as a customer number for a customer
Table	A collection of records for a single subject such as Customers, Products, or Sales
Relational database	Multiple tables that are linked together to address a business process such as managing trips, sales, and customers at Reason 2 Go
Objects	The parts of an Access database that help you view, edit, manage, and analyze the data: tables, queries, forms, reports, macros, and modules

Create Primary Keys

Learning Outcomes
- Set the primary key field
- Define one-to-many relationships

The **primary key field** of a table serves two important purposes. First, it contains data that uniquely identifies each record. No two records can have the exact same entry in the field designated as the primary key field. Second, the primary key field helps relate one table to another in a **one-to-many relationship**, where one record from one table may be related to many records in the second table. For example, one record in the Customers table may be related to many records in the Comments table. (One customer may have many comments.) The primary key field is always on the "one" side of a one-to-many relationship between two tables. **CASE** *Julia Rice asks you to check that a primary key field has been appropriately identified for each table in the new R2G database.*

STEPS

TROUBLE
Make sure the Design tab is selected on the Ribbon.

QUICK TIP
You can also click the Save button 💾 on the Quick Access Toolbar to save a table.

1. **Right-click the Comments table in the Navigation Pane, then click Design View**

   Table Design View for the Comments table opens. The field with the AutoNumber data type is generally the best candidate for the primary key field in a table because it automatically contains a unique number for each record.

2. **Click the CommentID field if it is not already selected, then click the Primary Key button in the Tools group on the Design tab**

   The CommentID field is now set as the primary key field for the Comments table, as shown in **FIGURE 1-10**.

3. **Right-click the Comments table tab, click Close, then click Yes to save the table**

   Any time you must save design changes to an Access object such as a table, Access displays a dialog box to remind you to save the object.

4. **Right-click the Customers table in the Navigation Pane, then click Design View**

   Access has already set CustID as the primary key field for the Customers table, as shown in **FIGURE 1-11**.

5. **Right-click the Customers table tab, then click Close**

   You were not prompted to save the Customers table because you did not make any design changes. Now that you're sure that each table in the R2G database has an appropriate primary key field, you're ready to link the tables. The primary key field plays a critical role in this relationship.

Object views

Each object has a number of **views** that allow you to complete different tasks. For example, to enter and edit data into the database, use **Datasheet View** for tables and queries and **Form View** for forms. To change the structure of an object, you most often work in **Design View**. Use **Print Preview** to see how a report will appear on a physical piece of paper. Click the arrow at the bottom of the View button on the Design tab of the Ribbon to see all of the available views for an object.

Learning about field properties

Properties are the characteristics that define the field. Two properties are required for every field: Field Name and Data Type. Many other properties, such as Field Size, Format, Caption, and Default Value, are defined in the Field Properties pane in the lower half of a table's Design View. As you add more property entries, you are generally restricting the amount or type of data that can be entered in the field, which increases data entry accuracy. For example, you might change the Field Size property for a State field to 2 to eliminate an incorrect entry such as FLL. Field properties change depending on the data type of the selected field. For example, date fields do not have a Field Size property because Access controls the size of fields with a Date/Time data type.

FIGURE 1-10: Creating a primary key field for the Comments table

FIGURE 1-11: Confirming the primary key field for the Customers table

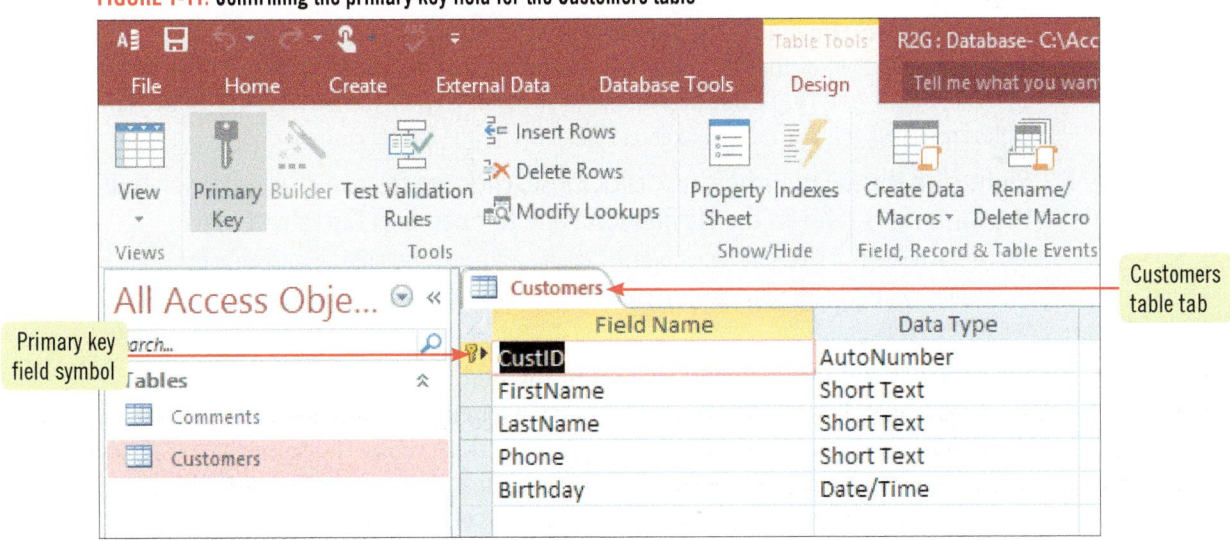

Relate Two Tables

Learning Outcomes
- Define foreign key field
- Create one-to-many relationships
- Set referential integrity

After you create tables and set primary key fields, you must connect the tables in one-to-many relationships to enjoy the benefits of a relational database. A one-to-many relationship between two tables means that one record from the first table is related to many records in the second table. You use a common field to make this connection. The common field is always the primary key field in the table on the "one" side of the relationship. **CASE** *Julia Rice explains that she has new comments to enter into the R2G database. To identify which customer is related to each comment, you define a one-to-many relationship between the Customers and Comments tables.*

STEPS

1. **Click the Database Tools tab on the Ribbon, then click the Relationships button**

TROUBLE

If the Show Table dialog box doesn't appear, click the Show Table button on the Design tab.

2. **In the Show Table dialog box, double-click Customers, double-click Comments, then click Close**

Each table is represented by a small **field list** window that displays the table's field names. A **key symbol** identifies the primary key field in each table. To relate the two tables in a one-to-many relationship, you connect them using a common field, which is always the primary key field on the "one" side of the relationship.

QUICK TIP

Drag a table's title bar to move the field list.

3. **Drag CustID in the Customers field list to the CustID field in the Comments field list**

The Edit Relationships dialog box opens, as shown in **FIGURE 1-12**. **Referential integrity**, a set of Access rules that governs data entry, helps ensure data accuracy.

TROUBLE

If you need to delete an incorrect relationship, right-click a relationship line, then click Delete.

4. **Click the Enforce Referential Integrity check box in the Edit Relationships dialog box, then click Create**

The **one-to-many line** shows the link between the CustID field of the Customers table (the "one" side) and the CustID field of the Comments table (the "many" side, indicated by the **infinity symbol**), as shown in **FIGURE 1-13**. The linking field on the "many" side is called the **foreign key field**. Now that these tables are related, it is much easier to enter comments for the correct customer.

QUICK TIP

To print the Relationships window, click the Relationship Report button on the Design tab, then click Print.

5. **Right-click the Relationships tab, click Close, click Yes to save changes, then double-click the Customers table in the Navigation Pane to open it in Datasheet View**

When you relate two tables in a one-to-many relationship, expand buttons appear to the left of each record in the table on the "one" side of the relationship. In this case, the Customers table is on the "one" side of the relationship.

6. **Click the expand button ⊞ to the left of the first record**

A **subdatasheet** shows the related comment records for each customer. In other words, the subdatasheet shows the records on the "many" side of a one-to-many relationship. The expand button ⊞ also changed to the collapse button ⊟ for the first customer. Widening the CommentText field allows you to see the entire entry in the Comments subdatasheet. Now the task of entering comments for the correct customer is much more straightforward.

TROUBLE

Be careful to enter complete comments for the correct customer, as shown in **FIGURE 1-14**.

7. **Enter two more comments, as shown in FIGURE 1-14**

Interestingly, the CustID field in the Comments table (the foreign key field) is not displayed in the subdatasheet. Behind the scenes, Access is entering the correct CustID value in the Comments table, which is the glue that ties each comment to the correct customer.

8. **Close the Customers table, then click Yes if prompted to save changes**

FIGURE 1-12: Edit Relationships dialog box

CustID field from the Customers table

CustID field from the Comments table

Enforce Referential Integrity check box

One-To-Many relationship, Customers to Comments

FIGURE 1-13: Linking the Customers and Comments tables

Relationships tab

Customers table field list

Comments table field list

CustID is a primary key field and the "one" side of the relationship

CommentID is a primary key field

Number 1 identifies the field on the "one" side of the relationship

One-to-many relationship line

Infinity symbol identifies the field on the "many" side of the relationship

FIGURE 1-14: Entering comments using the subdatasheet

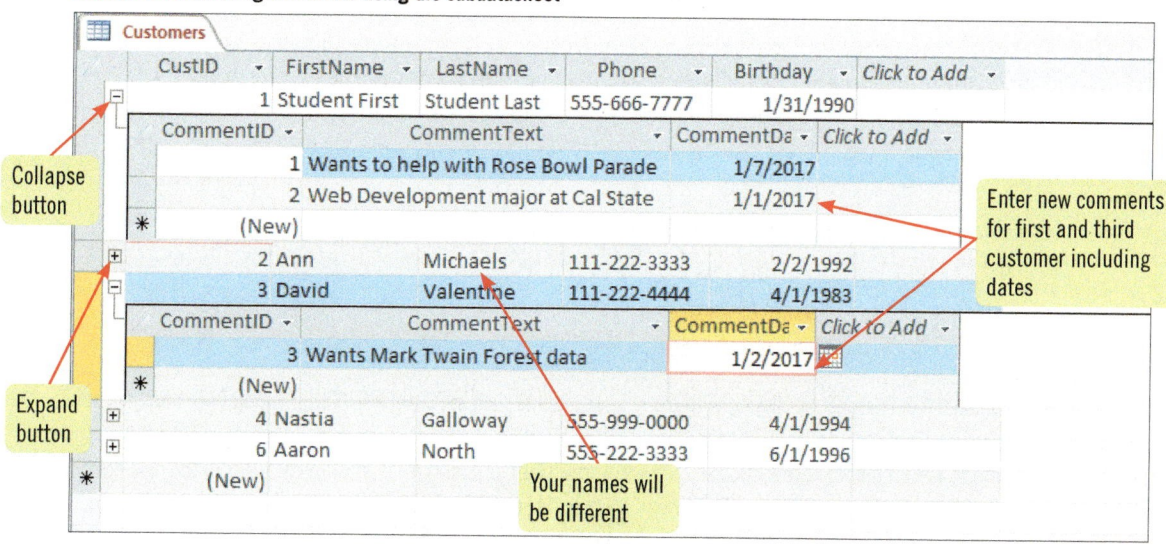

Collapse button

Enter new comments for first and third customer including dates

Expand button

Your names will be different

Enter Data

Learning Outcomes
• Navigate records in a datasheet
• Enter records in a datasheet

Your skill in navigating and entering new records is a key to your success with a relational database. You can use many techniques to navigate through the records in the table's datasheet. **CASE** ▶ *Even though you have already successfully entered some records, Julia Rice asks you to master this essential skill by entering several more customers in the R2G database.*

STEPS

1. **Double-click the Customers table in the Navigation Pane to open it, press [Tab] three times, then press [Enter] three times**

   The Customers table reopens. The Comments subdatasheets are collapsed. Both the [Tab] and [Enter] keys move the focus to the next field. The **focus** refers to which data you would edit if you started typing. When you navigate to the last field of the record, pressing [Tab] or [Enter] advances the focus to the first field of the next record. You can also use the Next record ▶ and Previous record ◀ **navigation buttons** on the navigation bar in the lower-left corner of the datasheet to navigate through the records. The **Current record** text box on the navigation bar tells you the number of the current record as well as the total number of records in the datasheet.

QUICK TIP

Press [Tab] in the CustID AutoNumber field.

2. **Click the FirstName field of the fourth record to position the insertion point to enter a new record**

   You can also use the New (blank) record button ▶✳ on the navigation bar to move to a new record. You enter new records at the end of the datasheet. You learn how to sort and reorder records later. A complete list of navigation keystrokes is shown in **TABLE 1-5**.

QUICK TIP

Access databases are multiuser with one important limitation: Two users cannot edit the same record at the same time. In that case, a message explains that the second user must wait until the first user moves to a different record.

3. **At the end of the datasheet, enter the last three records shown in FIGURE 1-15**

   The **edit record symbol** 🖉 appears to the left of the record you are currently editing. When you move to a different record, Access saves the data. Therefore, Access never prompts you to save data because it performs that task automatically. Saving data automatically allows Access databases to be **multiuser** databases, which means that more than one person can enter and edit data in the same database at the same time.

   Your CustID values might differ from those in **FIGURE 1-15**. Because the CustID field is an **AutoNumber** field, Access automatically enters the next consecutive number into the field as it creates the record. If you delete a record or are interrupted when entering a record, Access discards the value in the AutoNumber field and does not reuse it. Therefore, AutoNumber values do not represent the number of records in your table. Instead, they provide a unique value per record, similar to check numbers.

Changing from Navigation mode to Edit mode

If you navigate to another area of the datasheet by clicking with the mouse pointer instead of pressing [Tab] or [Enter], you change from **Navigation mode** to Edit mode. In **Edit mode**, Access assumes that you are trying to make changes to the current field value, so keystrokes such as [Ctrl][End], [Ctrl][Home], [←], and [→] move the insertion point within the field. To return to Navigation mode, press [Tab] or [Enter] (thus moving the focus to the next field), or press [↑] or [↓] (thus moving the focus to a different record).

FIGURE 1-15: New records in the Customers table

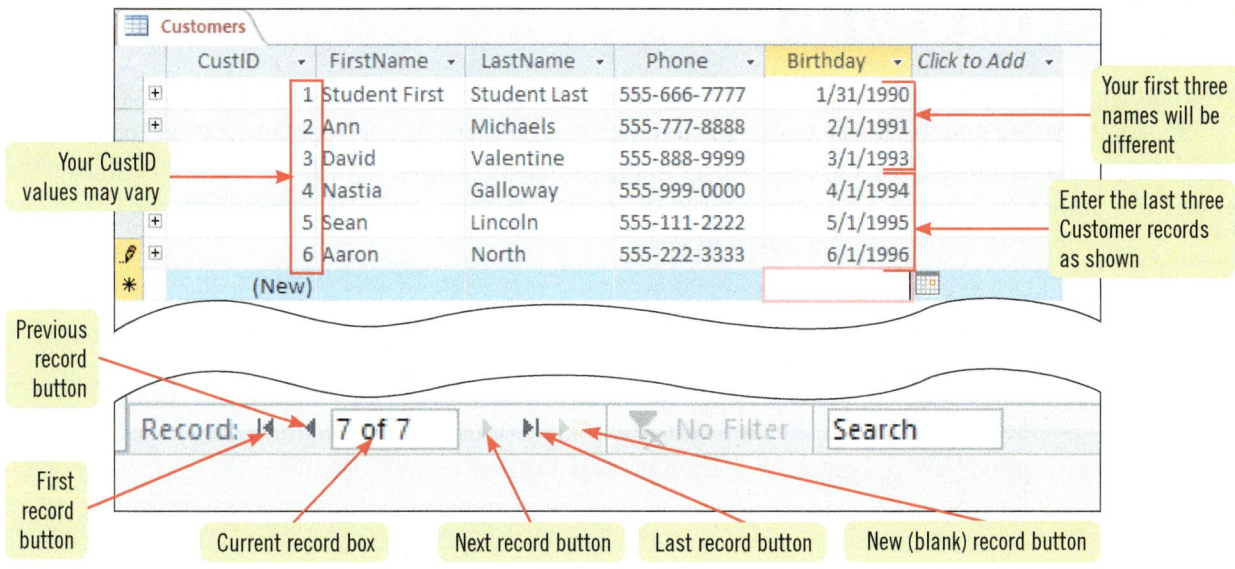

Your first three names will be different

Your CustID values may vary

Enter the last three Customer records as shown

Previous record button

First record button

Current record box

Next record button

Last record button

New (blank) record button

TABLE 1-5: Navigation mode keyboard shortcuts

shortcut key	moves to the
[Tab], [Enter], or [→]	Next field of the current record
[Shift][Tab] or [←]	Previous field of the current record
[Home]	First field of the current record
[End]	Last field of the current record
[Ctrl][Home] or [F5]	First field of the first record
[Ctrl][End]	Last field of the last record
[↑]	Current field of the previous record
[↓]	Current field of the next record

Cloud computing

Using **OneDrive**, a free service from Microsoft, you can store files in the "cloud" and retrieve them anytime you are connected to the Internet. Saving your files to the OneDrive is one example of cloud computing. **Cloud computing** means you are using an Internet resource to complete your work.

Access 2016

Edit Data

Updating existing data in a database is another critical database task. To change the contents of an existing record, navigate to the field you want to change and type the new information. You can delete unwanted data by clicking the field and using [Backspace] or [Delete] to delete text to the left or right of the insertion point. Other data entry keystrokes are summarized in TABLE 1-6. **CASE** *Julia Rice asks you to correct two records in the Customers table.*

STEPS

1. **Select the phone number in the Phone field of the second record, type 111-222-3333, press [Enter], type 2/2/92, then press [Enter]**

   You changed the telephone number and birth date of the second customer. When you entered the last two digits of the year value, Access inserted the first two digits after you pressed [Enter]. You'll also update the third customer.

2. **Press [Enter] enough times to move to the Phone field of the third record, type 111-222-4444, then press [Esc]**

   Pressing [Esc] once removes the current field's editing changes, so the Phone value changes back to the previous entry. Pressing [Esc] twice removes all changes to the current record. When you move to another record, Access saves your edits, so you can no longer use [Esc] to remove editing changes to the current record. You can, however, click the Undo button ↶ on the Quick Access Toolbar to undo changes to a previous record.

3. **Retype 111-222-4444, press [Enter], type 3/1/83 in the Birthday field, press [Enter], click the 3/1/83 date you just entered, click the Calendar icon 📅, then click April 1, 1983, as shown in FIGURE 1-16**

   When you are working in the Birthday field, which has a Date/Time data type, you can enter a date from the keyboard or use the **Calendar Picker**, a pop-up calendar, to find and select a date.

4. **Click the record selector for the fifth record (Sean Lincoln), click the Delete button in the Records group on the Home tab, then click Yes**

   A message warns that you cannot undo a record deletion. The Undo button ↶ is dimmed, indicating that you cannot use it. The Customers table now has five records, as shown in FIGURE 1-17. Keep in mind that your CustID values might differ from those in the figure because they are controlled by Access.

5. **Click the File tab, click Print, then click Print Preview to review the printout of the Customers table before printing**

6. **Click the Close Print Preview button, then click the Close button ✕ in the upper-right corner of the window to close the R2G.accdb database and Access 2016**

FIGURE 1-16: Editing customer records

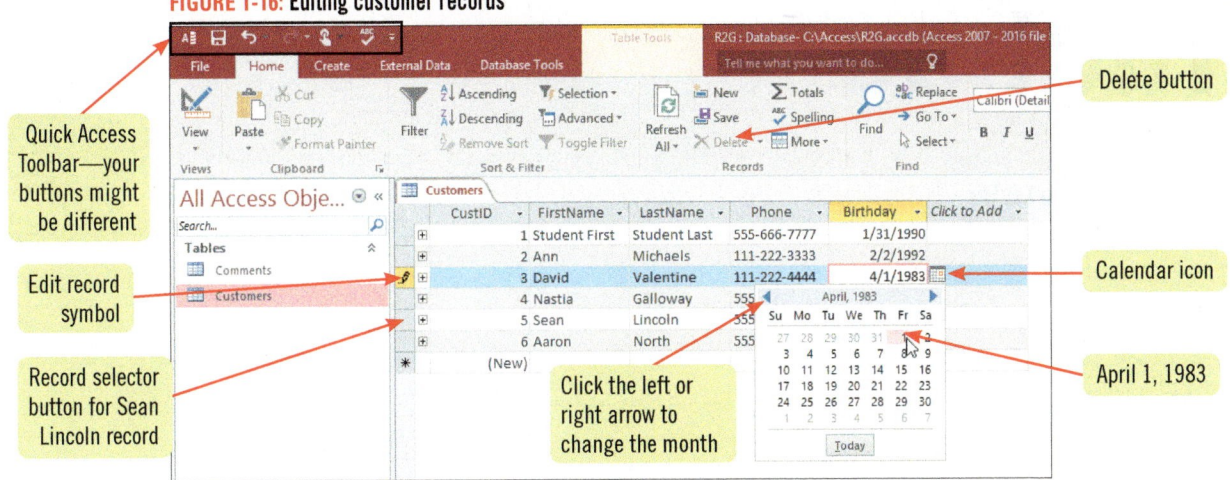

FIGURE 1-17: Final Customers datasheet

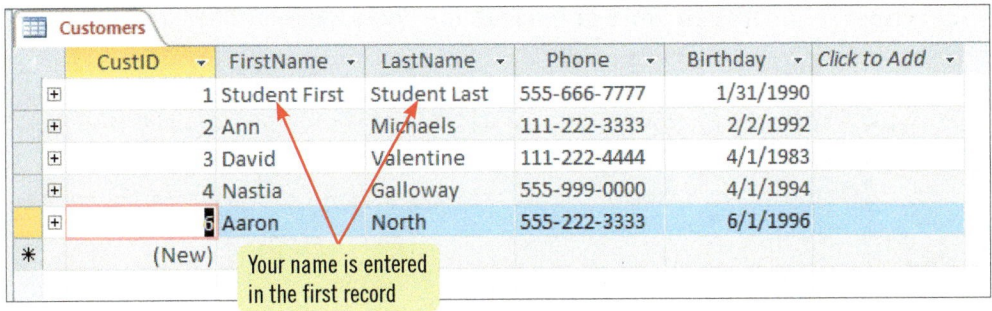

TABLE 1-6: Edit mode keyboard shortcuts

editing keystroke	action
[Backspace]	Deletes one character to the left of the insertion point
[Delete]	Deletes one character to the right of the insertion point
[F2]	Switches between Edit and Navigation mode
[Esc]	Undoes the change to the current field
[Esc][Esc]	Undoes all changes to the current record
[F7]	Starts the spell-check feature
[Ctrl][']	Inserts the value from the same field in the previous record into the current field
[Ctrl][;]	Inserts the current date in a Date field

Resizing and moving datasheet columns

You can resize the width of a field in a datasheet by dragging the column separator, the thin line that separates the field names to the left or right. The pointer changes to ↔ as you make the field wider or narrower. Release the mouse button when you have resized the field. To adjust the column width to accommodate the widest entry in the field, double-click the column separator. To move a column, click the field name to select the entire column, then drag the field name left or right.

Practice

Concepts Review

Label each element of the Access window shown in FIGURE 1-18.

FIGURE 1-18

Match each term with the statement that best describes it.

11. **Field**
12. **Record**
13. **Table**
14. **Datasheet**
15. **Query**
16. **Form**
17. **Report**

a. A subset of data from one or more tables

b. A collection of records for a single subject, such as all the customer records

c. A professional printout of database information

d. A spreadsheet-like grid that displays fields as columns and records as rows

e. A group of related fields for one item, such as all of the information for one customer

f. A category of information in a table, such as a company name, city, or state

g. An easy-to-use data entry screen

Select the best answer from the list of choices.

18. **When you create a new database, which object is created first?**
    a. Module
    b. Query
    c. Table
    d. Form

19. **Which of the following is *not* a typical benefit of relational databases?**
    a. Minimized duplicate data entry
    b. More accurate data
    c. Tables automatically create needed relationships
    d. More consistent data

20. **Which of the following is *not* an advantage of managing data with relational database software such as Access versus spreadsheet software such as Excel?**
    a. Allows multiple users to enter data simultaneously
    b. Uses a single table to store all data
    c. Provides data entry forms
    d. Reduces duplicate data entry

Skills Review

1. **Understand relational databases.**
   a. Write down five advantages of managing database information in Access versus using a spreadsheet.
   b. Write a sentence to explain how the terms field, record, table, and relational database relate to one another.

2. **Explore a database.**
   a. Start Access.
   b. Open the LakeHomes-1.accdb database from the location where you store your Data Files. Click Enable Content if a yellow Security Warning message appears.
   c. Open each of the four tables to study the data they contain. Complete the following table:

table name	number of records	number of fields

   d. Double-click the ListingsByRealtor query in the Navigation Pane to open it. Change any occurrence of Gordon Bono to *your* name. Move to another record to save your changes.
   e. Double-click the RealtorsMainForm in the Navigation Pane to open it. Use the navigation buttons to navigate through the 13 realtors to observe each realtor's listings.
   f. Double-click the RealtorListingReport in the Navigation Pane to open it. The records are listed in ascending order by realtor last name. Scroll through the report to make sure your name is positioned correctly.
   g. Close the LakeHomes-1 database, then close Access 2016.

3. **Create a database.**
   a. Start Access, click the Blank desktop database icon, use the Browse button to navigate to the location where you store your Data Files, type **LakeHomeMarketing** as the filename, click OK, and then click Create to create a new database named LakeHomeMarketing.accdb.

Skills Review (continued)

b. Switch to Table Design View, name the table **Prospects**, then enter the following fields and data types:

field name	data type
ProspectID	AutoNumber
ProspectFirst	Short Text
ProspectLast	Short Text
Phone	Short Text
Email	Hyperlink
Street	Short Text
City	Short Text
State	Short Text
Zip	Short Text

c. Save the table, switch to Datasheet View, and enter two records using your name in the first record and your instructor's name in the second. Tab through the ProspectID field, an AutoNumber field.

d. Enter **TN** (Tennessee) as the value in the State field for both records. Use school or fictitious (rather than personal) data for all other field data, and be sure to fill out each record completely.

e. Widen each column in the Prospects table so that all data is visible, then save and close the Prospects table.

4. Create a table.

a. Click the Create tab on the Ribbon, click the Table Design button in the Tables group, then create a new table with the following two fields and data types:

field name	data type
State2	Short Text
StateName	Short Text

b. Save the table with the name **States**. Click No when asked if you want Access to create the primary key field.

5. Create primary keys.

a. In Table Design View of the States table, set the State2 field as the primary key field.

b. Save the States table and open it in Datasheet View.

c. Enter one state record, using **TN** for the State2 value and **Tennessee** for the StateName value to match the State value of TN that you entered for both records in the Prospects table.

d. Close the States table.

6. Relate two tables.

a. From the Database Tools tab, open the Relationships window.

b. Add the States, then the Prospects table to the Relationships window.

c. Drag the bottom edge of the Prospects table to expand the field list to display all of the fields.

d. Drag the State2 field from the States table to the State field of the Prospects table.

e. In the Edit Relationships dialog box, click the Enforce Referential Integrity check box, then click Create. Your Relationships window should look like **FIGURE 1-19**. If you connect the wrong fields by mistake, right-click the line connecting the two fields, click Delete, then try again.

f. Close the Relationships window, and save changes when prompted.

FIGURE 1-19

Skills Review (continued)

7. Enter data.

a. Open the States table and enter the following records:

State2 field	StateName field
CO	Colorado
IA	Iowa
KS	Kansas
MO	Missouri
NE	Nebraska
OK	Oklahoma
WI	Wisconsin
TX	Texas

b. Add three more state records of your choice for a total of 12 records in the States table using the correct two-character abbreviation for the state and the correctly spelled state name.

c. Close and reopen the States table. Notice that Access automatically sorts the records by the values in the primary key field, the State2 field.

8. Edit data.

a. Click the Expand button for the TN record to see the two related records from the Prospects table.

b. Enter two more prospects in the TN subdatasheet using any fictitious but realistic data, as shown in **FIGURE 1-20**. Notice that you are not required to enter a value for the State field, the foreign key field in the subdatasheet.

c. If required by your instructor, print the States datasheet and the Prospects datasheet.

d. Click the Close button in the upper-right corner of the Access window to close all open objects as well as the LakeHomeMarketing.accdb database and Access 2016. If prompted to save any design changes, click Yes.

FIGURE 1-20

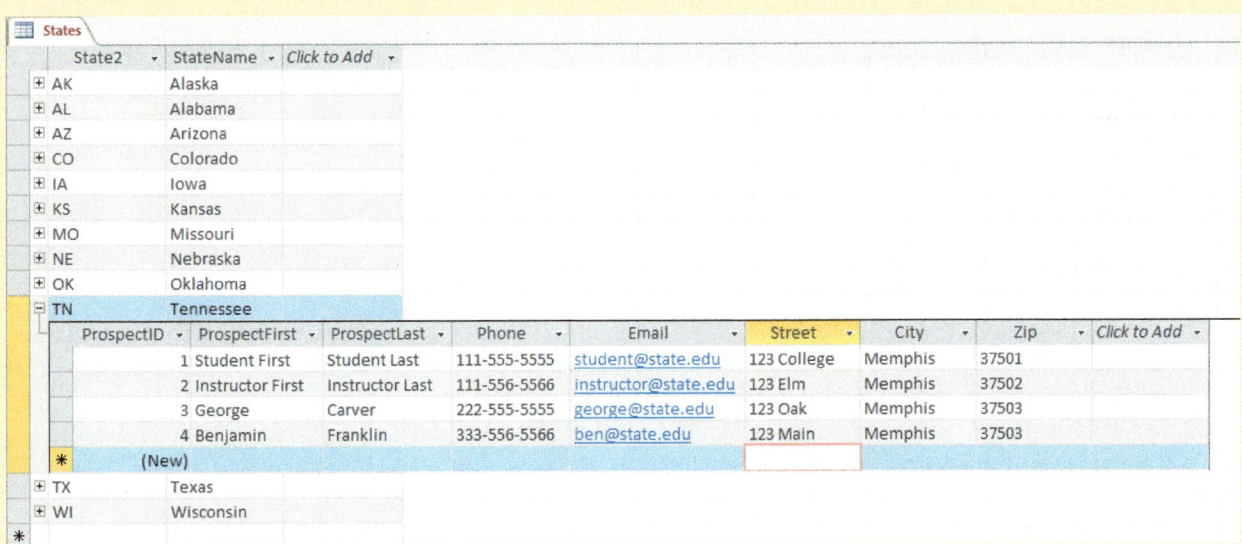

Independent Challenge 1 — For Fridays Class don't fuck up

Consider the following twelve subject areas:

- Telephone directory
- Islands of the Caribbean
- Members of the U.S. House of Representatives
- College course offerings
- Physical activities
- Ancient wonders of the world
- Restaurant menu
- Shopping catalog items
- Vehicles
- Conventions
- Party guest list
- Movie listings

a. For each subject, build a Word table with 4–7 columns and three rows. In the first row, enter field names that you would expect to see in a table used to manage that subject.

b. In the second and third rows of each table, enter two realistic records. The first table, Telephone Directory, is completed as an example to follow.

TABLE: Telephone Directory

FirstName	LastName	Street	Zip	Phone
Marco	Lopez	100 Main Street	88715	555-612-3312
Christopher	Stafford	253 Maple Lane	77824	555-612-1179

c. Consider the following guidelines as you build the table:

Make sure each record represents one item in that table. For example, in the Restaurant Menu table, the following table is a random list of categories of food. The records do not represent one item in a restaurant menu.

Beverage	Appetizer	Meat	Vegetable	Dessert
Milk	Chicken wings	Steak	Carrots	Chocolate cake
Tea	Onion rings	Salmon	Potato	Cheesecake

A better example of records that describe an item in the restaurant menu would be the following:

Category	Description	Price	Calories	Spicy
Appetizer	Chicken wings	$10	800	Yes
Beverage	Milk	$2	250	No

Do not put first and last names in the same field. This prevents you from easily sorting, filtering, or searching on either part of the name later.

For the same reasons, break street, city, state, zip, and country data into separate fields as well.

Do not put values and units of measure such as 5 minutes, 4 lbs, or 6 sq. miles in the same field. This also prevents you from sorting and calculating on the numeric part of the information. Make your field names descriptive such as TimeInMinutes or AreaInSquareMiles so that each record's entries are consistent.

Do not put these tables in one Access database. Putting all of these tables in one Access database would be analogous to putting a letter to your Congressman, a creative poem, and a cover letter to a future employer all in the same Word file. Just as that wouldn't make organizational sense, these tables do not belong together in the same Access database either. Create your sample tables in a Word document to stay focused on proper field and record construction versus the task of building Access tables.

Independent Challenge 2

You are working with several civic groups to coordinate a community-wide recycling effort. You have started a database called Salvage-1, which tracks the clubs, their recyclable material deposits, and the collection centers that are participating.

a. Start Access, then open the Salvage-1.accdb database from the location where you store your Data Files. Enable content if prompted.

b. Open each table's datasheet to study the number of fields and records per table. Notice that there are no expand buttons to the left of any records because relationships have not yet been established between these tables.

c. In a Word document, re-create the following table and fill in the blanks:

table name	number of records	number of fields

d. Close all table datasheets, then open the Relationships window and create the following one-to-many relationships. Drag the tables from the Navigation Pane to the Relationships window, and drag the title bars and borders of the field lists to position them as shown in **FIGURE 1-21**.

field on the "one" side of the relationship	field on the "many" side of the relationship
ClubNumber in Clubs table	ClubNumber in Deposits table
CenterNumber in Centers table	CenterNumber in Deposits table

e. Be sure to enforce referential integrity on all relationships. If you create an incorrect relationship, right-click the line linking the fields, click Delete, and try again. Your final Relationships window should look like **FIGURE 1-21**.

f. Click the Relationship Report button on the Design tab, and if required by your instructor, click Print to print a copy of the Relationships for Salvage-1 report. To close the report, right-click the Relationships for Salvage-1 tab and click Close. Click Yes when prompted to save changes to the report with the name **Relationships for Salvage-1**. Save and close the Relationships window.

g. Open the Clubs table and add a new record with fictitious but realistic data in all of the fields. Enter **8** as the ClubNumber value and your name in the FName (first name) and LName (last name) fields.

h. Expand the subdatasheets for each record in the Clubs table to see the related records from the Deposits table. Which club made the most deposits? Be ready to answer in class. Close the Clubs table.

i. Open the Centers table and add a new record with fictitious but realistic data in all of the fields. Enter your first and last names in the CenterName field and enter **5** as the CenterNumber.

j. Expand the subdatasheets for each record in the Centers table to see the related records from the Deposits table. Which center made the most deposits? Be ready to answer in class. Close the Centers table.

k. Close the Salvage-1.accdb database, then exit Access 2016.

FIGURE 1-21

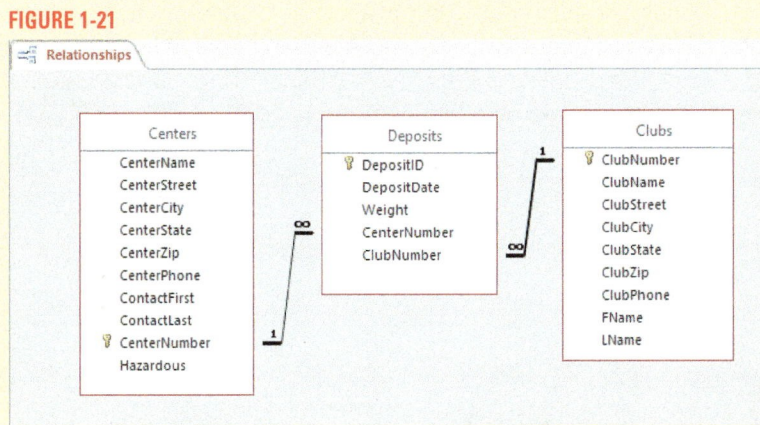

Access 2016

Independent Challenge 3

You are working for an advertising agency that provides social media consulting for small and large businesses in the midwestern United States. You have started a database called Contacts-1, which tracks your company's customers. (*Note*: To complete this Independent Challenge, make sure you are connected to the Internet.)

a. Start Access and open the Contacts-1.accdb database from the location where you store your Data Files. Enable content if prompted.

b. Add a new record to the Customers table, using any local business name, your first and last names, **$10,500** in the YTDSales field, and fictitious but reasonable entries for the rest of the fields.

c. Edit the Sprint Systems record (ID 1). Change the Company name to **A1 Cellular**, and change the Street value to **4455 Mastin St**.

d. Delete the record for EBC (ID 18), then close the Customers table.

e. Create a new table with two fields, **State2** and **StateName**. Assign both fields a Short Text data type. The State2 field will contain the two-letter abbreviation for state names. The StateName field will contain the Set the State2 field as the primary key field, then save the table as **States**.

f. Enter at least three records into the States table, making sure that all of the states used in the Customers datasheet are entered in the States table. This includes **KS Kansas**, **MO Missouri**, and any other state you entered in Step b when you added a new record to the Customers table.

g. Close all open tables. Open the Relationships window, add both the States and Customers field lists to the window, then expand the size of the Customers field list so that all fields are visible. (*Hint*: The field list will not show a vertical scroll bar when all fields in the list are visible.)

h. Build a one-to-many relationship between the States and Customers tables by dragging the State2 field from the States table to the State field of the Customers table to create a one-to-many relationship between the two tables. Enforce referential integrity on the relationship. If you are unable to enforce referential integrity, it means that a value in the State field of the Customers table doesn't have a perfect match in the State2 field of the States table. Open both table datasheets, making sure every state in the State field of the Customers table is also represented in the State2 field of the States table, close all datasheets, then reestablish the one-to-many relationship between the two tables with referential integrity.

i. Click the Relationship Report button on the Design tab, then if requested by your instructor, click Print to print the report.

j. Right-click the Relationships for Contacts-1 tab, then click Close. Click Yes when prompted to save the report with the name **Relationships for Contacts-1**.

k. Close the Relationships window, saving changes as prompted.

l. Close the Contacts-1.accdb database, then exit Access 2016.

Independent Challenge 4: Explore

Now that you've learned about Microsoft Access and relational databases, brainstorm how you might use an Access database in your daily life or career. Start by visiting the Microsoft website, and explore what's new in Access 2016.

(*Note*: To complete this Independent Challenge, make sure you are connected to the Internet.)

a. Using your favorite search engine, look up the keywords *benefits of a relational database* or *benefits of Microsoft Access* to find articles that discuss the benefits of organizing data in a relational database.

b. Read several articles about the benefits of organizing data in a relational database such as Access, identifying three distinct benefits. Use a Word document to record those three benefits. Also, copy and paste the website address of the article you are referencing for each benefit you have identified.

c. In addition, as you read the articles that describe relational database benefits, list any terminology unfamiliar to you, identifying at least five new terms.

d. Using a search engine or a website that provides a computer glossary such as www.whatis.com or www.webopedia.com, look up the definition of the new terms, and enter both the term and the definition of the term in your document as well as the website address where your definition was found.

e. Finally, based on your research and growing understanding of Access 2016, list three ways you could use an Access database to organize, enhance, or support the activities and responsibilities of your daily life or career. Type your name at the top of the document, and submit it to your instructor as requested.

Visual Workshop

Open the Basketball-1.accdb database from the location where you store your Data Files, then enable content if prompted. Open the Offense query datasheet, which lists offensive statistics by player by game. Modify any of the Matthew Douglas records to contain your first and last names, then move to a different record, observing the power of a relational database to modify every occurrence of that name throughout the database. Close the Offense query, then open the Players table. Note that there are no expand buttons to the left of the records, indicating that this table does not participate on the "one" side of a one-to-many relationship. Close the Players table and open the Relationships window. Drag the tables from the Navigation Pane and create the relationships with referential integrity, as shown in FIGURE 1-22. Note the one-to-many relationship between the Players and Stats table. Print the Relationships report if requested by your instructor and save it with the name **Relationships for Basketball-1**. Close the report and close and save the Relationships window. Now reopen the Players table noting the expand buttons to the left of each record. Expand the subdatasheet for your name and for several other players to observe the "many" records from the Stats table that are now related to each record in the Players table.

FIGURE 1-22

Building and Using Queries

CASE Julia Rice, trip developer for U.S. group travel at Reason 2 Go, has several questions about the customer and trip information in the R2G database. You'll develop queries to provide Julia with up-to-date answers.

Module Objectives

After completing this module, you will be able to:

- Use the Query Wizard
- Work with data in a query
- Use Query Design View
- Sort and find data

- Filter data
- Apply AND criteria
- Apply OR criteria
- Format a datasheet

Files You Will Need

R2G-2.accdb	HouseOfReps-2.accdb
Salvage-2.accdb	VetClinic-2.accdb
Service-2.accdb	Baseball-2.accdb

Use the Query Wizard

Learning Outcomes
- Describe the purpose for a query
- Create a query with the Simple Query Wizard

A **query** answers a question about the information in the database. A query allows you to select a subset of fields and records from one or more tables and then present the selected data as a single datasheet. A major benefit of working with data through a query is that you can focus on only the specific information you need, rather than navigating through all the fields and records from one or more large tables. You can enter, edit, and navigate data in a query datasheet just like a table datasheet. However, keep in mind that Access data is physically stored only in tables, even though you can select, view, and edit it through other Access objects such as queries and forms. Because a query doesn't physically store the data, a query data-sheet is sometimes called a **logical view** of the data. A query stores a set of **SQL (Structured Query Language)** instructions, but because you can use Access query tools such as Query Design View to create and modify the query, you are not required to write SQL statements to build or use Access queries. Access provides several tools to create a new query, one of which is the Simple Query Wizard. **CASE** *Julia Rice suggests that you use the Simple Query Wizard to create a query that displays fields from the Trips and Customers tables in one datasheet.*

STEPS

1. **Start Access, open the R2G-2.accdb database, enable content if prompted, then maximize the window**

   Access provides several tools to create a new query. One way is to use the **Simple Query Wizard**, which prompts you for the information it needs to create the query.

2. **Click the Create tab on the Ribbon, click the Query Wizard button in the Queries group, then click OK to start the Simple Query Wizard**

   The first Simple Query Wizard dialog box opens, prompting you to select the fields you want to view in the new query. You can select fields from one or more existing tables or queries.

3. **Click the Tables/Queries list arrow, click Table: Trips, double-click TripName, double-click City, double-click Category, then double-click Price**

   So far, you've selected four fields from the Trips table to display basic trip information in this query. You also want to add the first and last name information from the Customers table so you know which customers purchased each trip.

4. **Click the Tables/Queries list arrow, click Table: Customers, double-click FName, then double-click LName**

   You've selected four fields from the Trips table and two from the Customers table for your new query, as shown in **FIGURE 2-1**.

5. **Click Next, click Next to select Detail, select Trips Query in the title text box, type TripCustomerList as the name of the query, then click Finish**

   The TripCustomerList datasheet opens, displaying four fields from the Trips table and two from the Customers table, as shown in **FIGURE 2-2**. The query can show which customers have purchased which Trips because of the one-to-many table relationships established in the Relationships window.

Simple Query Wizard

The **Simple Query Wizard** is a series of dialog boxes that prompt you for the information needed to create a Select query. A **Select query** selects fields from one or more tables in your database and is by far the most common type of query. The other query wizards—Crosstab, Find Duplicates, and Find Unmatched—are used to create queries that do specialized types of data analysis and are covered in Module 10 on advanced queries.

FIGURE 2-1: Selecting fields using the Simple Query Wizard

FIGURE 2-2: TripCustomerList datasheet

TripName	City	Category	Price	FName	LName
Stanley Bay Cleanup	Captiva	Eco	$750	Ralph	Stewart
Stanley Bay Cleanup	Captiva	Eco	$750	Lisa	Gomez
Breckenridge Reconstruction	Breckenridge	Eco	$850	Kristen	Collins
Stanley Bay Cleanup	Captiva	Eco	$750	Kris	Shaw
Stanley Bay Cleanup	Captiva	Eco	$750	Lois	Gordon
Stanley Bay Cleanup	Captiva	Eco	$750	Naresh	Blackwell
Coastal Shore Cleanup	Captiva	Family	$1,000	Julia	Bouchart
Breckenridge Reconstruction	Breckenridge	Eco	$850	Tom	Camel
Golden Hands Venture	Orlando	Family	$900	Shirley	Cruz
Golden Hands Venture	Orlando	Family	$900	Zohra	Bell
Golden Hands Venture	Orlando	Family	$900	Kathryn	Hall
Golden Hands Venture	Orlando	Family	$900	Jose	Edwards
Red Reef Cleanup	Islamadora	Eco	$1,500	Jane	Taylor
Stanley Bay Cleanup	Captiva	Eco	$750	Kori	James
American Heritage Tour	Philadelphia	Educational	$1,200	Sharol	Wood
American Heritage Tour	Philadelphia	Educational	$1,200	Lois	Gordon
American Heritage Tour	Philadelphia	Educational	$1,200	Tim	Hayes
American Heritage Tour	Philadelphia	Educational	$1,200	Frank	Torres
Yosemite Park Cleanup	Sacramento	Eco	$1,250	Tom	Camel
American Heritage Tour	Philadelphia	Educational	$1,200	Jane	Taylor
Yosemite Park Cleanup	Sacramento	Eco	$1,250	Kristen	Collins
American Heritage Tour	Philadelphia	Educational	$1,200	Kris	Shaw
American Heritage Tour	Philadelphia	Educational	$1,200	Ralph	Stewart
American Heritage Tour	Philadelphia	Educational	$1,200	Nancy	Cole
American Heritage Tour	Philadelphia	Educational	$1,200	Brad	Long

Record: 1 of 106   No Filter   Search

106 records

Access 2016

Work with Data in a Query

You enter and edit data in a query datasheet the same way you do in a table datasheet. Because all data is stored in tables, any edits you make to data in a query datasheet are actually stored in the underlying tables and are automatically updated in all views of the data in other queries, forms, and reports. **CASE** ▶ *Julia Rice wants to change the name of one trip and update a city name. You can use the TripCustomerList query datasheet to make these edits.*

STEPS

TROUBLE
Be sure the final TripName is *Captiva Bay Cleanup*, not just *Captiva*.

1. **Double-click Stanley in the TripName field of the first or second record, type Captiva, then click any other record**

   All occurrences of Stanley Bay Cleanup automatically update to Captiva Bay Cleanup because this TripName field value is stored only once in the Trips table. See **FIGURE 2-3**. The TripName is selected from the Trips table and displayed in the TripCustomerList query for each customer who purchased this trip.

2. **Double-click Orlando in the City field of any record for the Golden Hands Venture trip, type College Park, then click any other record**

   All occurrences of Orlando automatically update to College Park for the Golden Hands Venture trip because this value is stored only once in the City field of the Trips table for the Golden Hands Venture record. The Golden Hands Venture trip is displayed in the TripCustomerList query for each customer who purchased that trip.

3. **Click the record selector button to the left of the first record, click the Home tab, click the Delete button in the Records group, then click Yes**

   You can delete records from a query datasheet the same way you delete them from a table datasheet. Notice that the navigation bar now indicates you have 105 records in the datasheet, as shown in **FIGURE 2-4**.

4. **Right-click the TripCustomerList query tab, then click Close**

   Each time a query is opened, it shows a current view of the data. This means that as new trips, customers, or sales are recorded in the database, the next time you open this query, the information will include all updates.

Hiding and unhiding fields in a datasheet

To hide a field in a datasheet, right-click the field name at the top of the datasheet and click the Hide Fields option on the shortcut menu. To unhide a field, right-click any field name, click Unhide Fields, and check the hidden field's check box in the Unhide Columns dialog box.

Freezing and unfreezing fields in a datasheet

In large datasheets, you may want to freeze certain fields so that they remain on the screen at all times. To freeze a field, right-click its field name in the datasheet, and then click Freeze Fields. To unfreeze a field, right-click any field name and click Unfreeze All Fields.

FIGURE 2-3: Working with data in a query datasheet

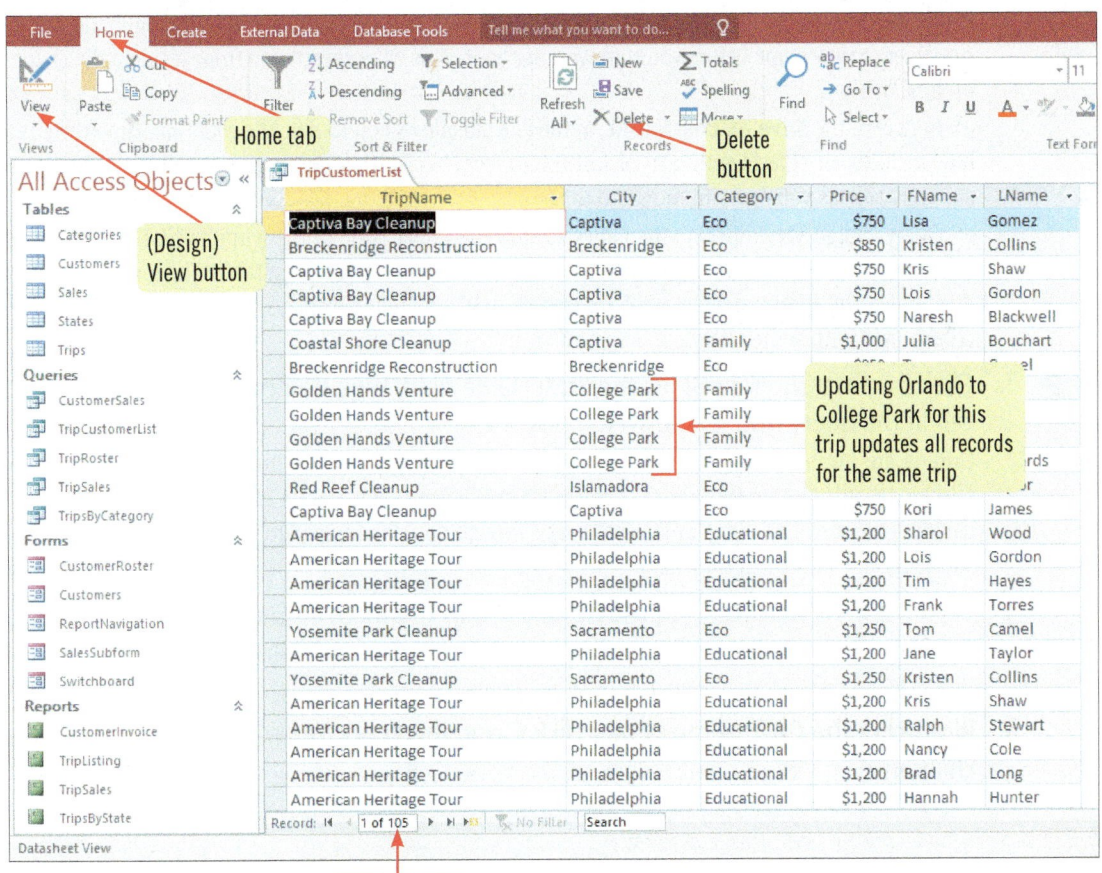

FIGURE 2-4: Final TripCustomerList datasheet

Use Query Design View

You use **Query Design View** to add, delete, or move the fields in an existing query; to specify sort orders; or to add **criteria** to limit the number of records shown in the resulting datasheet. You can also use Query Design View to create a new query from scratch. In the upper pane, Query Design View presents the fields you can use for that query in small windows called **field lists**. If you use the fields of two or more related tables in the query, the relationship between two tables is displayed with a **join line** (also called a **link line**) identifying which fields are used to establish the relationship. **CASE** ▶ *Julia Rice asks you to produce a list of trips in California. You use Query Design View to modify the existing TripsByState query to meet her request.*

STEPS

1. **Double-click the TripsByState query in the Navigation Pane to review the datasheet, then click the View button on the Home tab to switch to Query Design View**

   The TripsByState query contains the StateName field from the States table and the TripName, TripStartDate, and Price fields from the Trips table. This query contains two ascending sort orders: StateName and TripName. All records in California, for example, are further sorted by the TripName value.

2. **Click the File tab, click Save As, click Save Object As, click the Save As button, type CATrips to replace Copy of TripsByState, then click OK**

   If you want to build a new query starting from an existing query, use the Save As command and give the new query a new name before you start working on it. This will prevent you from accidentally changing the original query.

   In Access, the **Save As command** on the File tab allows you to save the *entire database* (the entire database includes all objects within it) or just the *current object* with a new name. Recall that Access saves *data* automatically as you move from record to record.

   Query Design View displays the tables used in the upper pane of the window. The link line shows that one record in the States table may be related to many records in the Trips table. The lower pane of the window, called the **query design grid** (or **query grid** for short), displays the field names, sort orders, and criteria used within the query.

3. **Click the first Criteria cell for the StateName field, type California, then click any other cell in the query grid as shown in FIGURE 2-5**

   Criteria are limiting conditions you set in the query design grid. In this case, the condition limits the selected records to only those with "California" in the StateName field. Criteria for a field with a Short Text data type are surrounded by "quotation marks" though you do not need to type the quotation marks. Access automatically adds them for you.

4. **Click the View button in the Results group to switch to Datasheet View**

   Now only 15 records are selected, because only 15 of the trips have "California" in the StateName field, as shown in FIGURE 2-6.

5. **Right-click the CATrips query tab, click Close, then click Yes when prompted to save changes**

Adding or deleting a table in a query

You might want to add a table's field list to the upper pane of Query Design View to select fields from that table for the query. To add a new table to Query Design View, drag it from the Navigation Pane to Query Design View, or click the Show Table button on the Design tab, then add the desired table(s). To delete an unneeded table from Query Design View, click its title bar, then press [Delete].

FIGURE 2-5: CATrips query in Design View

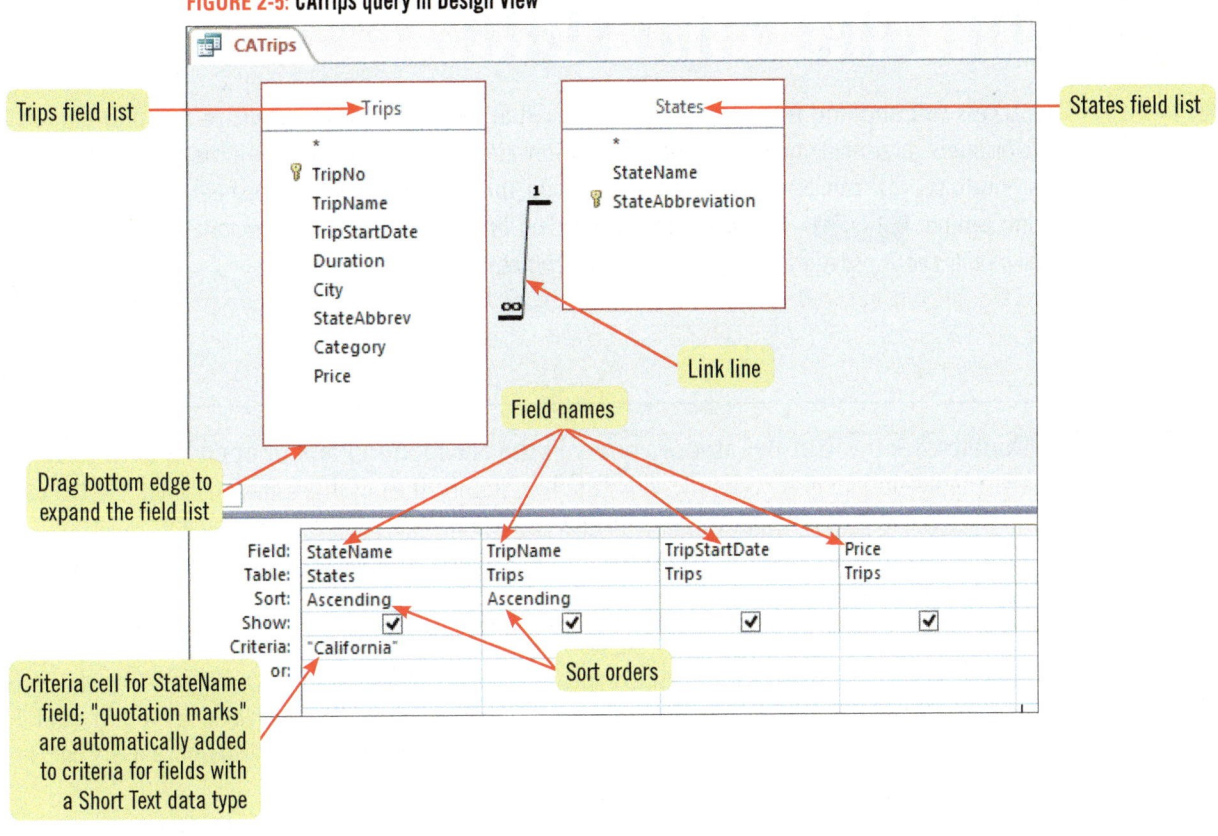

Trips field list

States field list

Link line

Field names

Drag bottom edge to expand the field list

Criteria cell for StateName field; "quotation marks" are automatically added to criteria for fields with a Short Text data type

Sort orders

FIGURE 2-6: CATrips query with California criterion

Only 15 California records are selected

TripName values are in ascending order

Sort and Find Data

The Access sort and find features are handy tools that help you quickly organize and find data in a table or query datasheet. **TABLE 2-1** describes the Sort and Find buttons on the Home tab. Besides using these buttons, you can also click the list arrow on the field name in a datasheet, and then click a sorting option. **CASE** *Julia asks you to provide a list of trips sorted by Category, and then by Price. You'll modify the TripsByCategory query to answer this request.*

STEPS

1. **Double-click the TripsByCategory query in the Navigation Pane to open its datasheet**

   The TripsByCategory query currently sorts Trips by Category, then by TripName. You'll add the Duration field to this query, then change the sort order for the records.

2. **Click the View button [icon] in the Views group to switch to Design View, then double-click the Duration field in the Trips field list**

   When you double-click a field in a field list, Access inserts it in the next available column in the query grid. You can also drag a field from a field list to a specific column of the query grid. To select a field in the query grid, you click its field selector. The **field selector** is the thin gray bar above each field in the query grid. To delete a field from a query, click its field selector, then press [Delete]. Deleting a field from a query does not delete it from the underlying table; the field is only deleted from the query.

   Currently, the TripsByCategory query is sorted by Category and then by TripName. Access evaluates sort orders from left to right. You want to change the sort order so that the records sort first by Category then by Price.

3. **Click Ascending in the TripName Sort cell, click the list arrow, click (not sorted), double-click the Price Sort cell, click the list arrow, then click Descending**

   The records are now set to be sorted in ascending order by Category, and within each Category, in a descending order by the Price field, as shown in **FIGURE 2-7**. Because sort orders always work from left to right, you might need to rearrange the fields before applying a sort order that uses more than one field. To move a field in the query design grid, click its field selector, then drag it left or right.

4. **Click the View button [icon] in the Results group to switch to Datasheet View**

   The new datasheet shows the Duration field in the fifth column. The records are now sorted in ascending order by the Category field, but for records in the same Category, they are further sorted in descending order by Price. Your next task is to replace all occurrences of "Tour" with "Trip" in the TripName field.

5. **Click in any TripName field, click the Replace button on the Home tab, type Tour in the Find What box, click in the Replace With box, type Trip, click the Match arrow button, then click Any Part of Field**

   The Find and Replace dialog box is shown in **FIGURE 2-8**.

6. **Click the Replace All button in the Find and Replace dialog box, click Yes to continue, then click Cancel to close the Find and Replace dialog box**

   Access replaced both occurrences of "Tour" with "Trip" in the TripName field, as shown in **FIGURE 2-9**.

7. **Right-click the TripsByCategory query tab, click Close, then click Yes if prompted to save changes**

FIGURE 2-7: Changing sort orders for the TripsByCategory query

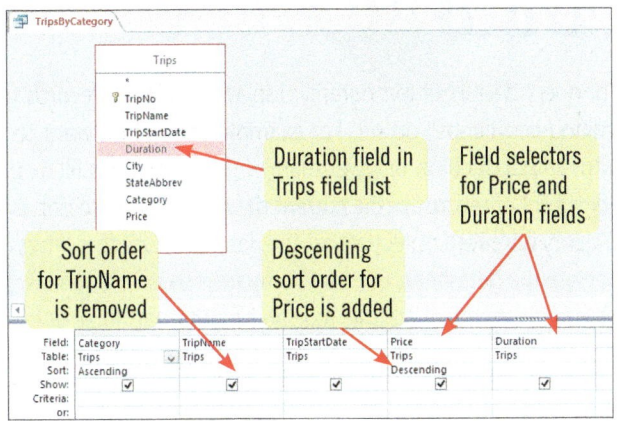

FIGURE 2-8: Find and Replace dialog box

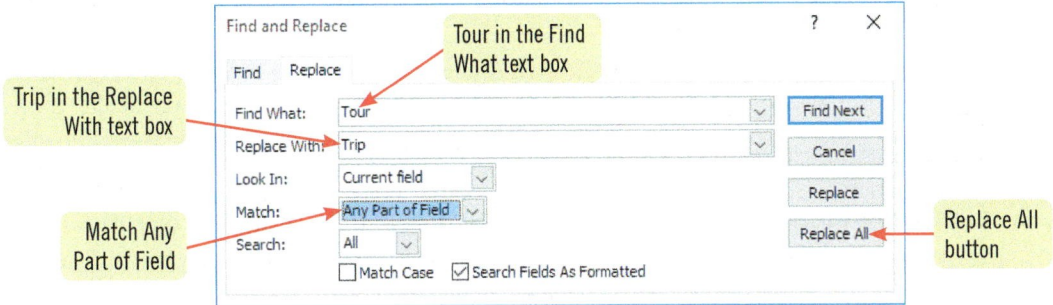

FIGURE 2-9: Final TripsByCategory datasheet with new sort orders

TABLE 2-1: Sort and Find buttons

name	button	purpose
Ascending		Sorts records based on the selected field in ascending order (0 to 9, A to Z)
Descending		Sorts records based on the selected field in descending order (Z to A, 9 to 0)
Remove Sort		Removes the current sort order
Find		Opens the Find and Replace dialog box to find data
Replace		Opens the Find and Replace dialog box to find and replace data
Go To		Helps you navigate to the first, previous, next, last, or new record
Select		Helps you select a single record or all records in a datasheet

Filter Data

Learning Outcomes
- Apply and remove filters in a query
- Use wildcards in criteria

Filtering a table or query datasheet temporarily displays only those records that match given criteria. Recall that criteria are limiting conditions you set. For example, you might want to show only trips in the state of Missouri, or only trips with a duration of fewer than 14 days. Although filters provide a quick and easy way to display a temporary subset of records in the current datasheet, they are not as powerful or flexible as queries. Most important, a query is a saved object within the database, whereas filters are temporary. Access removes all filters when you close the datasheet. **TABLE 2-2** compares filters and queries. **CASE** *Julia asks you to find all Family trips offered in the month of August. You can filter the Trips table datasheet to provide this information.*

STEPS

1. **Double-click the Trips table to open it, click any occurrence of Family in the Category field, click the Selection button in the Sort & Filter group on the Home tab, then click Equals "Family"**

   Six records are selected as shown in **FIGURE 2-10**. A filter icon appears to the right of the Category field. Filtering by the selected field value, called **Filter By Selection**, is a fast and easy way to filter the records for an exact match. To filter for comparative data (for example, where TripStartDate is equal to or greater than 7/1/2017), you must use the **Filter By Form** feature. Filter buttons are summarized in **TABLE 2-3**.

2. **Click the Advanced button in the Sort & Filter group, then click Filter By Form**

   The Filter by Form window opens. The previous Filter By Selection criterion, "Family" in the Category field, is still in the grid. Access places "quotation marks" around text criteria.

3. **Click the TripStartDate cell, then type 8/*/2017 as shown in FIGURE 2-11**

   Filter By Form also allows you to apply two or more criteria at the same time. An asterisk (*) in the day position of the date criterion works as a wildcard, selecting any date in the month of August in the year 2017.

4. **Click the Toggle Filter button in the Sort & Filter group**

   The datasheet selects one record that matches both filter criteria, as shown in **FIGURE 2-12**. Note that filter icons appear next to the TripStartDate and Category field names as both fields are involved in the filter.

5. **Close the Trips datasheet, then click Yes when prompted to save the changes**

   Saving changes to the datasheet saves the last sort order and column width changes. *Filters are not saved.*

Using wildcard characters

To search for a pattern, you can use a **wildcard** character to represent any character in the condition entry. Use a question mark (?) to search for any single character and an asterisk (*) to search for any number of characters. Wildcard characters are often used with the **Like** operator. For example, the criterion Like "12/*/17" would find all dates in December of 2017, and the criterion Like "F*" would find all entries that start with the letter F.

FIGURE 2-10: Filtering the Trips table

FIGURE 2-11: Filtering by Form criteria

FIGURE 2-12: Results of filtering by form

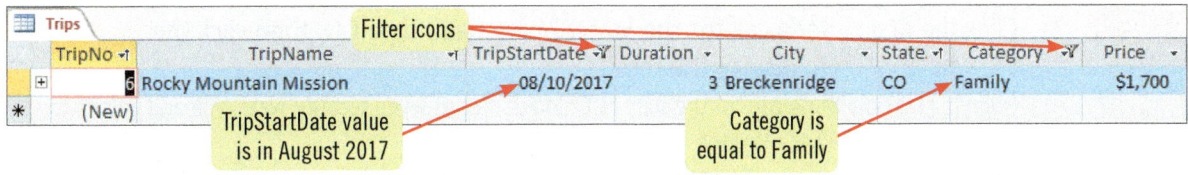

TABLE 2-2: Filters vs. queries

characteristics	filters	queries
Are saved as an object in the database		•
Can be used to select a subset of records in a datasheet	•	•
Can be used to select a subset of fields in a datasheet		•
Resulting datasheet used to enter and edit data	•	•
Resulting datasheet used to sort, filter, and find records	•	•
Commonly used as the source of data for a form or report		•
Can calculate sums, averages, counts, and other types of summary statistics across records		•
Can be used to create calculated fields		•

TABLE 2-3: Filter buttons

name	button	purpose
Filter	▼	Provides a list of values in the selected field that can be used to customize a filter
Selection	▼	Filters records that equal, do not equal, or are otherwise compared with the current value
Advanced	▦	Provides advanced filter features such as Filter By Form, Save As Query, and Clear All Filters
Toggle Filter	▦	Applies or removes the current filter

Apply AND Criteria

Learning Outcomes
- Enter AND criteria in a query
- Define criteria syntax
- Use comparison operators with criteria

You can limit the number of records that appear on a query datasheet by entering criteria in Query Design View. **Criteria** are tests, or limiting conditions, for which the record must be true to be selected for the query datasheet. To create **AND criteria**, which means that *all* criteria must be true to select the record, enter two or more criteria on the *same* Criteria row of the query design grid. **CASE** ▶ *Julia Rice asks you to provide a list of all Eco (ecological) trips in the state of Colorado with a duration of seven days or more. Use Query Design View to create the query with AND criteria to meet her request.*

STEPS

1. **Click the Create tab on the Ribbon, click the Query Design button, double-click Trips, then click Close in the Show Table dialog box**

   You want four fields from the Trips table in this query.

2. **Drag the bottom edge of the Trips field list down to display all of the fields, double-click TripName, double-click Duration, double-click StateAbbrev, then double-click Category to add these fields to the query grid**

   First add criteria to select only those records in Colorado. Because you are using the StateAbbrev field, you need to use the two-letter state abbreviation for Colorado, CO, as the Criteria entry.

TROUBLE

Access attempts to anticipate what you are entering in the criteria cell by providing a drop-down list of functions. Be careful to enter only CO as the criterion.

3. **Click the first Criteria cell for the StateAbbrev field, type CO, then click the View button ▦ to display the results**

   Querying for only those trips in the state of Colorado selects seven records. Next, you add criteria to select only the trips in the Eco category.

4. **Click the View button ⬗, click the first Criteria cell for the Category field, type Eco, then click the View button ▦ in the Results group**

   Criteria added to the same line of the query design grid are AND criteria. When entered on the same line, each criterion must be true for the record to appear in the resulting datasheet. Querying for both CO and Eco trips narrows the selection to three records. Every time you add AND criteria, you narrow the number of records that are selected because the record must be true for all criteria.

5. **Click the View button ⬗, click the first Criteria cell for the Duration field, then type >=7, as shown in FIGURE 2-13**

   Access assists you with **criteria syntax**, rules that specify how to enter criteria. Access automatically adds "quotation marks" around text criteria in Short Text and Long Text fields ("CO" and "Eco") and pound signs (#) around date criteria in Date/Time fields. The criteria in the Number, Currency, and Yes/No fields are not surrounded by any characters. See **TABLE 2-4** for more information about comparison operators such as >= (greater than or equal to).

TROUBLE

If your datasheet doesn't match **FIGURE 2-14**, return to Query Design View and compare your criteria with that of **FIGURE 2-13**.

6. **Click the View button ▦ in the Results group**

   The third AND criterion further narrows the number of records selected to two, as shown in **FIGURE 2-14**.

7. **Click the Save button 🖫 on the Quick Access Toolbar, type EcoCO7 as the query name, click OK, then close the query**

   The query is saved with the new name, EcoCO7, as a new object in the R2G-2 database. Criteria entered in Query Design View are permanently saved with the query (as compared to filters in the previous lesson, which are temporary and not saved with the object).

FIGURE 2-13: Query Design View with AND criteria

Drag bottom edge of Trips field list down to display all fields

AND criteria is in one row

FIGURE 2-14: Final datasheet of EcoCO7 query

Records meet all three criteria:
Duration >= 7
State = "CO"
Category = "Eco"

TABLE 2-4: Comparison operators

operator	description	expression	meaning
>	Greater than	>500	Numbers greater than 500
>=	Greater than or equal to	>=500	Numbers greater than or equal to 500
<	Less than	<"Elder"	Names from A to Elder, but not Elder
<=	Less than or equal to	<="Buehler"	Names from A through Buehler, inclusive
<>	Not equal to	<>"Bridgewater"	Any name except for Bridgewater

Searching for blank fields

Is Null and Is Not Null are two other types of common criteria. The **Is Null** criterion finds all records where no entry has been made in the field. **Is Not Null** finds all records where there is any entry in the field, even if the entry is 0. Primary key fields cannot have a null entry.

Apply OR Criteria

You use **OR criteria** when *any one criterion* must be true in order for the record to be selected. Enter OR criteria on *different* Criteria rows of the query design grid. As you add rows of OR criteria to the query design grid, you increase the number of records selected for the resulting datasheet because the record needs to match only one of the Criteria rows to be selected for the datasheet. **CASE** ▶ *Julia Rice asks you to add criteria to the previous query. She wants to include Adventure trips in the state of Colorado that are greater than or equal to seven days in duration. To do this, you make a copy of the EcoCO7 query to modify with OR criteria to add the new records for the Adventure trips.*

STEPS

1. **Right-click the EcoCO7 query in the Navigation Pane, click Copy, right-click a blank spot in the Navigation Pane, click Paste, type EcoAdventureCO7 in the Paste As dialog box, then click OK**

   By copying the EcoCO7 query before starting your modifications, you avoid changing the EcoCO7 query by mistake.

2. **Right-click the EcoAdventureCO7 query in the Navigation Pane, click Design View, click the second Criteria cell in the Category field, type Adventure, then click the View button to display the query datasheet**

   The query selected 11 records including all of the trips with Adventure in the Category field. Note that some of the Duration values are less than seven and some of the StateAbbrev values are not CO. Because each row of the query grid is evaluated separately, *all* Adventure trips are selected regardless of criteria in any other row. In other words, the criteria in one row have no effect on the criteria of other rows. To make sure that the Adventure trips are also in Colorado and have a duration of greater than or equal to seven days, you need to modify the second row of the query grid (the "or" row) to add that criteria.

3. **Click the View button, click the second Criteria cell in the Duration field, type >=7, click the second Criteria cell in the StateAbbrev field, type CO, then click in any other cell of the grid**

   Query Design View should look like **FIGURE 2-15**.

4. **Click the View button**

   Three records are selected that meet all three criteria as entered in row one or row two of the query grid, as shown in **FIGURE 2-16**.

5. **Right-click the EcoAdventureCO7 query tab, click Close, then click Yes to save and close the query datasheet**

FIGURE 2-15: Query Design View with OR criteria

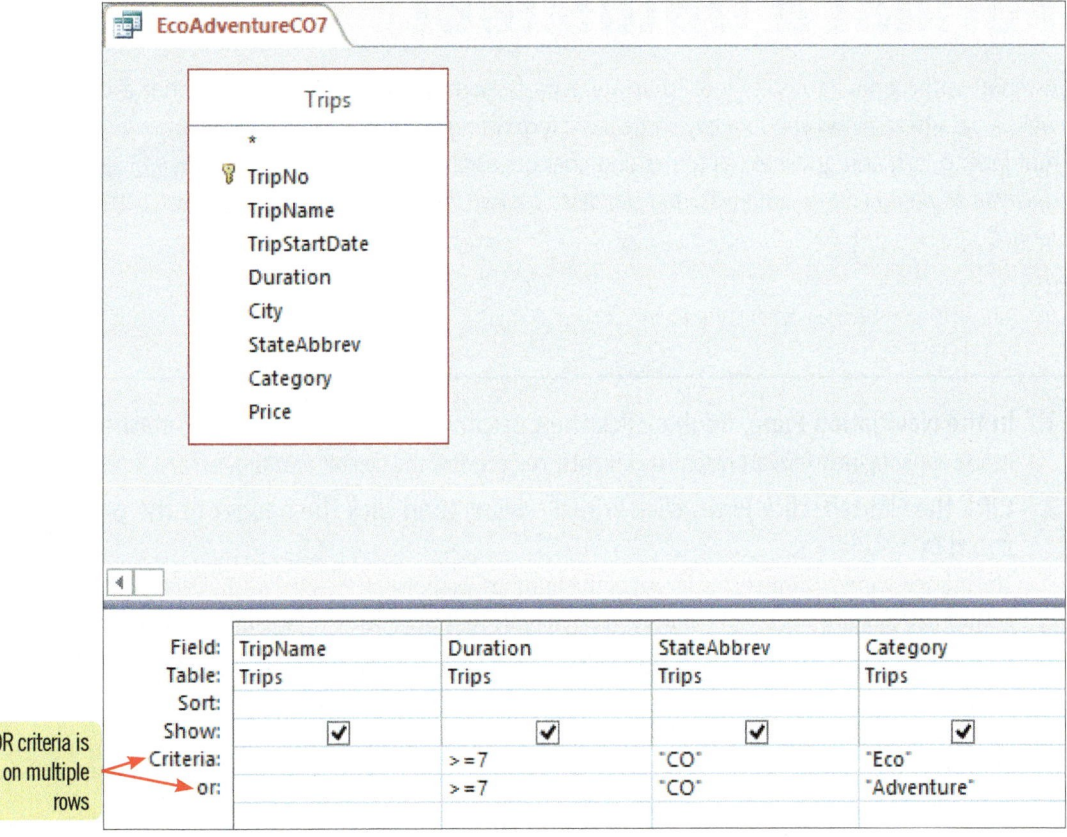

OR criteria is on multiple rows

Field:	TripName	Duration	StateAbbrev	Category
Table:	Trips	Trips	Trips	Trips
Sort:				
Show:	✔	✔	✔	✔
Criteria:		>=7	"CO"	"Eco"
or:		>=7	"CO"	"Adventure"

FIGURE 2-16: Final datasheet of EcoAdventureCO7 query

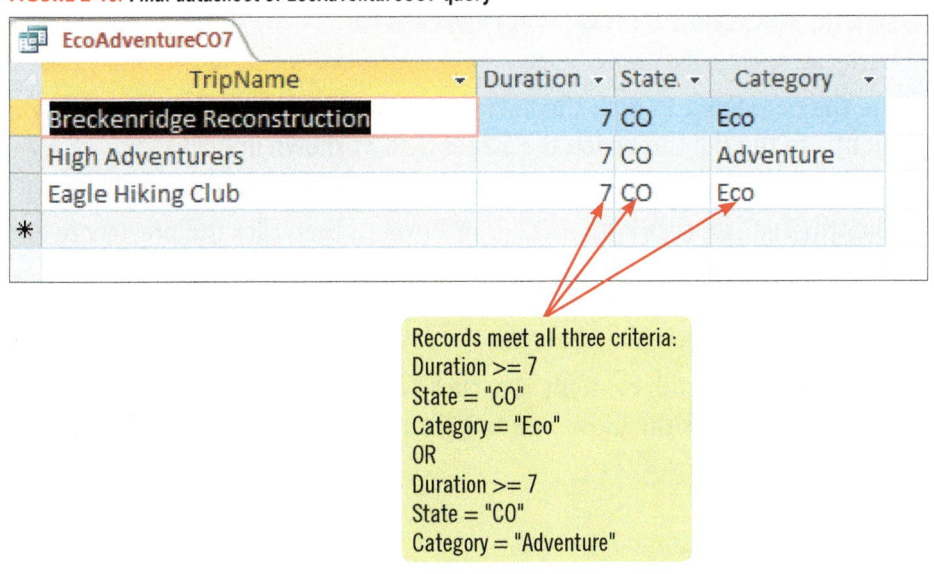

Records meet all three criteria:
Duration >= 7
State = "CO"
Category = "Eco"
OR
Duration >= 7
State = "CO"
Category = "Adventure"

Format a Datasheet

A report is the primary Access tool to create a professional printout, but you can print a datasheet as well. A datasheet allows you to apply some basic formatting modifications such as changing the font size, font face, colors, and gridlines. All formatting changes apply to the entire datasheet. **CASE** *Julia Rice asks you to print a list of customers. You decide to format the Customers table datasheet before printing it for her.*

STEPS

1. **In the Navigation Pane, double-click the Customers table to open it in Datasheet View**

   Before applying new formatting enhancements, you preview the default printout.

2. **Click the File tab, click Print, click Print Preview, then click the header of the printout to zoom in**

   The preview window displays the layout of the printout, as shown in **FIGURE 2-17**. By default, the printout of a datasheet contains the object name and current date in the header. The page number is in the footer.

3. **Click the Next Page button ▶ in the navigation bar to move to the next page of the printout**

   The last two fields, Phone and FirstContact, print on the second page because the first is not wide enough to accommodate them. You decide to switch the report to landscape orientation so that all of the fields print on one page, and then increase the size of the font before printing to make the text easier to read.

4. **Click the Landscape button on the Print Preview tab to switch the report to landscape orientation, then click the Close Print Preview button**

   You return to Datasheet View where you can make font face, font size, font color, gridline color, and background color choices.

5. **Click the Font list arrow [Calibri (Detail)] in the Text Formatting group, click Arial Narrow, click the Font Size list arrow [11], then click 12**

   You decide to widen the Street column.

6. **Use the ↔ pointer to drag the field separator between the Street and City field names slightly to the right to widen the Street field as shown in FIGURE 2-18**

   Double-clicking the field separators widens the columns as needed to display every entry in those fields.

7. **Click the File tab, click Print, click Print Preview, then click the preview to zoom in and out to review the information**

   All of the fields now fit across a page in landscape orientation. The preview of the printout is two pages, and in landscape orientation, it is easier to read.

8. **Right-click the Customers table tab, click Close, click Yes when prompted to save changes, then click the Close button ✕ on the title bar to close the R2G-2.accdb database and Access 2016**

FIGURE 2-17: Preview of Customers datasheet

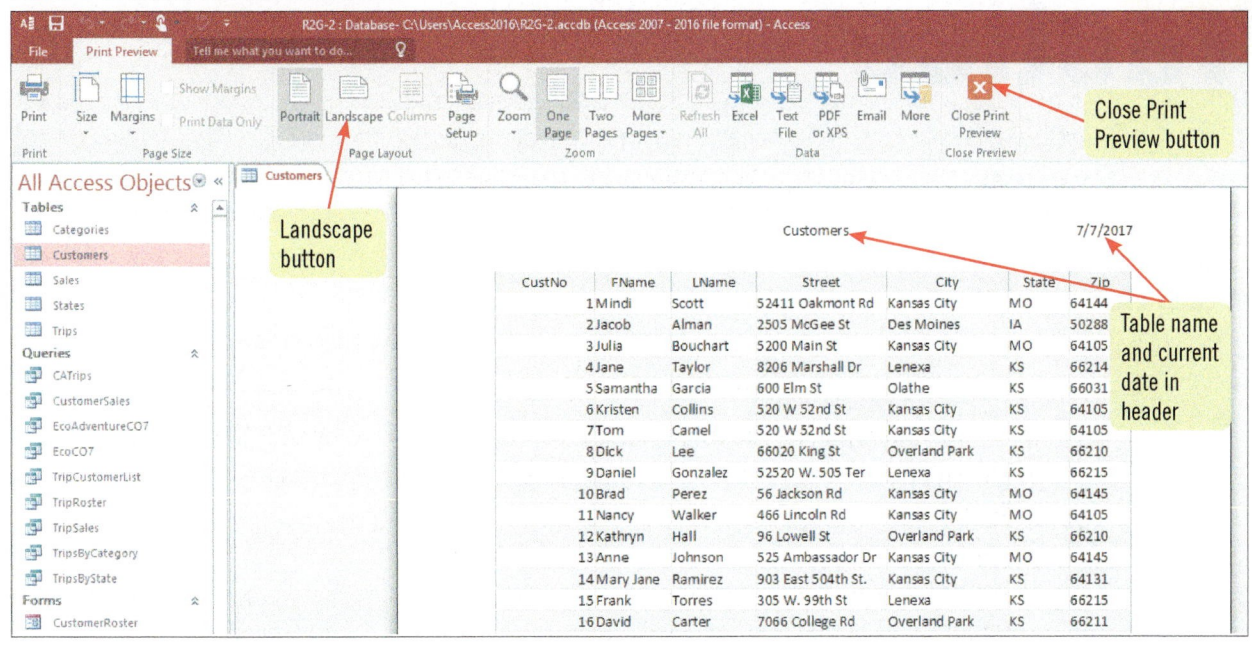

Landscape button

Close Print Preview button

Table name and current date in header

FIGURE 2-18: Formatting the Customers datasheet

Field separator

Font list arrow

Font Size list arrow

Drag or double-click with this pointer to resize columns

Practice

Concepts Review

Label each element of the Access window shown in FIGURE 2-19.

FIGURE 2-19

Match each term with the statement that best describes it.

6. **Query grid**   a. Putting records in ascending or descending order based on the values of a field
7. **Field selector**   b. Limiting conditions used to restrict the number of records that are selected in a query
8. **Filter**   c. The thin gray bar above each field in the query grid
9. **Filter By Selection** d. Creates a temporary subset of records
10. **Field lists**   e. Small windows that display field names
11. **Sorting**   f. Rules that determine how criteria are entered
12. **Join line**   g. Used to search for a pattern of characters
13. **Criteria**   h. The lower pane in Query Design View
14. **Syntax**   i. Identifies which fields are used to establish a relationship between two tables
15. **Wildcard**   j. A fast and easy way to filter the records for an exact match

Select the best answer from the list of choices.

16. AND criteria:
- **a.** determine sort orders.
- **b.** must all be true for the record to be selected.
- **c.** determine fields selected for a query.
- **d.** help set link lines between tables in a query.

17. SQL stands for which of the following?
- **a.** Structured Query Language
- **b.** Standard Query Language
- **c.** Special Query Listing
- **d.** Simple Query Listing

18. A query is sometimes called a logical view of data because:
- **a.** you can create queries with the Logical Query Wizard.
- **b.** queries contain logical criteria.
- **c.** query naming conventions are logical.
- **d.** queries do not store data—they only display a view of data.

19. Which of the following describes OR criteria?
- **a.** Selecting a subset of fields and/or records to view as a datasheet from one or more tables
- **b.** Using two or more rows of the query grid to select only those records that meet given criteria
- **c.** Reorganizing the records in either ascending or descending order based on the contents of one or more fields
- **d.** Using multiple fields in the query design grid

20. Which of the following is *not* true about a query?
- **a.** A query is the same thing as a filter.
- **b.** A query can select fields from one or more tables in a relational database.
- **c.** A query can be created using different tools.
- **d.** An existing query can be modified in Query Design View.

Skills Review

1. Use the Query Wizard.

   a. Open the Salvage-2.accdb database from the location where you store your Data Files. Enable content if prompted.

   b. Create a new query using the Simple Query Wizard. Select the CenterName field from the Centers table, the DepositDate and Weight fields from the Deposits table, and the ClubName field from the Clubs table. Select Detail, and enter **CenterDeposits** as the name of the query.

   c. Open the query in Datasheet View, then change any record with the Johnson Recycling value to a center name that includes your last name.

2. Work with data in a query.

   a. Delete the first record (A1 Salvage Center with a DepositDate value of 2/4/2014).

   b. Change any occurrence of JavaScript KC in the ClubName field to **Bootstrap Club**.

   c. Click any value in the DepositDate field, then click the Descending button on the Home tab to sort the records in descending order on the DepositDate field.

   d. Use the Calendar Picker to choose the date of **1/30/17** for the first record.

   e. Save and close the CenterDeposits query.

3. Use Query Design View.

   a. Click the Create tab, click the Query Design button, double-click Clubs, double-click Deposits, and then click Close to add the Clubs and Deposits tables to Query Design View.

   b. Drag the bottom edge of both field lists down as needed to display all of the field names in both tables.

   c. Add the following fields from the Clubs table to the query design grid in the following order: FName, LName, ClubName. Add the following fields from the Deposits table in the following order: DepositDate, Weight. View the results in Datasheet View, observing the number of records that are selected in the record navigation bar at the bottom of the datasheet.

   d. In Design View, enter criteria to display only those records with a Weight value of **>=100**, then observe the number of records that are selected in Datasheet View.

   e. Save the query with the name **100PlusDeposits**.

4. Sort and find data.

   a. In Query Design View of the 100PlusDeposits query, choose an ascending sort order for the ClubName field and a descending sort order for the Weight field.

   b. Display the query in Datasheet View, noting how the records have been resorted.

   c. In the ClubName field, change any occurrence of Boy Scout Troop 324 to Boy Scout Troop **6**.

   d. In the FName field, change any occurrence of Trey to *your* initials and save the query.

5. Filter data.

   a. Filter the 100PlusDeposits datasheet for only those records where the ClubName equals **Access Users Group**.

   b. Apply an advanced Filter By Form and use the >= operator to further narrow the records so that only the deposits with a DepositDate value on or after 1/1/2015 are selected.

   c. Apply the filter to see the datasheet and, if requested by your instructor, print the filtered 100PlusDeposits datasheet.

   d. Save and close the 100PlusDeposits query. Reopen the 100PlusDeposits query to confirm that filters are temporary (not saved), and then close the 100PlusDeposits query again.

Skills Review (continued)

6. Apply AND criteria.

 a. Right-click the 100PlusDeposits query, copy it, and then paste it as **100PlusDeposits2016**.

 b. Open the 100PlusDeposits2016 query in Query Design View.

 c. Modify the criteria to select all of the records with a DepositDate in **2016** and a Weight value **greater than or equal to 100**. (*Hint*: To select all records with a DepositDate in 2016, use a wildcard character for the month and day positions of the date criterion.)

 d. Display the results in Datasheet View. If requested by your instructor, print the 100PlusDeposits2016 datasheet, then save and close it.

7. Apply OR criteria.

 a. Right-click the 100PlusDeposits query, copy it, then paste it as **100PlusDeposits2Clubs**.

 b. Open the 100PlusDeposits2Clubs query in Design View, then add criteria to select the records with a ClubName of **Social Media Club** and a Weight value **greater than or equal to 100**.

 c. Add criteria to also include the records with a ClubName of **Access Users Group** with a Weight value **greater than or equal to 100**. FIGURE 2-20 shows the results.

 d. If requested by your instructor, print the 100PlusDeposits2Clubs datasheet, then save and close it.

FIGURE 2-20

Your initials will be in the FName field

8. Format a datasheet.

 a. In the Centers table datasheet, apply the Times New Roman font and a 14-point font size.

 b. Resize all columns so that all data and field names are visible.

 c. Display the Centers datasheet in Print Preview, switch the orientation to landscape, click the Margins button in the Page Size group, then click Narrow.

 d. If requested by your instructor, print the Centers datasheet.

 e. Save and close the Centers table, then close Access 2016.

Independent Challenge 1

You have built an Access database to track membership in a community service club. The database tracks member names and addresses as well as their community service hours.

a. Open the Service-2.accdb database from the location where you store your Data Files, enable content if prompted, then open the Activities, Members, and Zips tables to review their datasheets.

b. In the Zips table, click the expand button to the left of the 64111, Kansas City, MO record to display the two members linked to that zip code. Click the expand button to the left of the Jeremiah Hopper record to display the three activity records linked to Jeremiah.

c. Close all three datasheets, click the Database Tools tab, then click the Relationships button. The Relationships window shows you that one record in the Zips table is related to many records in the Members table through the common ZipCode field, and that one record in the Members table is related to many records in the Activities table through the common MemberNo field.

d. Click the Relationship Report button, then if requested by your instructor, print the Relationship report. Close and save the report with the default name **Relationships for Service-2**. Close the Relationships window.

e. Using Query Design View, build a query with the following fields: FirstName and LastName from the Members table and ActivityDate and HoursWorked from the Activities table.

f. View the datasheet, observe the number of records selected, then return to Query Design View.

g. Add criteria to select only those records where the ActivityDate is in March of 2017.

h. In Query Design View, apply an ascending sort order to the LastName and a descending sort order to the ActivityDate field, then view the datasheet.

i. Change the name Quentin Garden to your name, widen all columns so that all data and field names are visible, and save the query with the name **March2017**, as shown in FIGURE 2-21.

j. If requested by your instructor, print the March2017 datasheet, then close the March2017 query and close Access 2016.

FIGURE 2-21

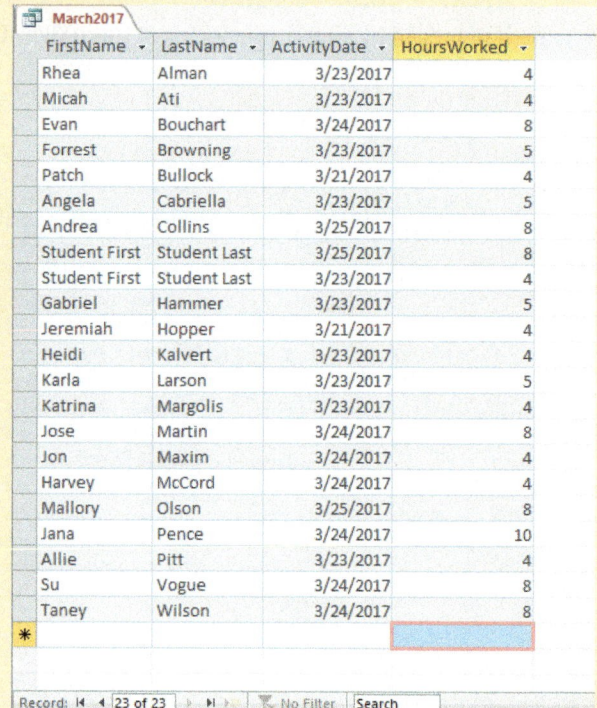

FirstName	LastName	ActivityDate	HoursWorked
Rhea	Alman	3/23/2017	4
Micah	Ati	3/23/2017	4
Evan	Bouchart	3/24/2017	8
Forrest	Browning	3/23/2017	5
Patch	Bullock	3/21/2017	4
Angela	Cabriella	3/23/2017	5
Andrea	Collins	3/25/2017	8
Student First	Student Last	3/25/2017	8
Student First	Student Last	3/23/2017	4
Gabriel	Hammer	3/23/2017	5
Jeremiah	Hopper	3/21/2017	4
Heidi	Kalvert	3/23/2017	4
Karla	Larson	3/23/2017	5
Katrina	Margolis	3/23/2017	4
Jose	Martin	3/24/2017	8
Jon	Maxim	3/24/2017	4
Harvey	McCord	3/24/2017	4
Mallory	Olson	3/25/2017	8
Jana	Pence	3/24/2017	10
Allie	Pitt	3/23/2017	4
Su	Vogue	3/24/2017	8
Taney	Wilson	3/24/2017	8

Record: I◄ ◄ 23 of 23 ► ►I ► No Filter Search

Independent Challenge 2

You work for a nonprofit agency that tracks voting patterns. You have developed an Access database with contact information for members of the House of Representatives. The director of the agency has asked you to create several state lists of representatives. You will use queries to extract this information.

a. Open the HouseOfReps-2.accdb database from the location where you store your Data Files, then enable content if prompted.

b. Open the Representatives and the States tables. Notice that one state is related to many representatives as evidenced by the expand buttons to the left of the records in the States tables.

c. Close both datasheets, then using Query Design View, create a query with the StateAbbrev, StateName, and Capital fields from the States table (in that order) as well as the FName and LName fields from the Representatives table.

d. Sort the records in ascending order on the StateName field, then in ascending order on the LName field.

e. Add criteria to select the representatives from Ohio or Pennsylvania. Use the StateAbbrev field to enter your criteria, using the two-character state abbreviations of **OH** and **PA**.

f. Save the query with the name **OhioAndPenn**, view the results, shown in FIGURE 2-22, then change the last name of Butterfield in the second record to *your* last name. Resize the columns as needed to view all the data and field names.

g. Print the OhioAndPenn datasheet if requested by your instructor, then close it and exit Access 2016.

FIGURE 2-22

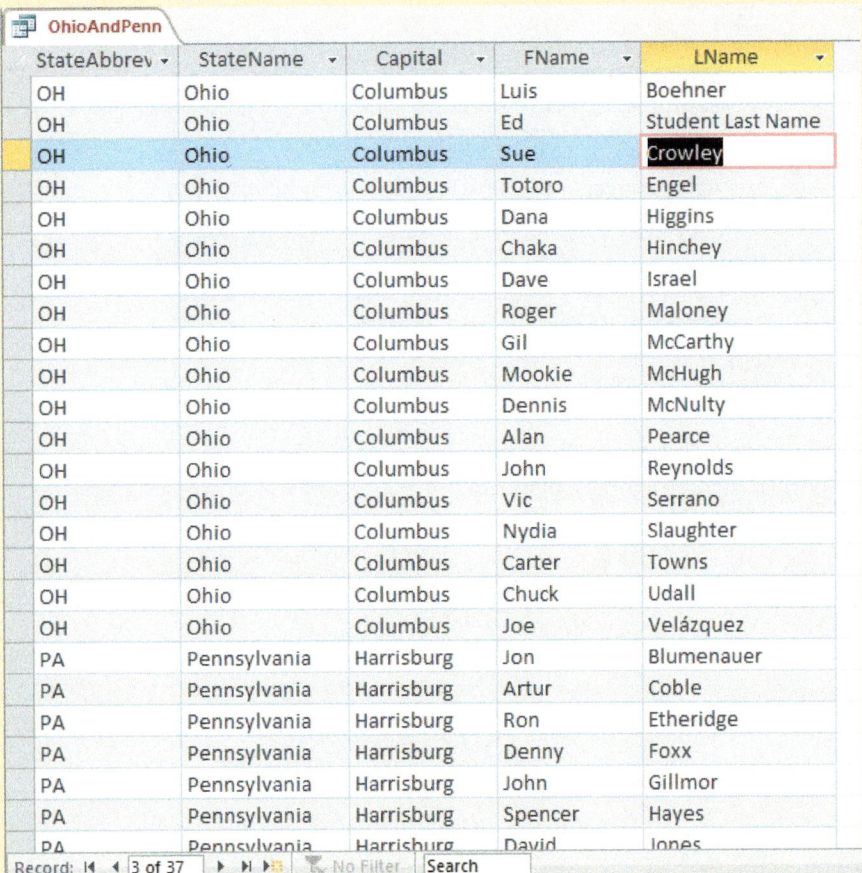

StateAbbrev	StateName	Capital	FName	LName
OH	Ohio	Columbus	Luis	Boehner
OH	Ohio	Columbus	Ed	Student Last Name
OH	Ohio	Columbus	Sue	Crowley
OH	Ohio	Columbus	Totoro	Engel
OH	Ohio	Columbus	Dana	Higgins
OH	Ohio	Columbus	Chaka	Hinchey
OH	Ohio	Columbus	Dave	Israel
OH	Ohio	Columbus	Roger	Maloney
OH	Ohio	Columbus	Gil	McCarthy
OH	Ohio	Columbus	Mookie	McHugh
OH	Ohio	Columbus	Dennis	McNulty
OH	Ohio	Columbus	Alan	Pearce
OH	Ohio	Columbus	John	Reynolds
OH	Ohio	Columbus	Vic	Serrano
OH	Ohio	Columbus	Nydia	Slaughter
OH	Ohio	Columbus	Carter	Towns
OH	Ohio	Columbus	Chuck	Udall
OH	Ohio	Columbus	Joe	Velázquez
PA	Pennsylvania	Harrisburg	Jon	Blumenauer
PA	Pennsylvania	Harrisburg	Artur	Coble
PA	Pennsylvania	Harrisburg	Ron	Etheridge
PA	Pennsylvania	Harrisburg	Denny	Foxx
PA	Pennsylvania	Harrisburg	John	Gillmor
PA	Pennsylvania	Harrisburg	Spencer	Hayes
PA	Pennsylvania	Harrisburg	David	Jones

Record: 3 of 37 — No Filter — Search

Independent Challenge 3

You have built an Access database to track the veterinarian clinics in your area.

a. Open the VetClinic-2.accdb database from the location where you store your Data Files, then enable content if prompted.

b. Open the Vets table and then the Clinics table to review the data in both datasheets.

c. Click the expand button next to the Animal Haven record in the Clinics table, then add your name as a new record to the Vets subdatasheet.

d. Close both datasheets.

e. Using the Simple Query Wizard, select the VetLast and VetFirst fields from the Vets table, and select the ClinicName and Phone fields from the Clinics table. Title the query **ClinicVetListing**, then view the datasheet.

f. Update any occurrence of Animal Haven in the ClinicName field to **Animal Emergency Shelter**.

g. In Query Design View, add criteria to select only **Animal Emergency Shelter** or **Veterinary Specialists** in the ClinicName field, then view the datasheet.

h. In Query Design View, move the ClinicName field to the first column, then add an ascending sort order on the ClinicName and VetLast fields.

i. Display the ClinicVetListing query in Datasheet View, resize the fields as shown in **FIGURE 2-23**, then print the datasheet if requested by your instructor.

j. Save and close the ClinicVetListing datasheet, then exit Access 2016.

FIGURE 2-23

ClinicName	VetLast	VetFirst	Phone
Animal Emergency Shelter	Chernoble	Selbert	(555) 555-7900
Animal Emergency Shelter	Kowalewski	Vicki	(555) 555-7900
Animal Emergency Shelter	Newhart	Darryl	(555) 555-7900
Animal Emergency Shelter	Sanderson	Anne	(555) 555-7900
Animal Emergency Shelter	Sellers	Kenneth	(555) 555-7900
Animal Emergency Shelter	StudentLast	StudentFirst	(555) 555-7900
Veterinary Specialists	Dyster	Mark	(555) 555-4000
Veterinary Specialists	Jovar	Thomas	(555) 555-4000
Veterinary Specialists	Krey	Mark	(555) 555-4000
Veterinary Specialists	Marsh	Frank	(555) 555-4000

Independent Challenge 4: Explore

An Access database is an excellent tool to help record and track job opportunities. For this exercise, you'll create a database from scratch that you can use to enter, edit, and query data in pursuit of a new job or career.

a. Create a new desktop database named **Jobs.accdb**.

b. Create a table named **Positions** with the following field names, data types, and descriptions:

Field name	Data type	Description
PositionID	AutoNumber	Primary key field
Title	Short Text	Title of position such as Accountant, Assistant Court Clerk, or Web Developer
CareerArea	Short Text	Area of the career field such as Accounting, Government, or Information Systems
AnnualSalary	Currency	Annual salary
Desirability	Number	Desirability rating of 1 = low to 5 = high to show how desirable the position is to you
EmployerID	Number	Foreign key field to the Employers table

c. Create a table named **Employers** with the following field names, data types, and descriptions:

Field name	Data type	Description
EmployerID	AutoNumber	Primary key field
CompanyName	Short Text	Company name of the employer
EmpStreet	Short Text	Employer's street address
EmpCity	Short Text	Employer's city
EmpState	Short Text	Employer's state
EmpZip	Short Text	Employer's zip code
EmpPhone	Short Text	Employer's phone, such as 111-222-3333

d. Be sure to set EmployerID as the primary key field in the Employers table and the PositionID as the primary key field in the Positions table.

e. Link the Employers and Positions tables together in a one-to-many relationship using the common EmployerID field. One employer record will be linked to many position records. Be sure to enforce referential integrity.

f. Using any valid source of potential employer data, enter five records into the Employers table.

g. Using any valid source of job information, enter five records into the Positions table by using the subdatasheets from within the Employers datasheet.

Because one employer may have many positions, all five of your Positions records may be linked to the same employer, you may have one position record per employer, or any other combination.

h. Build a query that selects CompanyName from the Employers table, and the Title, CareerArea, AnnualSalary, and Desirability fields from the Positions table. Sort the records in descending order based on Desirability. Save the query as **JobList**, and print it if requested by your instructor.

i. Close the JobList datasheet, then exit Access 2016.

Visual Workshop

Open the Baseball-2.accdb database from the location where you store your Data Files, and enable content if prompted. Create a query in Query Design View based on the Players and Teams tables, as shown in FIGURE 2-24. Add criteria to select only those records where the PlayerPosition field values are equal to 1 or 2 (representing pitchers and catchers). In Query Design View, set an ascending sort order on the TeamName and PlayerPosition fields. In the results, change the name of Aaron Campanella to your name. Save the query with the name **PitchersAndCatchers**, then compare the results with FIGURE 2-24, making changes and widening columns to display all of the data. Print the datasheet if requested by your instructor. Save and close the query and the Baseball-2.accdb database, then exit Access 2016.

FIGURE 2-24

TeamName	PlayerFirst	PlayerLast	Positic
Brooklyn Beetles	Student First	Student Last	1
Brooklyn Beetles	Cy	Young	2
Mayfair Monarchs	Luis	Durocher	1
Mayfair Monarchs	Carl	Mathewson	2
Rocky's Rockets	Andrew	Spalding	1
Rocky's Rockets	Sanford	Koufax	2
Snapping Turtles	Charles	Ford	1
Snapping Turtles	Greg	Perry	2

Using Forms

CASE Julia Rice, a trip developer at Reason 2 Go, asks you to create forms to make trip information easier to access, enter, and update.

Module Objectives

After completing this module, you will be able to:

- Use the Form Wizard
- Create a split form
- Use Form Layout View
- Add fields to a form

- Modify form controls
- Create calculations
- Modify tab order
- Insert an image

Files You Will Need

R2G-3.accdb	Service-3.accdb
R2GLogo.jpg	Salvage-3.accdb
LakeHomes-3.accdb	Jobs-3.accdb
LakeHome.jpg	Baseball-3.accdb
Scuba-3.accdb	

Use the Form Wizard

Learning
Outcomes
• Create a form with
  the Form Wizard
• Sort data in a form
• Describe form
  terminology and
  views

A **form** is an easy-to-use data entry and navigation screen. A form allows you to arrange the fields of a record in any layout so a database **user** can quickly and easily find, enter, edit, and analyze data. The database **designer** or **application developer** is the person responsible for building and maintaining tables, queries, forms, and reports for all of the users. **CASE** ▶ *Julia Rice asks you to build a form to enter and maintain trip information.*

STEPS

1. **Start Access, open the R2G-3.accdb database from the location where you store your Data Files, then enable content if prompted**

   You can use many methods to create a new form, but the Form Wizard is a fast and popular tool that helps you get started. The **Form Wizard** prompts you for information it needs to create a form, such as the fields, layout, and title for the form.

2. **Click the Create tab on the Ribbon, then click the Form Wizard button in the Forms group**

   The Form Wizard starts, prompting you to select the fields for this form. You want to create a form to enter and update data in the Trips table.

3. **Click the Tables/Queries list arrow, click Table: Trips, then click the Select All Fields button** `>>`

   You could now select fields from other tables, if necessary, but in this case, you have all of the fields you need.

4. **Click Next, click the Columnar option button, click Next, type Trips Entry Form as the title, then click Finish**

   The Trips Entry Form opens in **Form View**, as shown in **FIGURE 3-1**. Access provides three different views of forms, as summarized in **TABLE 3-1**. Each item on the form is called a **control**. A **label control** is used to describe the data shown in other controls such as text boxes. A label is also used for the title of the form, Trips Entry Form. A **text box** is used to display the data as well as enter, edit, find, sort, and filter the data. A **combo box** is a combination of two controls: a text box and a list. The Category data is displayed in a combo box control. You click the arrow button on a combo box control to display a list of values, or you can edit data directly in the combo box itself.

QUICK TIP
Click in the text box of the field you want to sort before clicking a sort button.

5. **Click Stanley Bay Cleanup in the TripName text box, click the Ascending button in the Sort & Filter group, then click the Next record button ▶ in the navigation bar to move to the second record**

   The Bass Habitat Project trip is the second record when the records are sorted in ascending order on the TripName data. Information about the current record number and total number of records appears in the navigation bar, just as it does in a datasheet.

6. **Click the Previous record button ◀ in the navigation bar to move back to the first record, click the TripName text box, then change American Legacy Project to American Heritage Project**

   Your screen should look like **FIGURE 3-2**. Forms displayed in Form View are the primary tool for database users to enter, edit, and delete data in an Access database.

7. **Right-click the Trips Entry Form tab, then click Close**

   When a form is closed, Access automatically saves any edits made to the current record.

FIGURE 3-1: Trips Entry Form in Form View

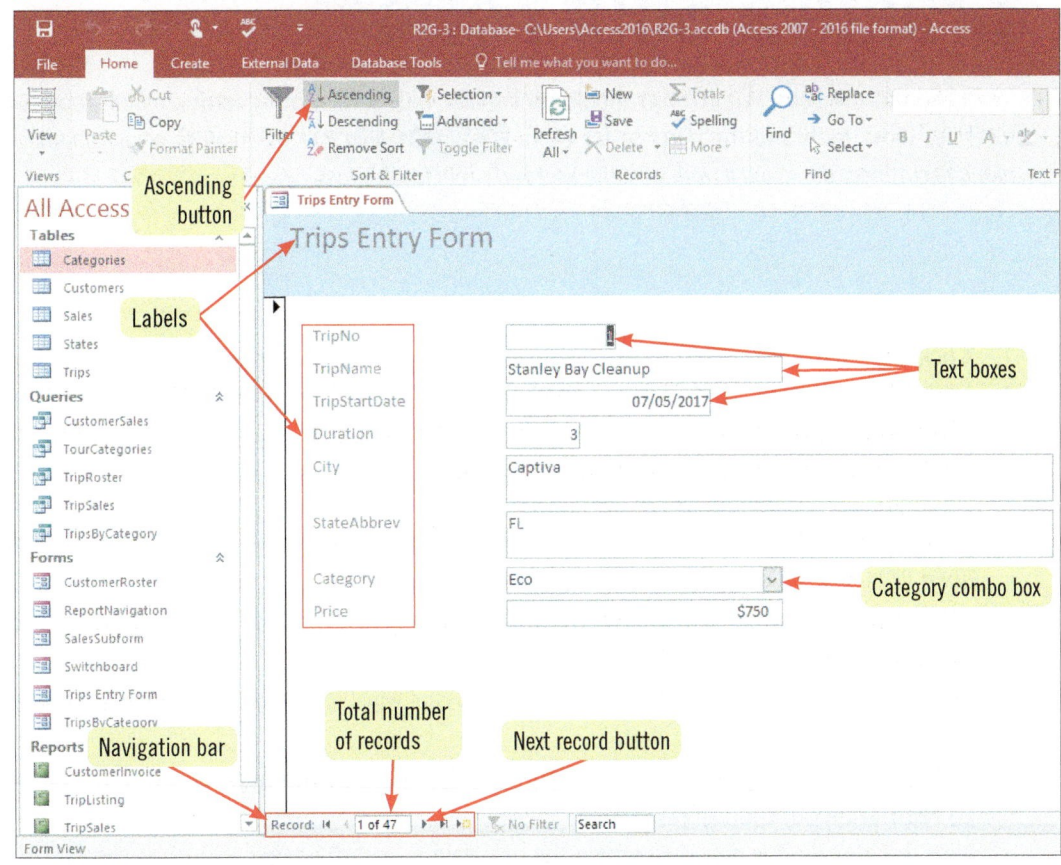

FIGURE 3-2: Editing data in Form View

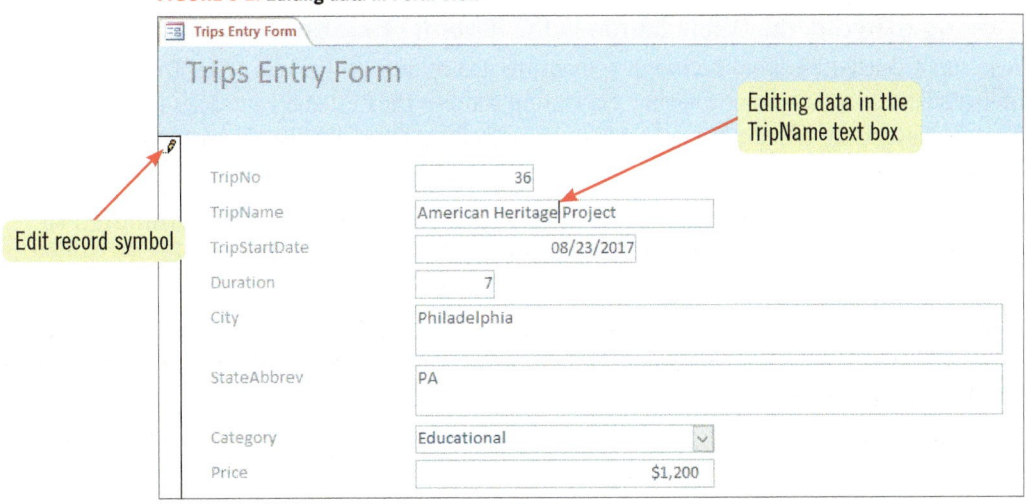

TABLE 3-1: Form views

view	primary purpose
Form	To find, sort, enter, and edit data
Layout	To modify the size, position, or formatting of controls; shows data as you modify the form, making it the tool of choice when you want to change the appearance and usability of the form while viewing data
Design	To modify the Form Header, Detail, and Footer section, or to access the complete range of controls and form properties; Design View does not display data

Create a Split Form

In addition to the Form Wizard, you should be familiar with several other form creation tools. **TABLE 3-2** identifies those tools and the purpose for each. **CASE** ▸ *Julia Rice asks you to create another form to manage customer data. You'll work with the Split Form tool for this task.*

Learning Outcomes
• Create a split form
• Enter and edit data in a form

STEPS

QUICK TIP
Layout View allows you to view and filter the data, but not edit it.

1. **Click the Customers table in the Navigation Pane, click the Create tab, click the More Forms button, click Split Form, then click the Add Existing Fields button in the Tools group on the Design tab to close the Field List if it opens**

   The Customers data appears in a split form with the top half in **Layout View**. The benefit of a **split form** is that the upper pane allows you to display the fields of one record in any arrangement, and the lower pane maintains a datasheet view of the first few records. If you edit, sort, or filter records in the upper pane, the lower pane is automatically updated, and vice versa.

2. **Click MO in the State text box in the upper pane, click the Home tab, click the Selection button in the Sort & Filter group, then click Does Not Equal "MO"**

   Thirty-seven records are filtered where the State field is not equal to MO. You also need to change a value in the Jacob Alman record.

TROUBLE
Make sure you edit the record in the datasheet in the lower pane.

3. **In the lower pane, select Des Moines in the City field of the first record, edit the entry to read Waukee, then press [Enter]**

   Note that "Waukee" is now the entry in the City field in both the upper and lower panes, as shown in **FIGURE 3-3**.

4. **Click the record selector for the Kristen Collins record in the lower pane as shown in FIGURE 3-4, then click the Delete button in the Records group on the Home tab**

   You cannot delete this record because it contains related records in the Sales table. This is a benefit of referential integrity on the one-to-many relationship between the Customers and Sales tables. Referential integrity prevents the creation of **orphan records**, records on the many side of a relationship that do not have a match on the one side.

5. **Click OK, right-click the Customers form tab, click Close, click Yes when prompted to save changes, then click OK to save the form with Customers as the name**

TABLE 3-2: Form creation tools

tool	icon	creates a form
Form		with one click based on the selected table or query
Form Design		from scratch in Form Design View
Blank Form		from scratch in Form Layout View
Form Wizard		by answering a series of questions provided by the Form Wizard dialog boxes
Navigation		used to navigate or move between different areas of the database
More Forms		based on Multiple Items, Datasheet, Split Form, or Modal Dialog arrangements
Split Form		with two panes, the upper showing one record at a time and the lower displaying a datasheet of many records

FIGURE 3-3: Customers table in a split form

FIGURE 3-4: Editing data in a split form

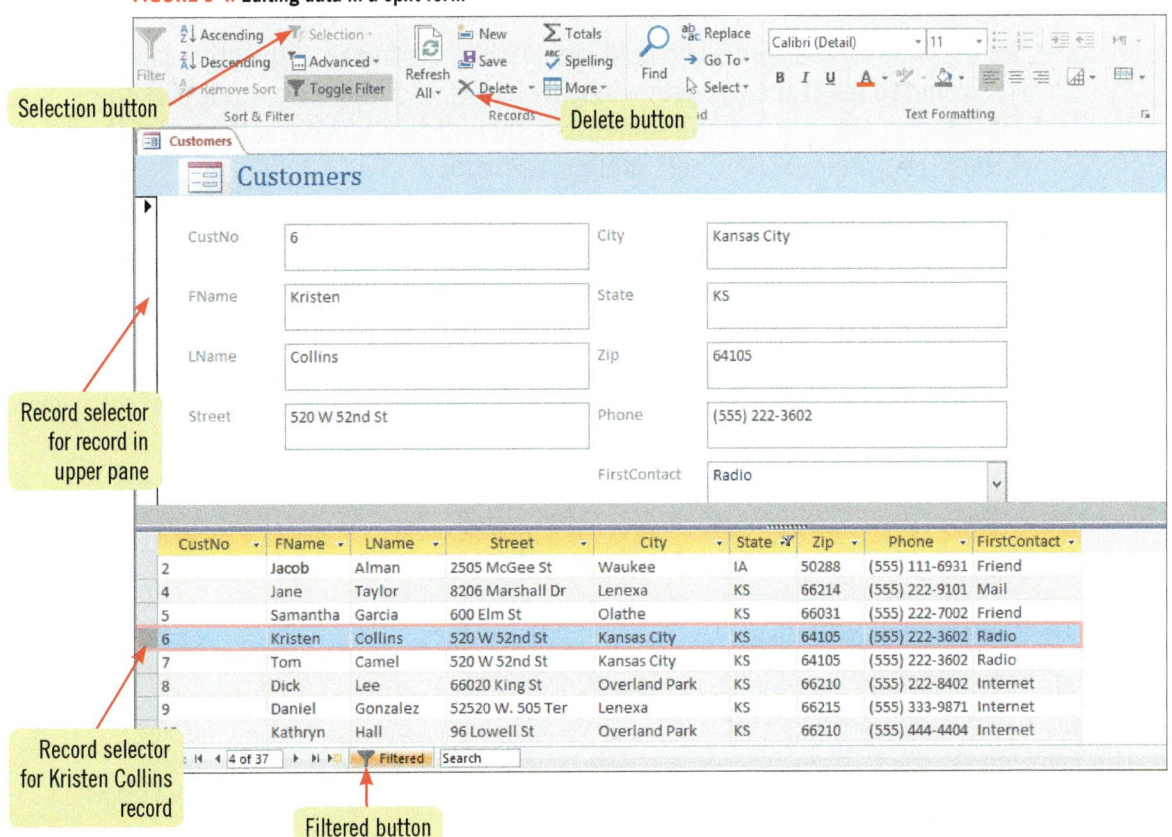

Use Form Layout View

Layout View lets you make some design changes to a form while you are browsing the data. For example, you can move and resize controls, add or delete a field on the form, filter and sort data, or change formatting characteristics, such as fonts and colors. TABLE 3-4 lists several of the most popular formatting commands found on the Format tab when you are working in Layout or Form Design View. **CASE** *Julia Rice asks you to make several design changes to the Trips Entry Form. You can make these changes in Layout View.*

STEPS

1. **Right-click Trips Entry Form in the Navigation Pane, then click Layout View**

   In Layout View, you can move through the records, but you cannot enter or edit the data as you can in Form View.

2. **Click the Next record button ▶ in the navigation bar twice to move to the third record, Bear Valley Adventures**

   You often use Layout View to make minor design changes, such as editing labels and changing formatting characteristics.

3. **Click the TripNo label to select it if it is not already selected, click between the words Trip and No, then press [Spacebar]**

   You also want to edit a few more labels.

4. **Continue editing the labels, as shown in FIGURE 3-5**

   You also want to change the text color of the labels to black to make them more noticeable.

5. **Click the Trip No label, press and hold [Shift] while clicking all of the other labels in the first column to select them together, release [Shift], click the Format tab, click the Font Color list arrow A in the Font group, then click Automatic at the top of the list**

   You also decide to narrow the City and StateAbbrev text boxes.

6. **Click Sacramento in the City text box, press and hold [Shift], click CA in the StateAbbrev text box to select the two text boxes at the same time, release [Shift], then use the ↔ pointer to drag the right edge of the selection to the left to make the text boxes approximately half as wide**

   Layout View for the Trips Entry Form should look like FIGURE 3-5. Mouse pointers in Form Layout and Form Design View are very important as they indicate what happens when you drag the mouse. Mouse pointers are described in TABLE 3-3.

TABLE 3-3: Mouse pointer shapes

shape	when does this shape appear?	action
▷	When you point to any unselected control on the form (the default mouse pointer)	Single-clicking with this mouse pointer selects a control
⊹	When you point to the upper-left corner or edge of a selected control in Form Design View or the middle of the control in Form Layout View	Dragging with this mouse pointer moves the selected control(s)
↕ ↔ ⤢ ⤡	When you point to any sizing handle (except the larger one in the upper-left corner in Form Design View)	Dragging with one of these mouse pointers resizes the control

FIGURE 3-5: Using Layout View to modify controls on the Trips Entry Form

TABLE 3-4: Useful formatting commands

button	button name	description
B	Bold	Toggles bold on or off for the selected control(s)
I	Italic	Toggles italic on or off for the selected control(s)
U	Underline	Toggles underline on or off for the selected control(s)
A	Font Color	Changes the text color of the selected control(s)
	Background Color or Shape Fill	Changes the background color of the selected control(s)
	Align Left	Left-aligns the selected control(s) within its own border
	Center	Centers the selected control(s) within its own border
	Align Right	Right-aligns the selected control(s) within its own border
	Alternate Row Color	Changes the background color of alternate records in the selected section
	Shape Outline	Changes the border color, thickness, or style of the selected control(s)
	Shape Effects	Changes the special visual effect of the selected control(s)

Table layouts

Layouts provide a way to group several controls together on a form or report to more quickly add, delete, rearrange, resize, or align controls. To insert a layout into a form or report, select the controls you want to group together, then choose the Stacked or Tabular button on the Arrange tab in Layout View. Each option applies a table layout to the controls so that you can insert, delete, merge, or split the cells in the layout to quickly rearrange or edit the controls in the layout. To remove a layout, use the Remove Layout button on the Arrange tab in Form Design View.

Add Fields to a Form

Adding and deleting fields in an existing form is a common activity. You can add or delete fields in a form in either Layout View or Design View using the Field List. The **Field List** lists the database tables and the fields they contain. To add a field to the form, drag it from the Field List to the desired location on the form. To delete a field on a form, click the field to select it, then press the [Delete] key. Deleting a field from a form does not delete it from the underlying table or have any effect on the data contained in the field. You can toggle the Field List on and off using the Add Existing Fields button on the Design tab in Layout or Design View. **CASE** ▸ *Julia Rice asks you to add the Trip description from the Categories table to the Trips Entry Form. You can use Layout View and the Field List to accomplish this goal.*

STEPS

1. **Click the Design tab on the Ribbon, click the Add Existing Fields button in the Tools group, then click the Show all tables link in the Field List**

   The Field List opens in Layout View, as shown in **FIGURE 3-6**. Notice that the Field List is divided into sections. The upper section shows the tables currently used by the form, the middle section shows directly related tables, and the lower section shows other tables in the database. The expand/collapse button to the left of the table names allows you to expand (show) the fields within the table or collapse (hide) them. The Description field is in the Categories table in the middle section.

   To move the Field List, drag its title bar. Double-click the title bar of the Field List to dock it to the right.

2. **Click the expand button ⊞ to the left of the Categories table, drag the Description field to the form, then use the ⬚ pointer to drag the new Description combo box and label below the Price text box**

   When you add a new field to a form, two controls are usually created: a label and a text box. The label contains the field name and the text box displays the data in the field. The Categories table moved from the middle to the top section of the Field List. You also want to align and format the new controls with others already on the form.

3. **Click the Description label, click the Format tab on the Ribbon, then click the Font color button 🅰 ▾ to change the text color from gray to black**

   With the new controls in position and formatted, you want to enter a new record. You must switch to Form View to edit, enter, or delete data.

4. **Click the Home tab, click the View button 🔲 to switch to Form View, click the New (blank) record button ▸ in the navigation bar, click the TripName text box, then enter a new record in the updated form, as shown in FIGURE 3-7**

   Be sure to enter the correct value for each field and note that when you select a value in the Category combo box, the Description is automatically updated. This is due to the one-to-many relationship between the Categories and Trips tables in the Relationships window.

FIGURE 3-6: Field List in Form Layout View

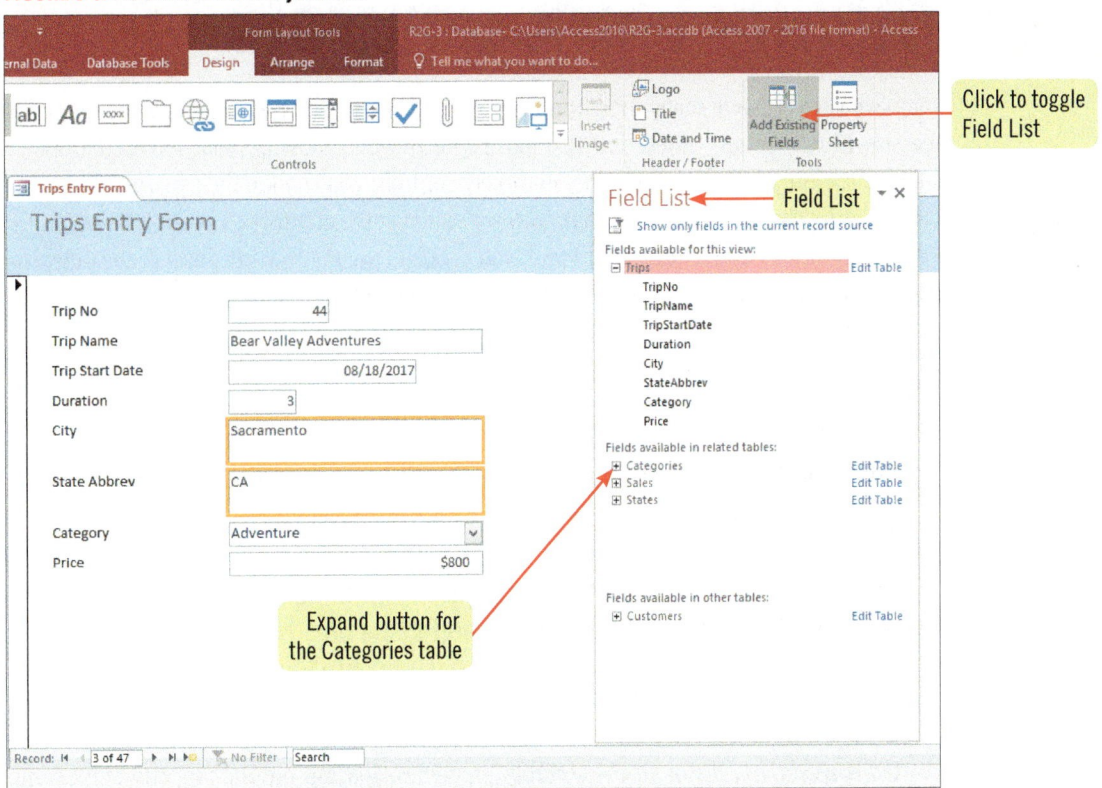

FIGURE 3-7: Entering a record in the updated Trips Entry Form in Form View

Bound versus unbound controls

Controls are either bound or unbound. **Bound controls** display values from a field such as text boxes and combo boxes. **Unbound controls** do not display data; unbound controls describe data or enhance the appearance of the form. Labels are the most common type of unbound control, but other types include lines, images, tabs, and command buttons. Another way to distinguish bound from unbound controls is to observe the form as you move from record to record. Because bound controls display data, their contents change as you move through the records, displaying data from the field of the current record. Unbound controls such as labels and lines do not change as you move through the records in a form.

Modify Form Controls

You have already made many modifications to form controls, such as changing the font color of labels and the size of text boxes. Labels and text boxes are the two most popular form controls. Other common controls are listed in **TABLE 3-5**. When you modify controls, you change their **properties** (characteristics). All of the control characteristics you can modify are stored in the control's **Property Sheet**. **CASE** ▶ *Because R2G is now focused on Eco (ecological) trips, you decide to use the Property Sheet of the Category field to modify the default value to be "Eco." Julia asks you to use the Property Sheet to make other control modifications to better size and align the controls.*

STEPS

1. **Right-click the Trips Entry Form tab, click Layout View, then click the Property Sheet button in the Tools group**

   The Property Sheet opens, replacing the Field List and showing you all of the properties for the selected item. Drag the title bar of the Property Sheet to move it. Double-click the title bar to dock it to the right.

2. **Click the Category combo box on the form, click the Data tab in the Property Sheet (if it is not already selected), click the Default Value box, type Eco, then press [Enter]**

   The Property Sheet should look like **FIGURE 3-8**. Access often helps you with the **syntax** (rules) of entering property values. In this case, Access added quotation marks around "Eco" to indicate that the default entry is text. Properties are categorized in the Property Sheet with the Format, Data, Event, and Other tabs. The All tab is a complete list of all the control's properties. You can use the Property Sheet to make all control modifications, although you'll probably find that some changes are easier to make using the Ribbon. The property values change in the Property Sheet as you modify a control using the Ribbon and vice versa.

   TROUBLE
   Be sure to click the Trip No label on the left, not the TripNo text box on the right.

3. **Click the Format tab in the Property Sheet, click the Trip No label in the form to select it, click the Home tab on the Ribbon, then click the Align Right button 🗏 in the Text Formatting group**

   Notice that the **Text Align property** on the Format tab in the Property Sheet is automatically updated from Left to Right even though you changed the property using the Ribbon instead of the Property Sheet.

4. **Click the Trip Name label, press and hold [Shift], then click each other label in the first column on the form**

   With all the labels selected, you can modify their Text Align property at the same time.

   TROUBLE
   You may need to click 🗏 twice.

5. **Click 🗏 in the Text Formatting group**

   Don't be overwhelmed by the number of properties available for each control on the form or the number of ways to modify each property. Over time, you will learn about most of these properties. At this point, it's only important to know the purpose of the Property Sheet and understand that properties are modified in various ways.

   TROUBLE
   Your Trip No value might not match **FIGURE 3-9**. It is an AutoNumber value, controlled by Access.

6. **Click the Save button 🖫 on the Quick Access Toolbar, click the Form View button 🖽 to switch to Form View, click the New (blank) record button ▶❋ in the navigation bar, then enter the record shown in FIGURE 3-9**

   For new records, "Eco" is provided as the default value for the Category combo box, but you can change it by typing a new value or selecting one from the list. With the labels right-aligned, they are much closer to the data in the text boxes that they describe.

FIGURE 3-8: Using the Property Sheet

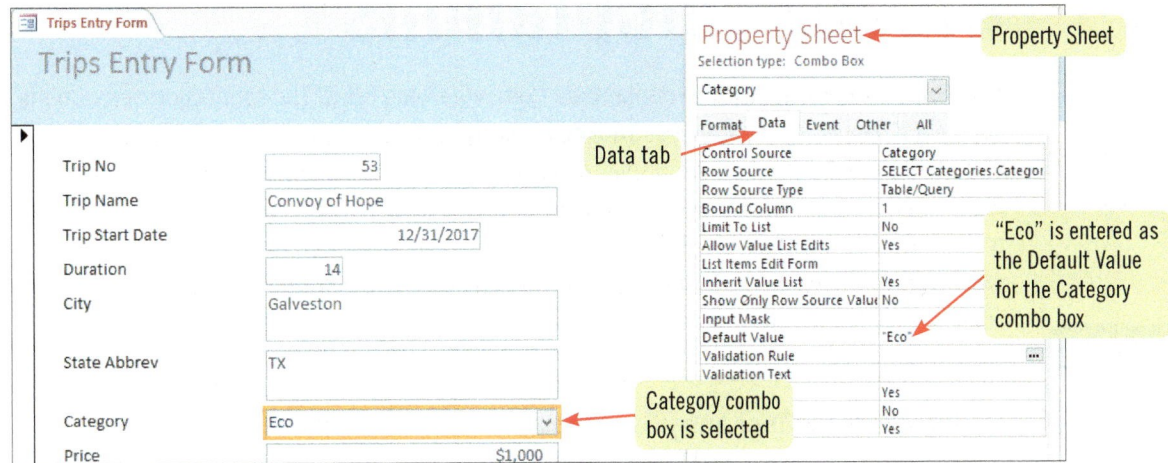

FIGURE 3-9: Modified Trips Entry Form

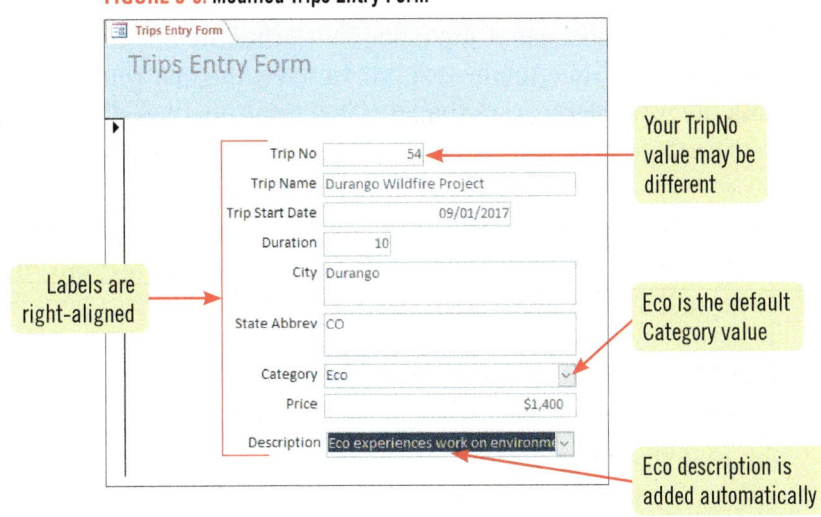

TABLE 3-5: Common form controls

name	used to	bound	unbound
Label	Provide consistent descriptive text as you navigate from record to record; the label is the most common type of unbound control and can also be used as a hyperlink to another database object, external file, or webpage		•
Text box	Display, edit, or enter data for each record from an underlying record source; the text box is the most common type of bound control	•	
List box	Display a list of possible data entries	•	
Combo box	Display a list of possible data entries for a field, and provide a text box for an entry from the keyboard; combines the list box and text box controls	•	
Tab control	Create a three-dimensional aspect on a form		•
Check box	Display "yes" or "no" answers for a field; if the box is checked, it means "yes"	•	
Toggle button	Display "yes" or "no" answers for a field; if the button is pressed, it means "yes"	•	
Option button	Display a choice for a field	•	
Option group	Display and organize choices (usually presented as option buttons) for a field	•	
Line and Rectangle	Draw lines and rectangles on the form		•
Command button	Provide an easy way to initiate a command or run a macro		•

Create Calculations

Text boxes are generally used to display data from underlying fields. The connection between the text box and field is defined by the **Control Source property** on the Data tab of the Property Sheet for that text box. A text box control can also display a calculation. To create a calculation in a text box, you enter an expression instead of a field name in the Control Source property. An **expression** is a combination of field names, operators (such as +, –, /, and *), and functions (such as Sum, Count, or Avg) that results in a single value. Sample expressions are shown in TABLE 3-6. **CASE** *Julia Rice asks you to add a text box to the Trips Entry Form to calculate the trip end date. You can add a text box in Form Design View to accomplish this.*

STEPS

1. **Right-click the Trips Entry Form tab, then click Design View**

   You want to add the trip end date calculation just below the Duration text box. First, you'll resize the City and State Abbrev fields.

2. **Click the City label, press and hold [Shift], click the City text box, click the State Abbrev label, click the StateAbbrev text box to select the four controls together, release [Shift], click the Arrange tab, click the Size/Space button, then click To Shortest**

   With the City and StateAbbrev fields resized, you're ready to move them to make room for the new control to calculate the tour end date.

3. **Click a blank spot on the form to deselect the four controls, click the StateAbbrev text box, use the ⬚ pointer to move it down, click the City text box, then use the ⬚ pointer to move it down**

   To add the calculation to determine the trip end date (the trip start date plus the duration), start by adding a new text box to the form between the Duration and City text boxes.

4. **Click the Design tab, click the Text Box button 🔲 in the Controls group, then click between the Duration and City text boxes to insert the new text box**

   Adding a new text box automatically adds a new label to the left of the text box.

5. **Double-click Text23, type Trip End Date, click the Home tab, click the Font Color button 🅰 ▾, then press [Enter]**

   With the label updated to correctly identify the text box to the right, you're ready to enter the expression to calculate the tour end date.

6. **Click the new text box to select it, click the Data tab in the Property Sheet, click the Control Source property, type =[TripStartDate]+[Duration], then press [Enter] to update the form as shown in FIGURE 3-10**

   All expressions entered in a control must start with an equal sign (=). When referencing a field name within an expression, [square brackets]—(not parentheses) and not {curly braces}—surround the field name. In an expression, you must type the field name exactly as it was created in Table Design View, but you do not need to match the capitalization.

7. **Click the View button 🔲 to switch to Form View, tab three times to the Duration field, type 5, then press [Enter]**

   Note that the trip end date, calculated by an expression, automatically changed to five days after the trip start date to reflect the new duration value. The updated Trips Entry Form with the trip end date calculation for the Bikers for Ecology is shown in FIGURE 3-11.

FIGURE 3-10: Adding a text box to calculate a value

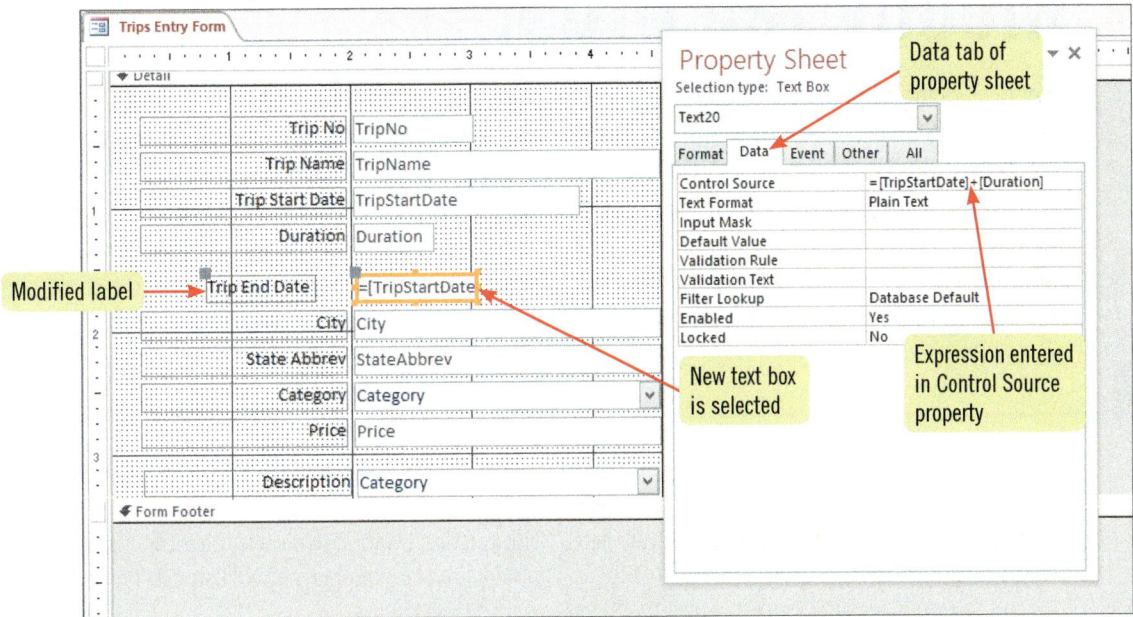

FIGURE 3-11: Displaying the results of a calculation in Form View

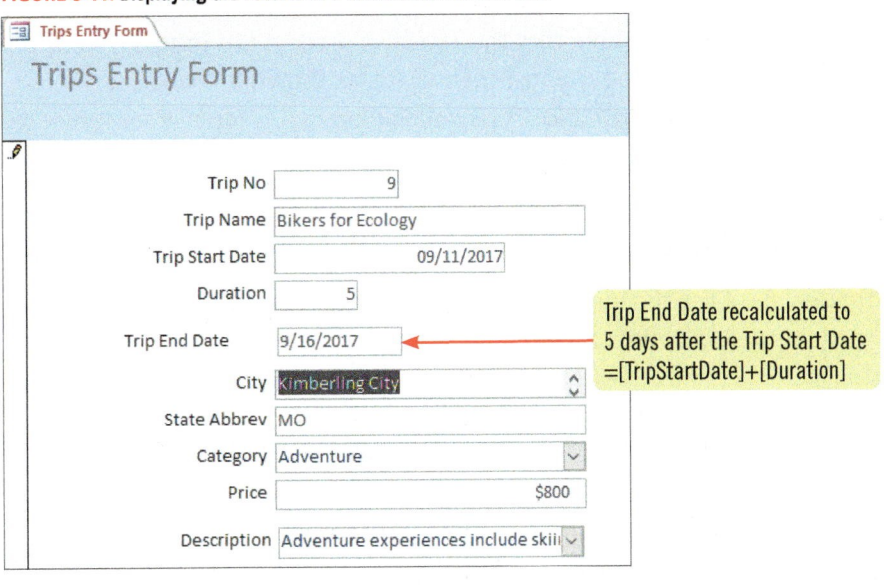

TABLE 3-6: Sample expressions

sample expression	description
=Sum([Salary])	Uses the **Sum** function to add the values in the Salary field
=[Price] * 1.05	Multiplies the Price field by 1.05 (adds 5% to the Price field)
=[Subtotal] + [Shipping]	Adds the value of the Subtotal field to the value of the Shipping field
=Avg([Freight])	Uses the **Avg** function to display an average of the values in the Freight field
=Date()	Uses the **Date** function to display the current date in the form of mm-dd-yy
="Page " &[Page]	Displays the word Page, a space, and the result of the [Page] field, an Access field that contains the current page number
=[FirstName]& " " &[LastName]	Displays the value of the FirstName and LastName fields in one control, separated by a space
=Left([ProductNumber],2)	Uses the **Left** function to display the first two characters in the ProductNumber field

Modify Tab Order

After positioning all of the controls on the form, you should check the tab order and tab stops. **Tab order** is the order the focus moves as you press [Tab] in Form View. A **tab stop** refers to whether a control can receive the focus in the first place. By default, the Tab Stop property for all text boxes and combo boxes is set to Yes, but some text boxes, such as those that contain expressions, will not be used for data entry. Therefore, the Tab Stop property for a text box that contains a calculation should be set to No. Unbound controls such as labels and lines do not have a Tab Stop property because they cannot be used to enter or edit data. **CASE** *Julia suggests that you check the tab order of the Trips Entry Form, then change tab stops and tab order as necessary.*

STEPS

1. **Press [Tab] enough times to move through several records, watching the focus move through the bound controls of the form**

   Because the Trip End Date text box is a calculated field, you don't want it to receive the focus. To prevent the Trip End Date text box from receiving the focus, you set its Tab Stop property to No using its Property Sheet. You can work with the Property Sheet in either Layout or Design View.

QUICK TIP
You can also switch between views using the View buttons in the lower-right corner of the window.

2. **Right-click the Trips Entry Form tab, click Design View, click the text box with the Trip End Date calculation if it is not already selected, click the Other tab in the Property Sheet, double-click the Tab Stop property to toggle it from Yes to No, then change the Name property to TripEndDate, as shown in FIGURE 3-12**

   The Other tab of the Property Sheet contains the properties you need to change the tab stop and tab order. The **Tab Stop property** determines whether the field accepts focus, and the **Tab Index property** indicates the numeric tab order for all controls on the form that have the Tab Stop property set to Yes. The **Name property** on the Other tab is also important as it identifies the name of the control, which is used in other areas of the database. To review your tab stop changes, return to Form View.

QUICK TIP
In Form Design View, press [Ctrl][.] to switch to Form View. In Form View, press [Ctrl][,] to switch to Form Design View.

3. **Click the View button [icon] to switch to Form View, then press [Tab] nine times to move to the next record**

   Now that the tab stop has been removed from the TripEndDate text box, the tab order flows correctly from the top to the bottom of the form, skipping the calculated field. To review the tab order for the entire form in one dialog box, you must switch to Form Design View.

4. **Right-click the Trips Entry Form tab, click Design View, then click the Tab Order button in the Tools group to open the Tab Order dialog box**

   The Tab Order dialog box allows you to view and change the tab order by dragging fields up or down using the **field selector** to the left of the field name. Moving fields up and down in this list also renumbers the Tab Index property for the controls in their respective Property Sheets. If you want Access to create a top-to-bottom and left-to-right tab order, click **Auto Order**.

TROUBLE
If the order of your fields does not match those in **FIGURE 3-13**, move a field by clicking the field selector and then dragging the field up or down.

5. **Click the Auto Order button to make sure your tab order goes top to bottom as shown in FIGURE 3-13, click OK to close the Tab Order dialog box, click the Property Sheet button to toggle it off, click the Save button [icon] on the Quick Access Toolbar to save your work, then click a blank spot on the form to deselect the text box**

FIGURE 3-12: Using the Property Sheet to set tab properties

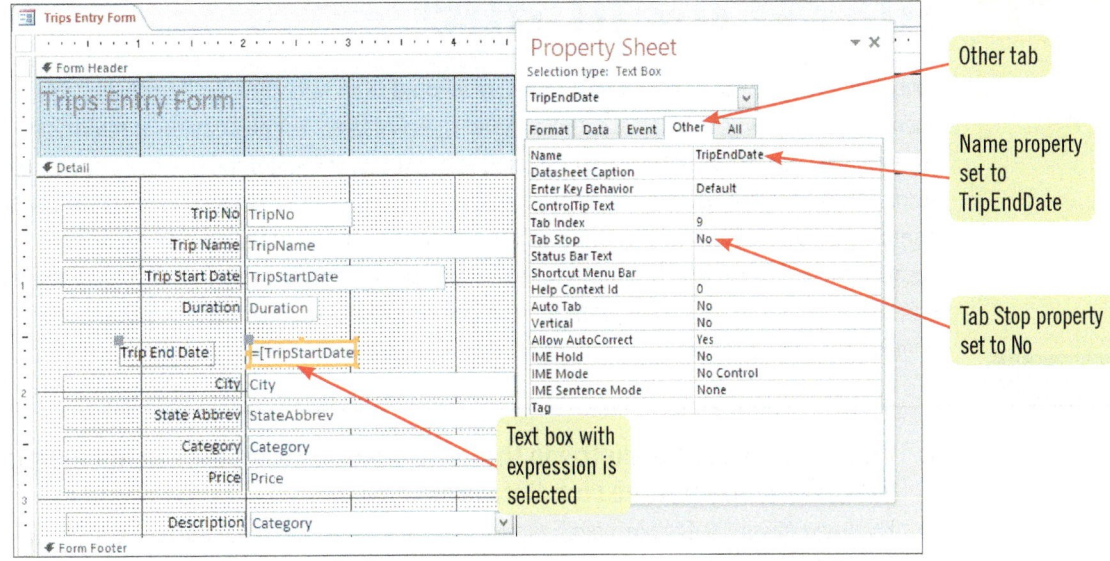

FIGURE 3-13: Tab Order dialog box

Form layouts

A **layout** helps you keep the controls on a form organized as a group. You can apply a stacked or tabular layout to the controls on your form by clicking the Stacked or Tabular buttons on the Arrange tab in Form Design View. Remove a layout by clicking the Remove Layout button. You can also modify a layout by modifying the margins, padding, and anchoring options of the layout using buttons found in the Position group on the Arrange tab in Form Design View. **Margin** refers to the space between the outer edge of the control and the data displayed inside the control. **Padding** is the space between the controls. **Anchoring** allows you to tie controls together so you can work with them as a group. Some of the Form Wizards automatically apply a layout to the controls that you can modify or remove as needed.

Insert an Image

Graphic images, such as pictures, logos, or clip art, can add style and professionalism to a form. The form section in which you place the images is significant. **Form sections** determine where controls are displayed and printed; they are described in TABLE 3-7. For example, if you add a company logo to the Form Header section, the image appears at the top of the form in Form View as well as at the top of a printout. If you add the same image to the Detail section, it prints next to each record in the printout because the Detail section is printed for every record. **CASE** *Julia Rice suggests that you add the R2G logo to the top of the Trips Entry Form. You can add the control in either Layout or Design View, but if you want to place it in the Form Header section, you have to work in Design View.*

STEPS

1. **Click the Insert Image button in the Controls group, click Browse, then navigate to the location where you store your Data Files**

   The Insert Picture dialog box opens, prompting you for the location of the image.

2. **Click the Web-Ready Image Files button, click All Files, double-click R2GLogo.jpg, then click at the top of the Form Header section at about the 3" mark on the ruler**

   The R2GLogo image is added to the right side of the Form Header section. When an image or control is selected in Design View, you can use **sizing handles**, which are small squares at the corners of the selection box. Drag a handle to resize the image or control. You use the pointer to move a control.

3. **Use the pointer to move the logo to the top edge of the Form Header section, then drag the top edge of the Detail section up using the pointer**

   You also want to align the Trip End Date label with the other labels in the first column.

4. **Click the Trip End Date label, click the Home tab on the Ribbon, click the Align Right button, press and hold [Shift], click the Duration label, click the Arrange tab on the Ribbon, click the Align button, then click Right as shown in FIGURE 3-14**

   With the form completed, you open it in Form View to observe the changes.

5. **Click the Save button on the Quick Access Toolbar, click the Home tab, then click the View button to switch to Form View**

   You decide to add one more record with your final Trips Entry Form.

6. **Click the New (blank) record button in the navigation bar, then enter the new record shown in FIGURE 3-15, using your last name in the Trip Name field**

   Now print only this single new record.

7. **Click the File tab, click Print in the navigation bar, click Print, click the Selected Record(s) option button, then click OK**

8. **Close the Trips Entry Form, click Yes if prompted to save it, close the R2G-3.accdb database, then exit Access 2016**

FIGURE 3-14: Adding an image to the Form Header section

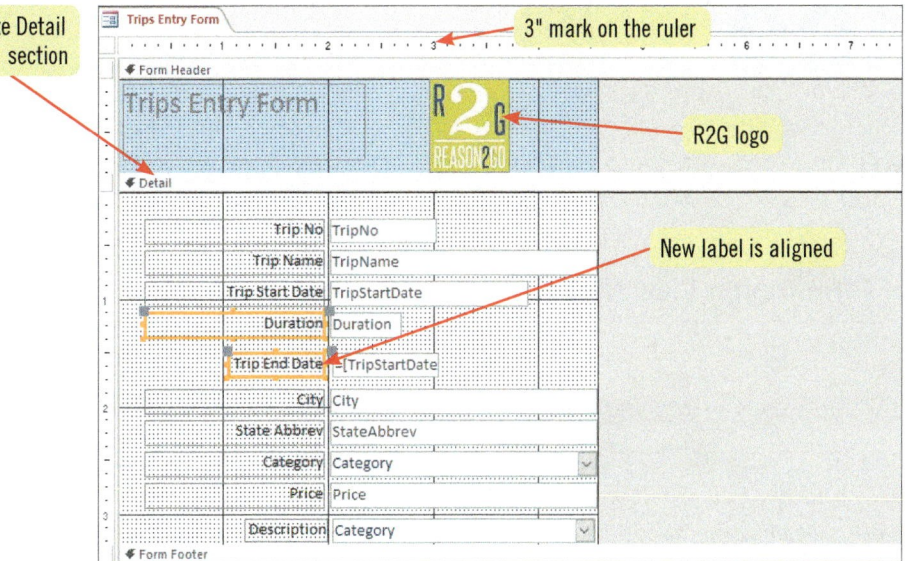

FIGURE 3-15: Final Trips Entry Form with new record

TABLE 3-7: Form sections

section	controls placed in this section print
Form Header	Only once at the top of the first page of the printout
Detail	Once for every record
Form Footer	Only once at the end of the last page of the printout

Applying a background image

A **background image** is an image that fills the entire form or report, appearing "behind" the other controls. A background image is sometimes called a watermark image. To add a background image, use the Picture property for the form or report to browse for the image that you want to use in the background.

Practice

Concepts Review

Label each element of Form Design View shown in FIGURE 3-16.

FIGURE 3-16

Match each term with the statement that best describes it.

10. **Tab order**
11. **Calculated control**
12. **Detail section**
13. **Form Footer section**
14. **Bound control**
15. **Database designer**

a. Created by entering an expression in a text box
b. Controls placed here print once for every record in the underlying record source
c. Used on a form to display data from a field
d. Controls placed here print only once at the end of the printout
e. The way the focus moves from one bound control to the next in Form View
f. Responsible for building and maintaining tables, queries, forms, and reports

Select the best answer from the list of choices.

16. **Every element on a form is called a(n):**
    a. property.
    b. item.
    c. control.
    d. tool.

17. **Which of the following is probably *not* a graphic image?**
    a. Logo
    b. Clip art
    c. Calculation
    d. Picture

18. **The most common bound control is the:**
    - **a.** combo box.
    - **b.** label.
    - **c.** list box.
    - **d.** text box.

19. **The most common unbound control is the:**
    - **a.** text box.
    - **b.** combo box.
    - **c.** label.
    - **d.** command button.

20. **Which form view cannot be used to view data?**
    - **a.** Layout
    - **b.** Design
    - **c.** Datasheet
    - **d.** Preview

Skills Review

1. **Use the Form Wizard.**
   - **a.** Start Access and open the LakeHomes-3.accdb database from the location where you store your Data Files. Enable content if prompted.
   - **b.** Click the Create tab, then use the Form Wizard to create a form based on all of the fields in the Realtors table. Use a Columnar layout and type **Realtor Entry Form** to title the form.
   - **c.** Add a *new record* with your name in the RFirst and RLast text boxes. Note that the RealtorNo field is an AutoNumber field that is automatically incremented as you enter your first and last names. Enter your school's telephone number for the RPhone field value, and enter **4** as the AgencyNo field value.
   - **d.** Save and close the Realtor Entry Form.

2. **Create a split form.**
   - **a.** Click the Agencies table in the Navigation Pane, click the Create tab, click the More Forms button, then click Split Form.
   - **b.** Close the Property Sheet if it opens then switch to Form View.
   - **c.** Click the record selector in the lower pane for AgencyNo 3, Green Mountain Realty, then click the Delete button in the Records group to delete this realtor. Click OK when prompted that you cannot delete this record because there are related records in the Realtors table.
   - **d.** Navigate to the AgencyNo 4 record, Shepherd of the Hills Realtors, in either the upper or lower pane of the split form. Change 7744 Pokeberry Lane to **800 Lake Shore Drive**.
   - **e.** Right-click the Agencies form tab, click Close, click Yes when prompted to save changes, type **Agencies Split Form** as the name of the form, then click OK.

3. **Use Form Layout View.**
   - **a.** Open the Realtor Entry Form in Layout View.
   - **b.** Modify the labels on the left to read: **Realtor Number**, **Realtor First Name**, **Realtor Last Name**, **Realtor Cell**, **Agency Number**.
   - **c.** Modify the text color of the labels to be black.
   - **d.** Resize all of the text boxes on the right to be the same width as the RealtorNo text box.
   - **e.** Save the Realtor Entry Form.

4. **Add fields to a form.**
   - **a.** Open the Field List, show all the tables, then expand the Agencies table to display its fields.
   - **b.** Drag the AgencyName field to the form, then move the AgencyName label and combo box below the Agency Number controls.
   - **c.** Modify the AgencyName label to read **Agency Name**.
   - **d.** Modify the text color of the Agency Name label to black.
   - **e.** Close the Field List and save and close the Realtor Entry Form.

Skills Review (continued)

5. Modify form controls.

  a. Reopen the Realtor Entry Form in Layout View, then select all of the labels in the left column and use the Align Right button on the Home tab to right-align them.

  b. Save the form, switch to Form View, navigate to Realtor No 5 (Jane Ann Welch), then use the Agency Name combo box to change the Agency Name to **Big Cedar Realtors**.

  c. In Layout View, resize and align all controls so that the labels are lined up on the left and the text boxes are lined up on the right, as shown in **FIGURE 3-17**.

FIGURE 3-17

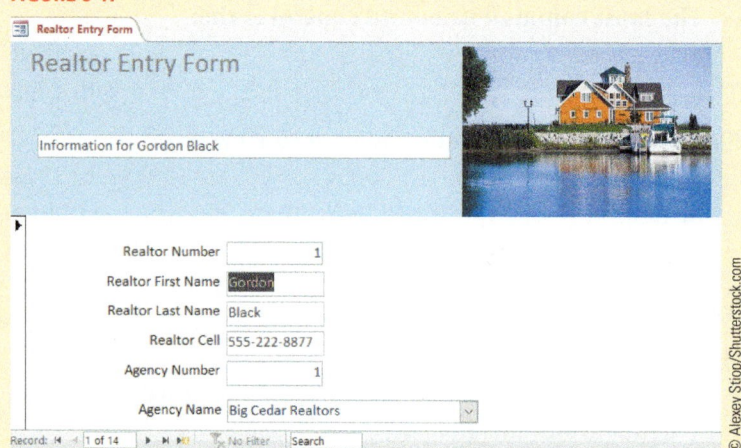

6. Create calculations.

  a. Switch to Form Design View, expand the size of the Form Header section by dragging the top edge of the Detail section down about 0.5", then add a text box at about the 1" mark below the Realtor Entry Form label in the Form Header section.

  b. Delete the Text14 label that is created when you add a new text box. The number in your label is based on previous work done to the form, so it might vary.

  c. Widen the text box to be almost as wide as the entire form, then enter the following expression into the text box, which will add the words *Information for* to the realtor's first name, a space, and then the realtor's last name.

    ="Information for "&[RFirst]&" "&[RLast]

  d. Save the form, then view it in Form View. Be sure the new text box correctly displays a space before and after the realtor's first name. If #Name? appears, which indicates that the expression was entered incorrectly, return to Design View to correct the expression.

  e. In Form View, change the Realtor Last Name for Realtor Number 1 from Bono to **Black**. Tab to the RPhone text box to observe how the expression in the Form Header automatically updates.

  f. Tab through several records, observing the expression in the Form Header section.

7. Modify tab order.

  a. Switch to Form Design View, then open the Property Sheet.

  b. Select the new text box with the expression in the Form Header section, then change the Tab Stop property from Yes to **No**.

  c. Select the RealtorNo text box in the Detail section, then change the Tab Stop property from Yes to **No**. (AutoNumber fields cannot be edited, so they do not need to have a tab stop.)

  d. Close the Property Sheet.

  e. Open the Tab Order dialog box and click the Auto Order button to make sure the focus moves from top to bottom through the form.

  f. Save the form and view it in Form View. Tab through the form to make sure that the tab order is sequential and skips the expression in the Form Header as well as the Realtor Number text box. Use the Tab Order button on the Design tab in Form Design View to modify the tab order, if necessary.

Skills Review (continued)

8. **Insert an image.**

   a. Switch to Design View, then click the Form Header section bar.

   b. Add the LakeHome.jpg image to the right side of the Form Header, then resize the image to be about 2.5" × 1.5". Remember to search for All files.

   c. Remove the extra blank space in the Form Header section by dragging the top edge of the Detail section up as far as possible.

   d. Drag the right edge of the form as far as possible to the left.

   e. Save the form, then switch to Form View as shown in **FIGURE 3-17**. Move through the records, observing the calculated field from record to record to make sure it is calculating correctly.

   f. Find the record with your name, and if requested by your instructor, print only that record.

   g. Close the Realtor Entry Form, close the LakeHomes-3.accdb database, then exit Access.

Independent Challenge 1

As a volunteer for a scuba divers' club, you have developed a database to help manage scuba dives. In this exercise, you'll create a data entry form to manage the dive trips.

   a. Start Access, then open the Scuba-3.accdb database from the location where you store your Data Files. Enable content if prompted.

   b. Using the Form Wizard, create a form that includes all the fields in the DiveTrips table and uses the Columnar layout, then type **Dive Trip Entry** as the title of the form.

   c. Switch to Layout View, then delete the ID text box and label.

   d. Using Form Design View, use the [Shift] key to select all of the text boxes except the last one for TripReport, then resize them to the shortest size using the To Shortest option on the Size/Space button on the Arrange tab.

   e. Using Form Design View, resize the Location, City, State/Province, Country, and Lodging text boxes to be no wider than the Rating text box.

   f. Using Form Design View, move and resize the controls, as shown in **FIGURE 3-18**. This will require several steps. Once the controls are resized, drag the top of the Form Footer section up to remove the extra blank space in the Detail section.

   g. Using Form Layout View, modify the labels and alignment of the labels, as shown in **FIGURE 3-18**. Note that there are spaces between the words in the labels, the labels are right-aligned, and the text boxes are left-aligned.

   h. In Form View, sort the records in ascending order on the Dive Master ID field, which will order the Great Barrier Reef tour as the first record. Edit the Certification Diving and Trip Report fields, as shown in **FIGURE 3-18** for the TripReport field using your name.

   i. Save the form, then if requested by your instructor, print only the record with your name.

   j. Close the Dive Trip Entry form, close the Scuba-3.accdb database, then exit Access 2016.

FIGURE 3-18

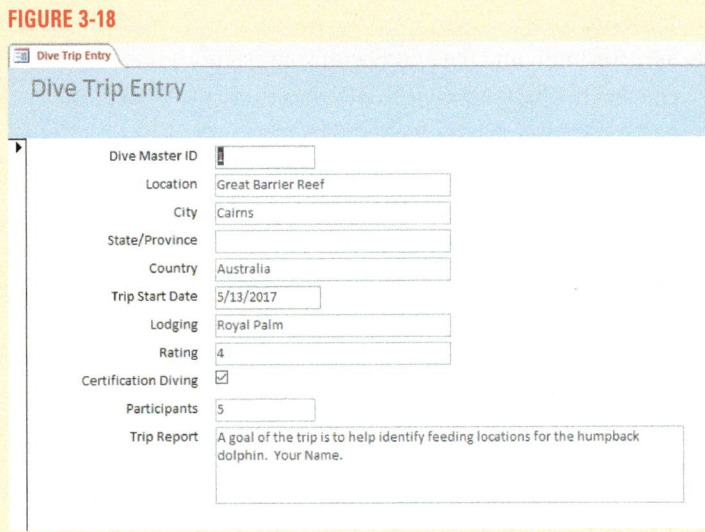

Independent Challenge 2

You have built an Access database to track membership in a community service club. The database tracks member names and addresses as well as their status in the club.

a. Start Access, then open the Service-3.accdb database from the location where you store your Data Files. Enable content if prompted.

b. Using the Form Wizard, create a form based on all of the fields of the Members table and the DuesOwed field in the Status table.

c. View the data by Members, use a Columnar layout, then enter **Member Information** as the title of the form.

d. Enter a new record with your name and the school name, and address of your school for the Company and address fields. Give yourself a StatusNo entry of **1**. In the DuesPaid field, enter **50**. The DuesOwed field automatically displays 100 because that value is pulled from the Status table and is based on the entry in the StatusNo field, which links the Members table to the Status table.

e. In Layout View, add a text box to the form and move it below the DuesOwed text box.

f. Open the Property Sheet for the new text box, display the Data tab, and in the Control Source property of the new text box, enter **=[DuesOwed]-[DuesPaid]**, the expression that calculates the balance between DuesOwed and DuesPaid.

g. Open the Property Sheet for the new label, and change the Caption property on the Format tab for the new label to **Balance**. Resize the label to be as wide as the labels above it.

h. Right-align all of the labels in the first column.

i. Set the Tab Stop property for the text box that contains the calculated Balance to **No**.

j. In Layout or Design View, resize DuesPaid and DuesOwed text boxes to be the same width as the new Balance text box, then right-align all data within the three text boxes because numbers are clearer when they align on the decimal point.

k. Make sure that the Format property on the Format tab is Currency for the DuesPaid, DuesOwed, and Balance expression text boxes. Close the Property Sheet.

l. In Form Design View, make sure that the right edge of the form is at or less than the 7" mark on the horizontal ruler. The horizontal ruler is located just above the Form Header section.

m. Save the form, find the record with your name, change the DuesPaid value to **60**, then move and resize controls as necessary to match **FIGURE 3-19**.

n. If requested by your instructor, print only the record with your name.

o. Save and close the Member Information form, then close the Service-3.accdb database and exit Access 2016.

FIGURE 3-19

Independent Challenge 3

You have built an Access database to organize the deposits at a salvage and recycling center. Various clubs regularly deposit recyclable material, which is measured in pounds when the deposits are made.

a. Open the Salvage-3.accdb database from the location where you store your Data Files. Enable content if prompted.

b. Using the Form Wizard, create a form based on all of the fields in the CenterDeposits query. View the data by Deposits, use the Columnar layout, and title the form **Deposit Listing**.

c. Switch to Layout View, then make each label bold.

d. Modify the labels so that CenterName is **Center Name**, DepositDate is **Deposit Date**, and ClubName is **Club Name**.

e. Switch to Form Design View and resize the CenterName and ClubName text boxes so they are the same height and width as the Weight text box, as shown in **FIGURE 3-20**.

f. Switch to Form View, find and change any entry of A1 Salvage Center to *your* last name, then print one record with your name if requested by your instructor.

g. Using Form View of the Deposit Listing form, filter for all records with your last name in the CenterName field.

h. Using Form View of the Deposit Listing form, sort the filtered records in descending order on the DepositDate field.

i. In Form Design View, narrow the form by dragging the right edge as far left as possible.

j. Preview the first record, as shown in **FIGURE 3-20**. If requested by your instructor, print the first record.

k. Save and close the Deposit Listing form, close the Salvage-3.accdb database, then exit Access.

FIGURE 3-20

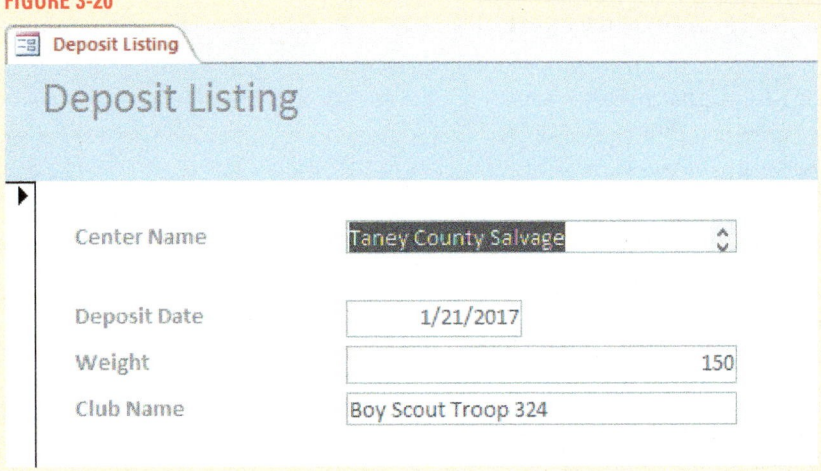

Independent Challenge 4: Explore

One way you can use an Access database on your own is to record and track your job search efforts. In this exercise, you will develop a form to help you enter data into your job-tracking database.

a. Start Access and open the Jobs-3.accdb database from the location where you store your Data Files. Enable content if prompted.

b. Click the Create tab, then use the Form Wizard to create a new form based on all the fields of both the Employers and Positions tables.

c. View the data by Employers, use a Datasheet layout for the subform, accept the default names for the form and subform, then open the form to view information.

d. Use Layout View and Design View to modify the form labels, text box positions, alignment, and sizes, as shown in FIGURE 3-21. Also note that the columns within the subform have been resized to display all of the data in the subform.

FIGURE 3-21

Independent Challenge 4: Explore (continued)

e. Change the CompanyName of IBM in the first record to ***Your* Last Name Software**, and if instructed to create a printout, print only that record. Close the Employers form.

f. Click the Employers table in the Navigation Pane, then use the Split Form option on the More Forms button of the Create tab to create a split form on the Employers table. Close and save the split form with the name **Employers Split Form**.

g. Open the Employers Split Form in Form View, change the address and phone number information for EmployerID 1 to your school's address and phone information, as shown in **FIGURE 3-22**.

h. Navigate through all five records, then back to EmployerID 1, observing both the upper and lower panes of the split form as you move from record to record.

i. Open the Employers form and navigate forward and backward through all five records to study the difference between the Employers form, which uses a form/subform versus the Employers Split Form. Even though both the Employers form and Employers Split Form show datasheets in the bottom halves of the forms, they are fundamentally very different. The split form is displaying the records of only the Employers table, whereas the Employers form is using a subform to display related records from the Positions table in the lower datasheet. You will learn more about forms and subforms in later modules.

j. Close the Jobs-3.accdb database, then exit Access.

FIGURE 3-22

Visual Workshop

Open the Baseball-3.accdb database, enable content if prompted, then use the Split Form tool to create a form named **Players**, as shown in FIGURE 3-23, based on the Players table. Switch to Form Design View, remove the layout, and resize the controls as shown. Modify the labels as shown and note that they are all right-aligned. View the data in Form View, and sort the records in ascending order by last name. Change the first, last, and nickname of the John Bench record in the first record to your name, and if instructed to create a printout, print only that record. Save and close the Players form, close the Baseball-3.accdb database, then exit Access.

FIGURE 3-23

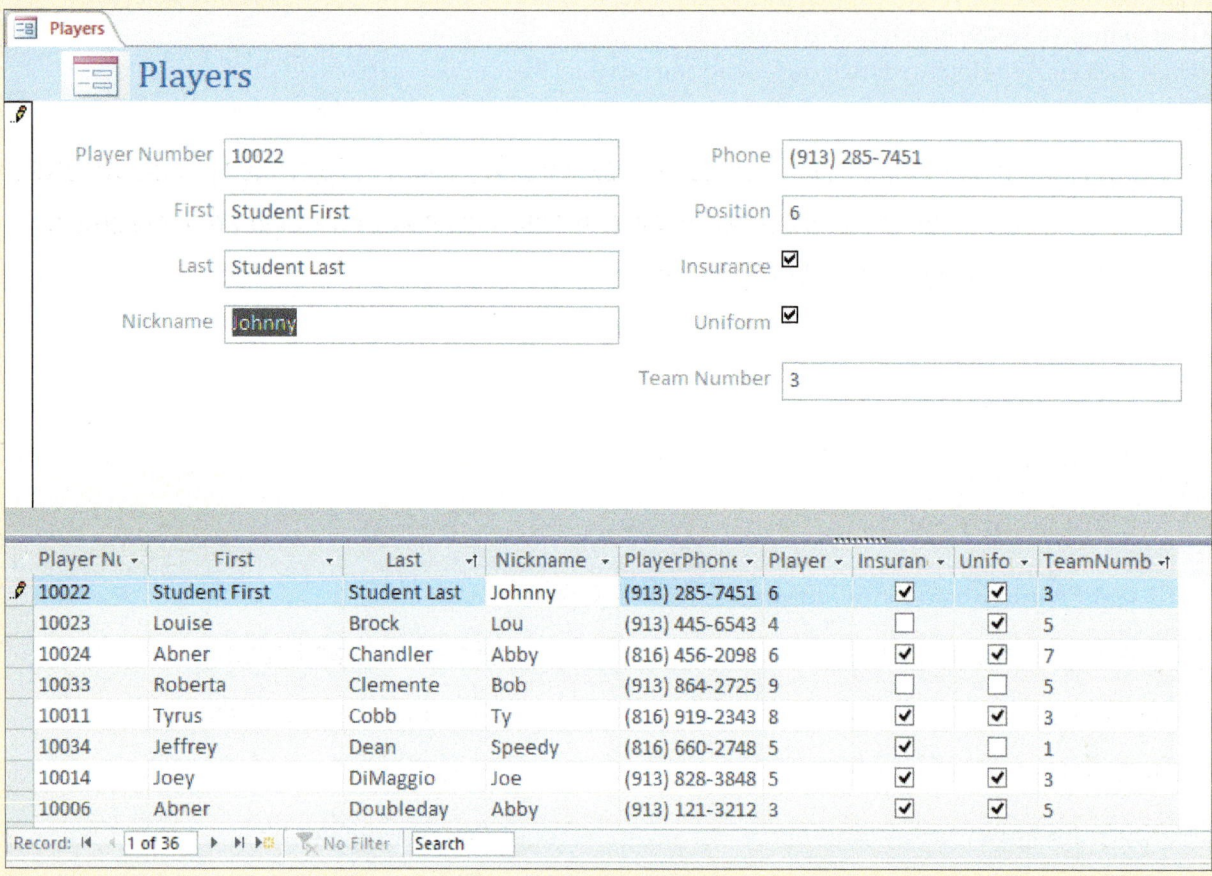

Using Reports

CASE Julia Rice, a trip developer at Reason 2 Go, asks you to produce some reports to help her share and analyze data. A report is an Access object that creates a professional-looking printout.

Module Objectives

After completing this module, you will be able to:

- Use the Report Wizard
- Use Report Layout View
- Review report sections
- Apply group and sort orders
- Add subtotals and counts
- Resize and align controls
- Format a report
- Create mailing labels

Files You Will Need

R2G-4.accdb	Salvage-4.accdb
LakeHomes-4.accdb	JobSearch-4.accdb
Conventions-4.accdb	Basketball-4.accdb
Service-4.accdb	

Use the Report Wizard

Learning Outcomes
- Create a report with the Report Wizard
- Change page orientation

A **report** is the primary object you use to print database content because it provides the most formatting, layout, and summary options. A report may include various fonts and colors, clip art and lines, and multiple headers and footers. A report can also calculate subtotals, averages, counts, and other statistics for groups of records. You can create reports in Access by using the **Report Wizard**, a tool that asks questions to guide you through the initial development of the report. Your responses to the Report Wizard determine the record source, style, and layout of the report. The **record source** is the table or query that defines the fields and records displayed on the report. The Report Wizard also helps you sort, group, and analyze the records. **CASE** ▶ *Julia Rice asks you to use the Report Wizard to create a report to display the trips within each state.*

STEPS

1. **Start Access, open the R2G-4.accdb database, enable content if prompted, click the Create tab on the Ribbon, then click the Report Wizard button in the Reports group**

   The Report Wizard starts, prompting you to select the fields you want on the report. You can select fields from one or more tables or queries.

2. **Click the Tables/Queries list arrow, click Table: States, double-click the StateName field, click the Tables/Queries list arrow, click Table: Trips, click the Select All Fields button ⬚ >> ⬚, click StateAbbrev in the Selected Fields list, then click the Remove Field button ⬚ < ⬚**

   By selecting the StateName field from the States table, and all fields from the Trips table except the StateAbbrev field, you have all of the fields you need for the report, as shown in **FIGURE 4-1**.

3. **Click Next, then click by States if it is not already selected**

   Choosing "by States" groups the records for each state. In addition to record-grouping options, the Report Wizard later asks if you want to sort the records within each group. You can use the Report Wizard to specify up to four fields to sort in either ascending or descending order.

4. **Click Next, click Next again to include no additional grouping levels, click the first sort list arrow, click TripName, then click Next**

   The last questions in the Report Wizard deal with report appearance and the report title.

5. **Click the Stepped option button, click the Landscape option button, click Next, type State Trips for the report title, then click Finish**

   The State Trips report opens in **Print Preview**, which displays the report as it appears when printed, as shown in **FIGURE 4-2**. The records are grouped by state, the first state being California, and then sorted in ascending order by the TripName field within each state. Reports are **read-only** objects, meaning you can use them to read and display data but not to change (write to) data. As you change data using tables, queries, or forms, reports constantly display those up-to-date edits just like all of the other Access objects.

6. **Scroll down to see the second grouping section on the report for the state of Colorado, then click the Next Page button ▶ in the navigation bar to see the second page of the report**

   Even in **landscape orientation** (11" wide by 8.5" tall as opposed to **portrait orientation**, which is 8.5" wide by 11" tall), the fields on the State Trips report may not fit on one sheet of paper. The labels in the column headings and the data in the columns need to be resized to improve the layout. Depending on your monitor, you might need to scroll to the right to display all the fields on this page.

FIGURE 4-1: Selecting fields for a report using the Report Wizard

FIGURE 4-2: State Trips report in Print Preview

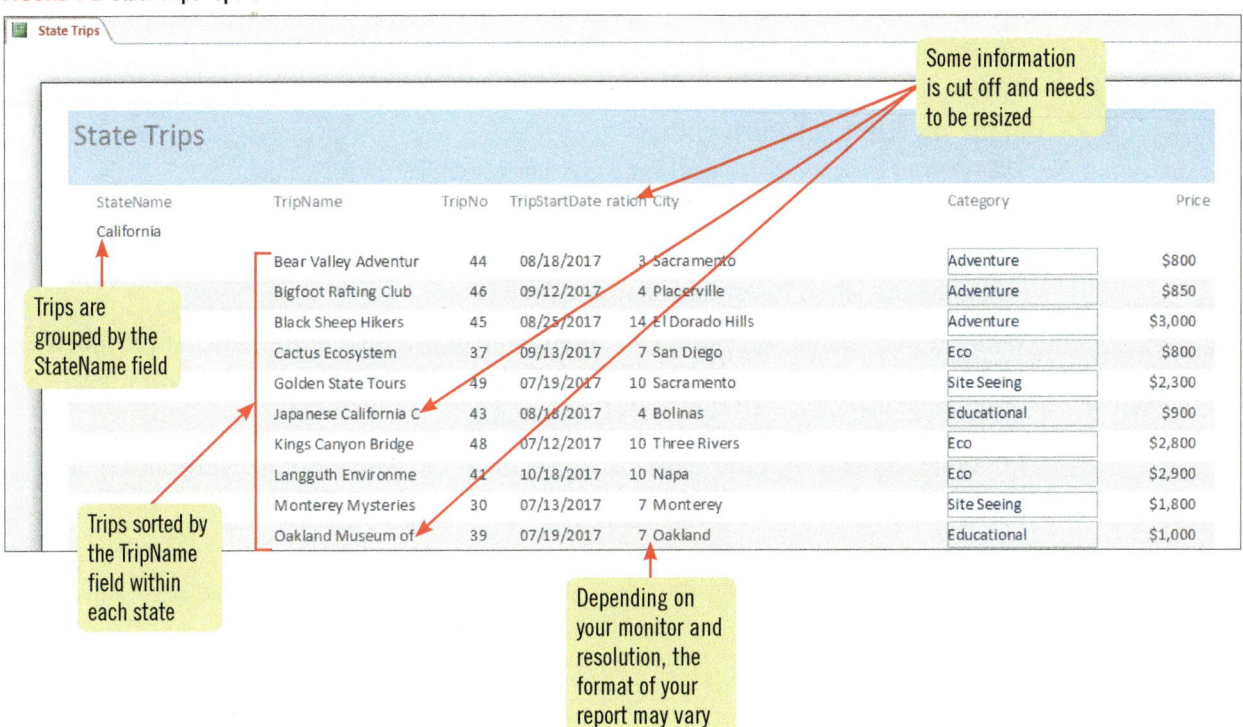

Changing page orientation

To change page orientation from Portrait (8.5" wide by 11" tall) to Landscape (11" wide by 8.5" tall) and vice versa, click the Portrait or Landscape button on the Print Preview tab when viewing the report in Print Preview. To switch to Print Preview, right-click the report in the Navigation Pane, and then choose Print Preview on the shortcut menu.

Use Report Layout View

Reports have multiple views that you use for various report-building and report-viewing activities. Although some tasks can be accomplished in more than one view, each view has a primary purpose to make your work with reports as easy and efficient as possible. The different report views are summarized in TABLE 4-1. **CASE** *Julia Rice asks you to modify the State Trips report so that all of the fields fit comfortably across one sheet of paper in landscape orientation.*

STEPS

TROUBLE
If the Field List or Property Sheet window opens, close it.

1. **Right-click the State Trips report tab, then click Layout View**
   Layout View opens and applies a grid to the report that helps you resize, move, and position controls. You decide to narrow the City column to make room for the Price data.

2. **Click Sacramento (or any value in the City column), then use the ↔ pointer to drag the left edge of the City column to the right to narrow it to about half of its current size, as shown in FIGURE 4-3**
   By narrowing the City column, you create extra space in the report.

QUICK TIP
If you select the entire row, just click again directly on the label to select it.

3. **Click the City label, then use ↔ to drag the left edge to the right to position it above the column of City data**
   You use the extra room to better display the data on the report.

QUICK TIP
You can use the Undo button ↶ to undo multiple actions in Layout View.

4. **Continue to use ↔ to resize the columns of data and labels so that the entire trip name in the TripName column is visible**
   The TripName column now has more space to completely display the trip names.

5. **Click the StateName label, click between the words State and Name, press the [Spacebar] so that the label reads State Name, then modify the TripName, TripNo, and TripStartDate labels to contain spaces as well**

6. **Click the StateName label, press and hold [Shift], click each of the other seven labels to select them as a group, release [Shift], click the Format tab, click the Font Color drop-down list arrow A ⋅, then click Automatic**

7. **Continue working with the columns so that all of the data is visible and your report looks like FIGURE 4-4**

FIGURE 4-3: Modifying the column width in Report Layout View

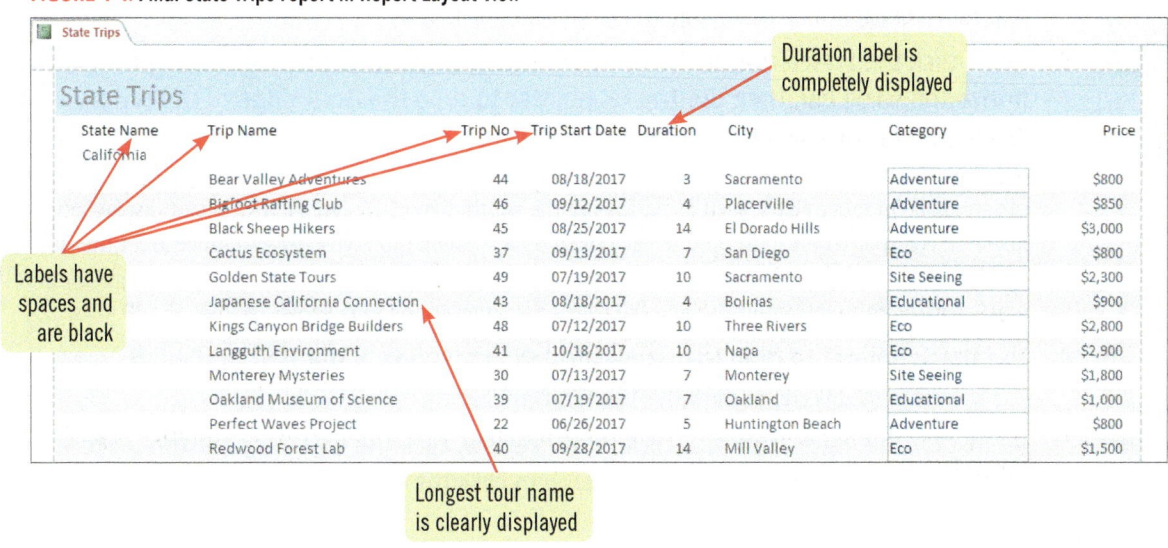

FIGURE 4-4: Final State Trips report in Report Layout View

TABLE 4-1: Report views

view	primary purpose
Report View	To quickly review the report without page breaks
Print Preview	To review each page of an entire report as it will appear if printed
Layout View	To modify the size, position, or formatting of controls; shows live data as you modify the report, making it the tool of choice when you want to change the appearance and positioning of controls on a report while also reviewing live data
Design View	To work with report sections or to access the complete range of controls and report properties; Design View does not display data

Review Report Sections

Report **sections** determine where and how often controls in that section print in the final report. For example, controls in the Report Header section print only once at the beginning of the report, but controls in the Detail section print once for every record the report displays. **TABLE 4-2** describes report sections. **CASE** *You and Julia Rice preview the State Trips report to review and understand report sections.*

STEPS

1. **Right-click the State Trips tab, click Print Preview, then scroll up as needed and click the light blue bar at the top of the report above the Trip Start Date label until you display the first page of the report, as shown in FIGURE 4-5**

   The first page shows four report sections: Report Header, Page Header, StateAbbreviation Header, and Detail.

2. **Click the Next Page button ▶ on the navigation bar to move to the second page of the report**

   If the second page of the report does not contain data, it means that the report may be too wide to fit on a single sheet of paper. You fix that problem in Report Design View.

   QUICK TIP
   If your report is too wide, you will see a green error indicator in the upper-left corner of the report. Pointing to the error icon ⚠ ▾ displays a message about the error.

3. **Right-click the State Trips tab, click Design View, scroll to the far right using the bottom horizontal scroll bar, then use the ↔ pointer to drag the right edge of the report as far as you can to the left, as shown in FIGURE 4-6**

   In Report Design View, you can work with the report sections and make modifications to the report that you cannot make in other views, such as narrowing the width. Report Design View does not display any data, however. For your report to fit on one page in landscape orientation, you need to move all of the controls to the left of the 10.5" mark on the horizontal **ruler** using the default 0.25" left and right margins. You will practice fixing this problem by moving the page calculation in the Page Footer section.

4. **Use the ⬚ pointer to drag the page calculation text box about 0.5" to the left**

   To review your modifications, show the report in Print Preview.

   QUICK TIP
   You can also use the View buttons in the lower-right corner of a report to switch views.

5. **Right-click the State Trips tab, click Print Preview, click the Last Page button ▶| to navigate to the last page of the report, then click the report to zoom in and out to examine the page, as shown in FIGURE 4-7**

   Previewing each page of the report helps you confirm that no blank pages are created and allows you to examine how the different report sections print on each page.

TABLE 4-2: Report sections

section	where does this section print?
Report Header	At the top of the first page
Page Header	At the top of every page (but below the Report Header on the first page)
Group Header	Before every group of records
Detail	Once for every record
Group Footer	After every group of records
Page Footer	At the bottom of every page
Report Footer	At the end of the report

Using Reports

FIGURE 4-5: State Trips in Print Preview

FIGURE 4-6: State Trips report in Design View

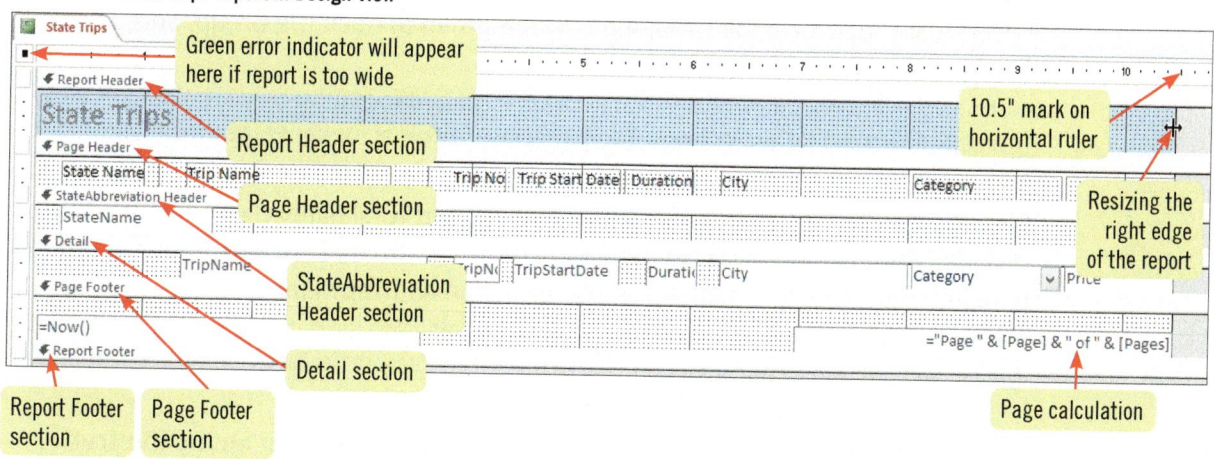

FIGURE 4-7: Last page of State Trips report in Print Preview

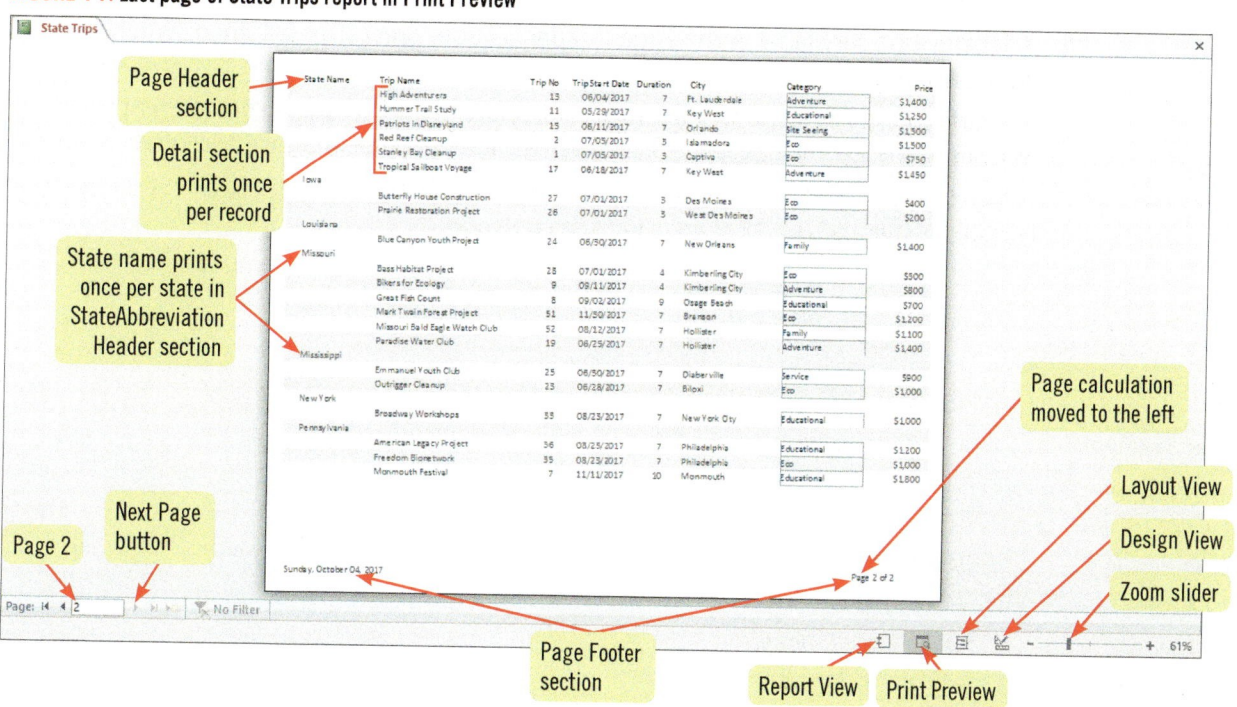

Using Reports

Apply Group and Sort Orders

Learning
Outcomes
• Group and sort
  records in a report
• Cut and paste
  controls

Grouping means to sort records by a particular field plus provide a header and/or footer section before or after each group of sorted records. For example, if you group records by the StateAbbreviation field, the Group Header is called the StateAbbreviation Header and the Group Footer is called the StateAbbreviation Footer. The StateAbbreviation Header section appears once for each state in the report, immediately before the records in that state. The StateAbbreviation Footer section also appears once for each state in the report, immediately after the records for that state. **CASE** *The records in the State Trips report are currently grouped by the StateAbbreviation field. Julia Rice asks you to further group the records by the Category field (Adventure, Eco, Educational, and Family, for example) within each state.*

STEPS

1. **Click the Close Print Preview button to return to Report Design View, then click the Group & Sort button in the Grouping & Totals group to open the Group, Sort, and Total pane**

   Currently, the records are grouped by the StateAbbreviation field and further sorted by the TripName field. To add the Category field as a grouping field within each state, you work with the Group, Sort, and Total pane in Report Design View.

2. **Click the Add a group button in the Group, Sort, and Total pane, click Category, then click the Move up button ◈ on the right side of the Group, Sort, and Total pane so that Category is positioned between StateAbbreviation and TripName**

   A Category Header section is added to Report Design View just below the StateAbbreviation Header section. You move the Category control from the Detail section to the Category Header section so it prints only once for each new Category instead of once for each record in the Detail section.

TROUBLE
Use the Move up
◈ and Move
down ◈ buttons
as needed to make
sure your Group,
Sort, and Total pane
looks exactly like
FIGURE 4-8.

3. **Right-click the Category combo box in the Detail section, click Cut on the shortcut menu, right-click the Category Header section, click Paste, then use the ⬚ pointer to drag the Category combo box to the right to position it as shown in FIGURE 4-8**

   Now that you've moved the Category combo box to the Category Header, it will print only once per category within each state. You no longer need the Category label in the Page Header section.

4. **Click the Category label in the Page Header section, press [Delete], then switch to Print Preview and zoom to 100%**

   The State Trips report should look like **FIGURE 4-9**. Notice that the records are now grouped by category within state. Detail records are further sorted in ascending order by the TripName field value.

FIGURE 4-8: Group, Sort, and Total pane and new Category Header section

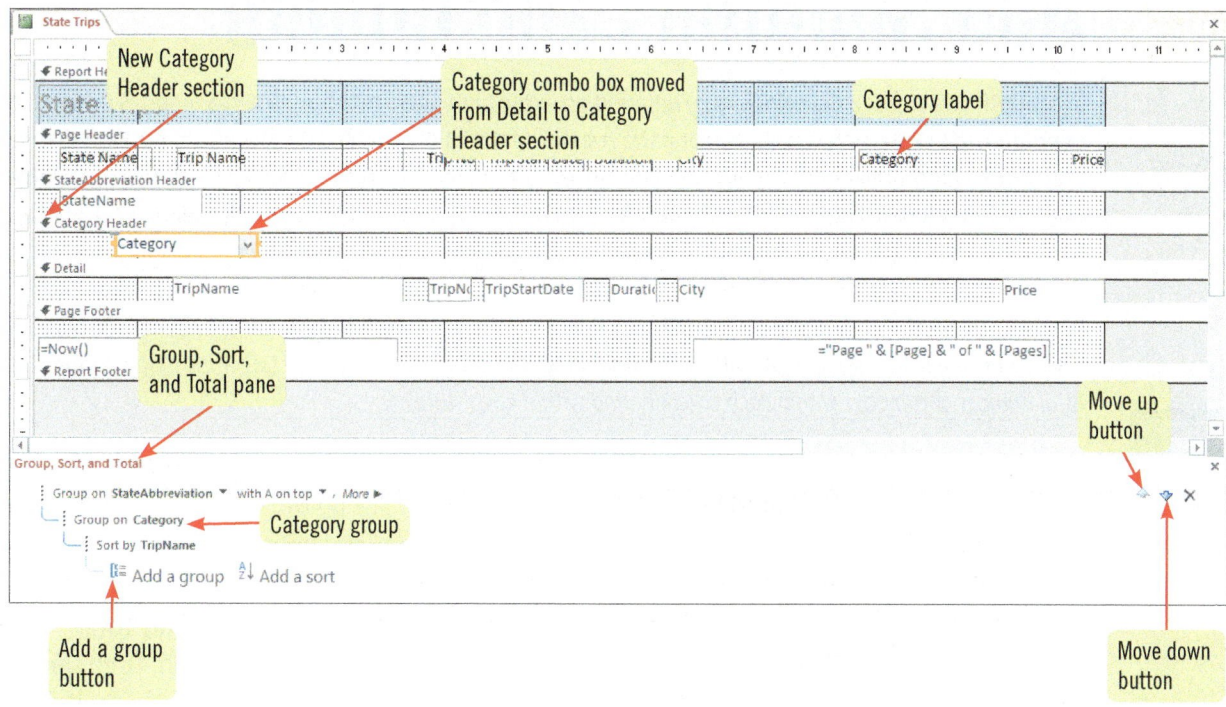

FIGURE 4-9: State Trips report grouped by category within state

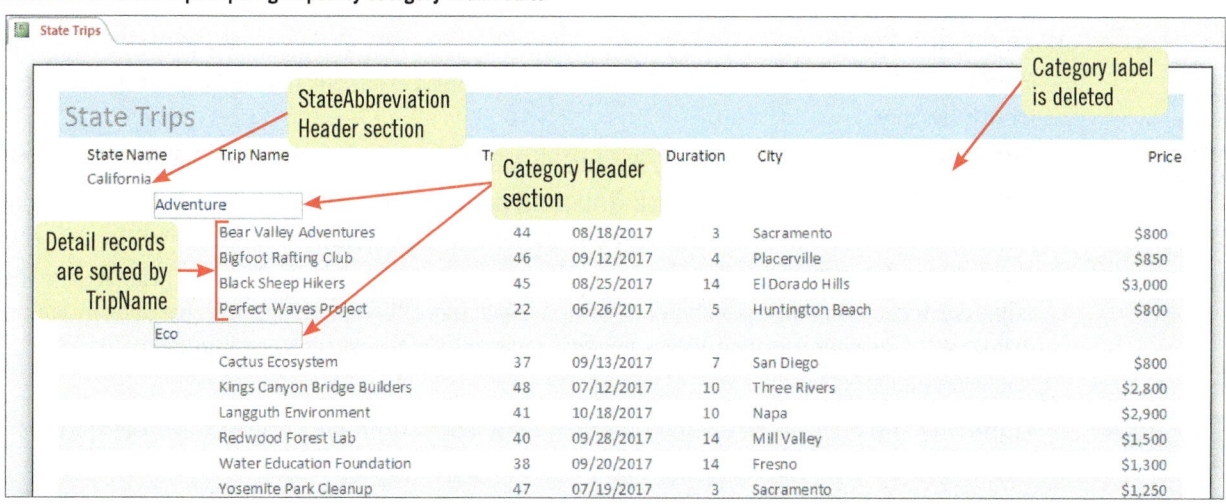

Record Source Property

The **Record Source property** of a report or form determines what fields and records that report or form will display. It is the first property on the Data tab of the Property Sheet for a report or form. The value of the Record Source property may be the name of a table or query. The Record Source property can also be a SELECT statement, which is SQL (Structured Query Language) code. In the Property Sheet for a report, click the Record Source property, and then click the Build button ⋯ to enter Query Design View, where you can change the Record Source property or save it as a query object within the database.

Add Subtotals and Counts

In a report, you create a **calculation** by entering an expression into a text box. When a report is previewed or printed, the expression is evaluated and the resulting calculation is placed on the report. An **expression** is a combination of field names, operators (such as +, −, /, and *), and functions that results in a single value. A **function** is a built-in formula, such as Sum or Count, that helps you quickly create a calculation. Notice that every expression starts with an equal sign (=), and when it uses a function, the arguments for the function are placed in (parentheses). **Arguments** are the pieces of information that the function needs to create the final answer. When an argument is a field name, the field name must be surrounded by [square brackets].   **CASE**   *Julia Rice asks you to add a calculation to the State Trips report to sum the total number of trip days within each category and within each state.*

STEPS

1. **Switch to Report Design View**

   A logical place to add subtotals for each group is right after that group of records prints, in the Group Footer section. You use the Group, Sort, and Total pane to open Group Footer sections.

2. **Click the More button for the StateAbbreviation field in the Group, Sort, and Total pane, click the without a footer section list arrow, click with a footer section, then do the same for the Category field, as shown in FIGURE 4-10**

   With the StateAbbreviation Footer and Category Footer sections open, you're ready to add controls to calculate the total number of trip days within each category and within each state. You use a text box control with an expression to make this calculation.

3. **Click the Text Box button [abl] in the Controls group, then click just below the Duration text box in the Category Footer section**

   Adding a new text box automatically adds a new label to its left. First, you modify the label to identify the information; then you modify the text box to contain the correct expression to sum the number of trip days for that category.

4. **Click the Text20 label to select it, double-click Text20, type Total days:, click the Unbound text box to select it, click Unbound again, type =Sum([Duration]), press [Enter], then widen the text box to view the entire expression**

   The expression =Sum([Duration]) uses the Sum function to add the days in the Duration field. Because the expression is entered in the Category Footer section, it will sum all Duration values for that category within that state. To sum the Duration values for each state, the expression also needs to be inserted in the StateAbbreviation Footer.

5. **Right-click the =Sum([Duration]) text box, click Copy, right-click the StateAbbreviation Footer section, click Paste, then press [→] enough times to position the controls in the StateAbbreviation Footer section just below those in the Category Footer section, as shown in FIGURE 4-11**

   With the expression copied to the StateAbbreviation Footer section, you're ready to preview your work.

6. **Switch to Print Preview, navigate to the last page of the report, then click to zoom so you can see all of the Pennsylvania trips**

   As shown in **FIGURE 4-12**, seven trip days are totaled for the Eco category, and 17 for the Educational category, which is a total of 24 trip days for the state of Pennsylvania. The summary data would look better if it were aligned more directly under the trip Duration values. You resize and align controls in the next lesson.

FIGURE 4-10: Opening group footer sections

FIGURE 4-11: Adding subtotals to group footer sections

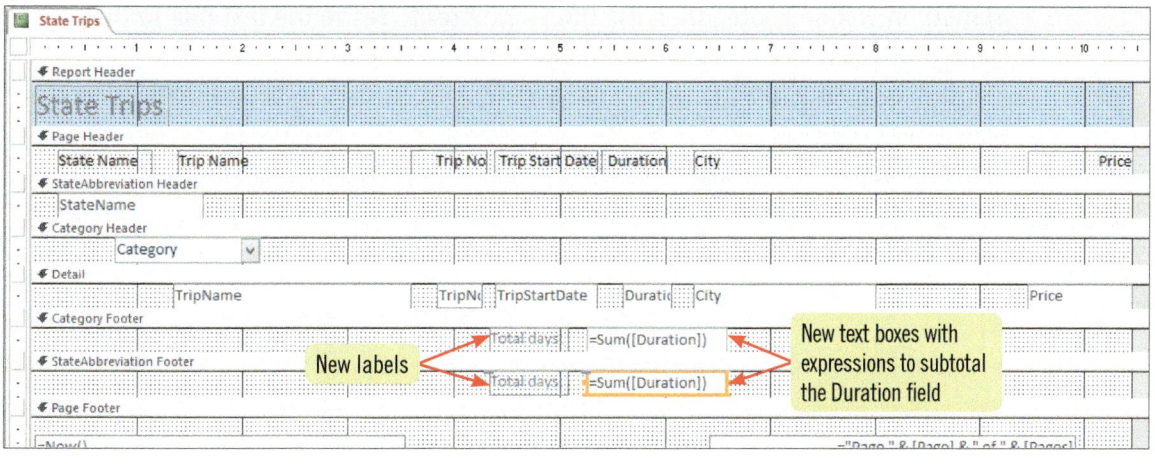

FIGURE 4-12: Previewing the new group footer calculations

Resize and Align Controls

After you add information to the appropriate section of a report, you might also want to align the data in precise columns and rows to make the information easier to read. To do so, you can use two different types of **alignment** commands. You can left-, right-, or center-align a control within its own border using the Align Left ☰, Center ☰, and Align Right ☰ buttons on the Home tab. You can also align the edges of controls with respect to one another using the Left, Right, Top, and Bottom commands on the Align button of the Arrange tab in Report Design View. **CASE** ▶ *You decide to resize and align several controls to improve the readability of the State Trips report. Layout View is a good choice for these tasks.*

STEPS

1. **Switch to Layout View, click the Design tab on the Ribbon, then click the Group & Sort button to toggle off the Group, Sort, and Total pane**

   You decide to align the expressions that subtotal the number of trip days for each category within the Duration column to make the report easier to read and more professional.

2. **Click the Total days text box in the Category Footer, then use the ↔ pointer to resize the text box so that the data is aligned in the Duration column, as shown in FIGURE 4-13**

   If the value in your Total days text box is not right-aligned, click the Align Right button (shown in **FIGURE 4-13**). With the calculation formatted as desired in the Category Footer, you can quickly apply those modifications to the calculation in the StateAbbreviation Footer as well.

3. **Scroll down the report far enough to find and then click the Total days text box in the StateAbbreviation Footer, then use the ↔ pointer to resize the text box so that it is the same width as the text box in the Category Footer section**

   With both expressions resized so they line up under the Duration values in the Detail section, they are easier to read on the report.

4. **Scroll the report so you can see all of the Colorado trips, as shown in FIGURE 4-14**

   You can apply resize, alignment, or formatting commands to more than one control at a time. **TABLE 4-3** provides techniques for selecting more than one control at a time in Report Design View.

Precisely moving and resizing controls

You can move and resize controls using the mouse or other pointing device, but you can move controls more precisely using the keyboard. Pressing the arrow keys while holding [Ctrl] moves selected controls one **pixel** (picture element) at a time in the direction of the arrow. Pressing the arrow keys while holding [Shift] resizes selected controls one pixel at a time.

FIGURE 4-13: Resizing controls in Layout View

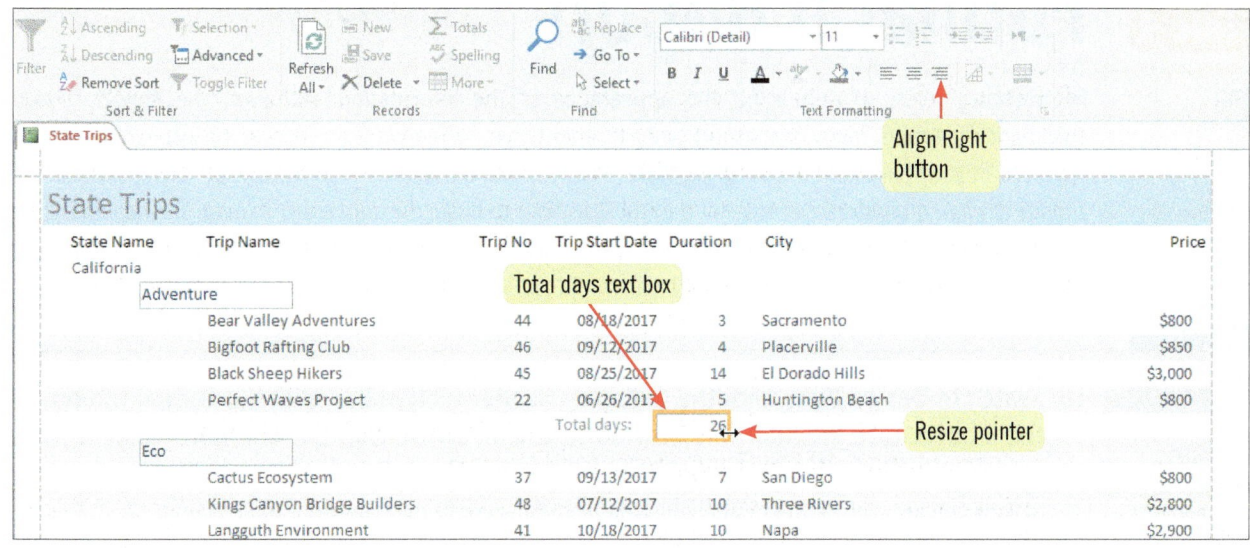

FIGURE 4-14: Reviewing the aligned and resized controls

TABLE 4-3: Selecting more than one control at a time in Report Design View

technique	description
Click, [Shift]+click	Click a control, and then press and hold [Shift] while clicking other controls; each one is selected
Drag a selection box	Drag a selection box (an outline box you create by dragging the pointer in Report Design View); every control that is in or is touched by the edges of the box is selected
Click in the ruler	Click in either the horizontal or vertical ruler to select all controls that intersect the selection line
Drag in the ruler	Drag through either the horizontal or vertical ruler to select all controls that intersect the selection line as it is dragged through the ruler

Format a Report

Learning Outcomes
• Format controls and sections of a report
• Add labels to a report

Formatting refers to enhancing the appearance of the information. Although the Report Wizard automatically applies many formatting embellishments, you often want to change the appearance of the report to fit your particular needs. **CASE** ▶ *When reviewing the State Trips report with Julia, you decide to change the background color of some of the report sections to make the data easier to read. The Report Wizard applied alternating formats, which you want to change. You want to shade each Category Header and Category Footer section using the same color. To make changes to entire report sections, you work in Report Design View.*

STEPS

1. **Switch to Design View, click the Category Header section bar, click the Format tab on the Ribbon, click the Alternate Row Color button arrow, click the Maroon 2 color square as shown in FIGURE 4-15, click the Shape Fill button, then click the Maroon 2 color square**

   Make a similar modification by applying a different fill color to the Category Footer section.

2. **Click the Category Footer section bar, click the Alternate Row Color button arrow, click the Maroon 1 color square (just above Maroon 2 in the Standard Colors section), click the Shape Fill button, then click the Maroon 1 color square**

   When you use the Alternate Row Color and Shape Fill buttons, you're actually modifying the **Back Color** and **Alternate Back Color** properties in the Property Sheet of the section or control you selected. Background shades can help differentiate parts of the report, but be careful with dark colors, as they may print as solid black on some printers and fax machines.

3. **Switch to Layout View to review your modifications**

   The category sections are clearer, but you decide to make one more modification to emphasize the report title.

4. **Click the State Trips label in the Report Header section, click the Home tab, then click the Bold button B in the Text Formatting group**

   The report in Layout View should look like FIGURE 4-16. You also want to add a label to the Report Footer section to identify yourself.

5. **Switch to Report Design View, drag the bottom edge of the Report Footer down about 0.5", click the Label button Aa in the Controls group, click at the 1" mark in the Report Footer, type Created by *your* name, press [Enter], click the Home tab, then click B in the Text Formatting group**

6. **Save and preview the State Trips report**

7. **If required by your instructor, print the report, and then close it**

FIGURE 4-15: Formatting section backgrounds

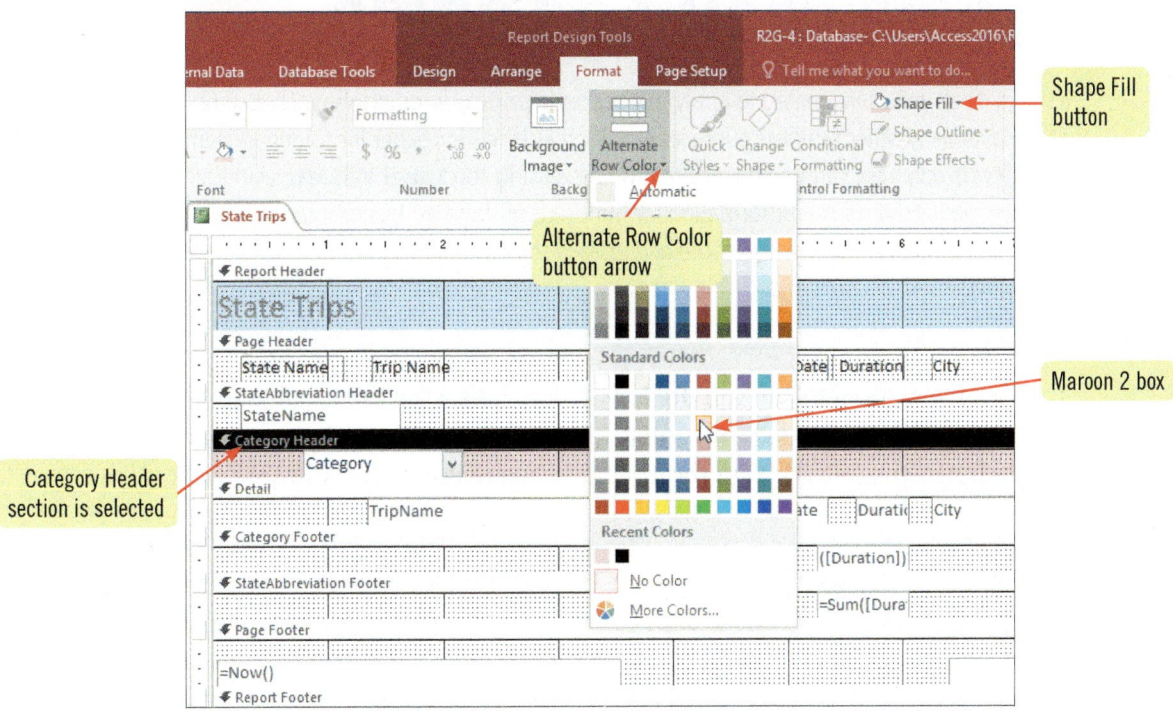

FIGURE 4-16: Final formatted State Trips report

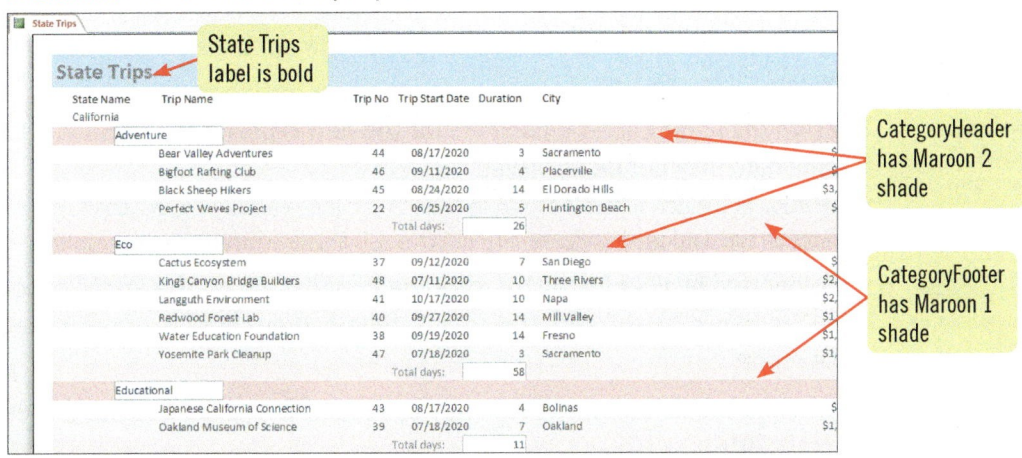

Create Mailing Labels

Learning Outcomes
• Create a report of labels
• Print specific pages of a report

Mailing labels are often created to apply to envelopes, postcards, or letters when assembling a mass mailing. They have many other business purposes too, such as labels for paper file folders or name tags. Any data in your Access database can be converted into labels using the **Label Wizard**, a special report wizard that precisely positions and sizes information for hundreds of standard business labels. **CASE** ▶ *Julia Rice asks you to create mailing labels for all of the addresses in the Customers table. You use the Label Wizard to handle this request.*

STEPS

1. **Click the Customers table in the Navigation Pane, click the Create tab, then click the Labels button in the Reports group**

   The first Label Wizard dialog box opens. The Filter by manufacturer list box provides over 30 manufacturers of labels. Avery is the default choice. With the manufacturer selected, your next task is to choose the product number of the labels you will feed through the printer. The cover on the box of labels you are using provides this information. In this case, you'll be using Avery 5160 labels, a common type of sheet labels used for mailings and other purposes.

2. **Scroll through the Product number list, then click 5160 as shown in FIGURE 4-17**

   Note that by selecting a product number, you also specify the dimensions of the label and number of columns.

3. **Click Next, then click Next again to accept the default font and color choices**

   The third question of the Label Wizard asks how you want to construct your label. You'll add the fields from the Customers table with spaces and line breaks to pattern a standard mailing format.

4. **Double-click FName, press [Spacebar], double-click LName, press [Enter], double-click Street, press [Enter], double-click City, type a comma (,) and press [Spacebar], double-click State, press [Spacebar], then double-click Zip**

   If your prototype label doesn't look exactly like **FIGURE 4-18**, delete the fields in the Prototype label box and try again. Be careful to put a space between the FName and LName fields in the first row, a comma and a space between the City and State fields, and a space between the State and Zip fields.

5. **Click Next, double-click LName to select it as a sorting field, click Next, click Finish to accept the name Labels Customers for the new report, then click OK if prompted that some data may not be displayed**

   A portion of the new report is shown in **FIGURE 4-19**. It is generally a good idea to print the first page of the report on standard paper to make sure everything is aligned correctly before printing on labels.

6. **If requested by your instructor, click the Print button on the Print Preview tab, click the From box, type 1, click the To box, type 1, then click OK to print the first page of the report**

7. **Close the Labels Customers report, close the R2G-4.accdb database, then exit Access 2016**

FIGURE 4-17: Label Wizard dialog box

FIGURE 4-18: Building a prototype label

FIGURE 4-19: Labels Customers report

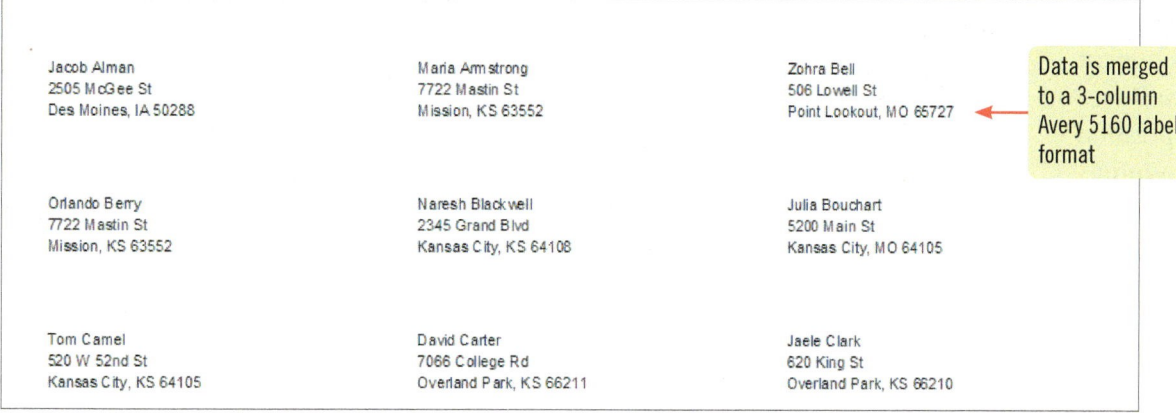

Practice

Concepts Review

Label each element of the Report Design View window shown in FIGURE 4-20.

FIGURE 4-20

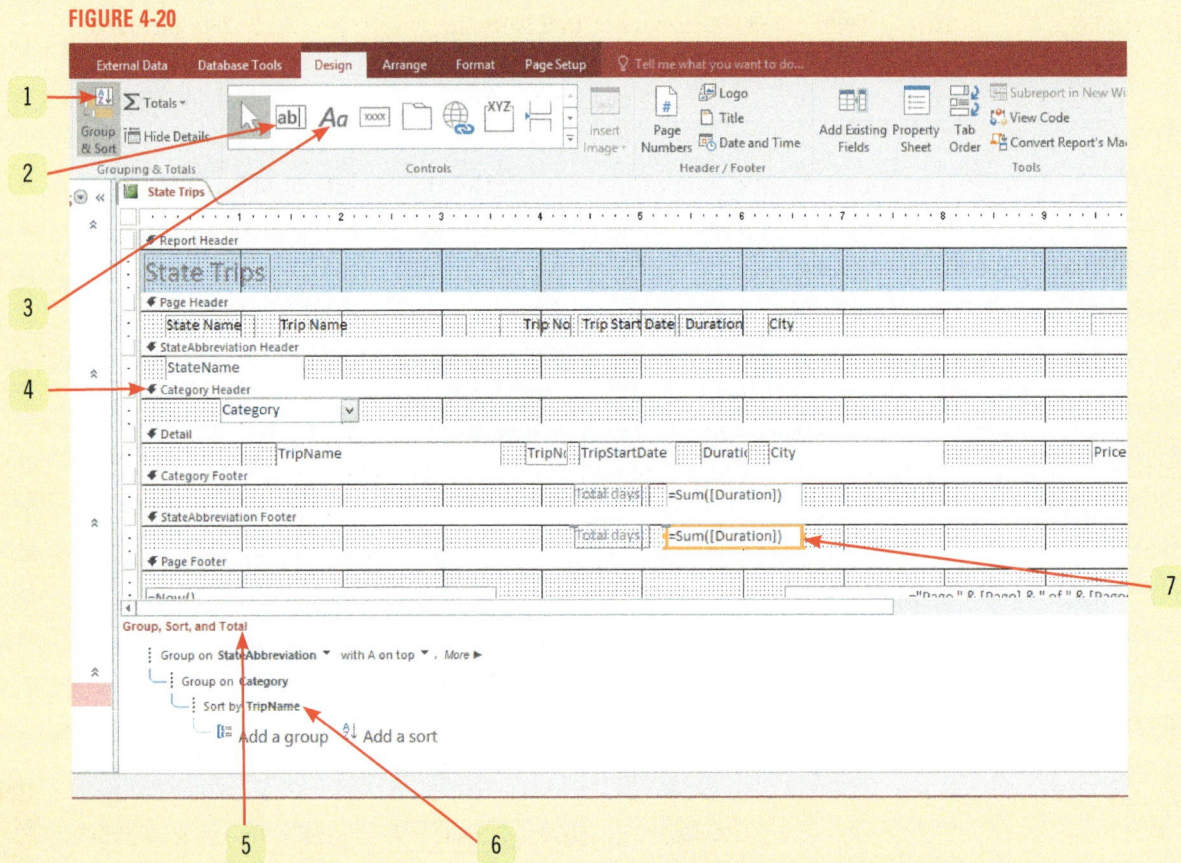

Match each term with the statement that best describes it.

8. **Record source**
9. **Alignment**
10. **Detail section**
11. **Expression**
12. **Grouping**
13. **Section**
14. **Formatting**

a. Left, center, or right are common choices
b. Prints once for every record
c. Used to identify which fields and records are passed to the report
d. Sorting records *plus* providing a header or footer section
e. Determines how controls are positioned on the report
f. A combination of field names, operators, and functions that results in a single value
g. Enhancing the appearance of information displayed in the report

Select the best answer from the list of choices.

15. **Which type of control is most commonly placed in the Detail section?**
    a. Image
    b. Line
    c. Text box
    d. Label

16. **Which of the following is not a valid report view?**
    a. Print Preview
    b. Section View
    c. Layout View
    d. Design View

17. **A title for a report would most commonly be placed in which report section?**
    a. Group Footer
    b. Detail
    c. Report Header
    d. Report Footer

18. **A calculated expression that presents page numbering information would probably be placed in which report section?**
    a. Report Header
    b. Detail
    c. Group Footer
    d. Page Footer

19. **To align the edges of several controls with each other, you use the alignment commands on the:**
    a. Formatting tab.
    b. Design tab.
    c. Print Preview tab.
    d. Arrange tab.

20. **Which of the following expressions counts the number of records using the FirstName field?**
    a. =Count([FirstName])
    b. =Count[FirstName]
    c. =Count((FirstName))
    d. =Count{FirstName}

21. **What is the difference between grouping and sorting in a report?**
    a. Grouping allows you to add a Group Header and/or Group Footer section to a report.
    b. Grouping means to sort in ascending order.
    c. Grouping means to sort by more than one field.
    d. You can have more than one grouping field, but you can only have one sorting field.

Skills Review

1. **Use the Report Wizard.**
    a. Start Access and open the LakeHomes-4.accdb database from the location where you store your Data Files. Enable content if prompted.
    b. Use the Report Wizard to create a report based on the RLast and RPhone fields from the Realtors table and the Type, SqFt, BR, Bath, and Asking fields from the Listings table. (*Hint*: Make sure your fields are added in the order listed.)
    c. View the data by Realtors, do not add any more grouping levels, and sort the records in descending order by the Asking field. (*Hint*: Click the Ascending button to toggle it to Descending.)
    d. Use a Stepped layout and a Landscape orientation. Title the report **Listings by Realtor**.
    e. Preview the first and second pages of the new report.

2. **Use Report Layout View.**
    a. Switch to Layout View and close the Field List and Property Sheet if they are open.
    b. Drag the right edge of the Asking column and label to the left to provide a little more space between the Asking column and Type column.
    c. Modify the RLast label to read **Realtor**, the RPhone label to read **Cell**, the SqFt label to read **Square Ft**, the BR label to read **Bedrooms**, and the Bath label to read **Baths**.
    d. Switch to Print Preview to review your changes.

Skills Review (continued)

3. **Review report sections.**

   a. Switch to Report Design View.

   b. Drag the text box that contains the Page calculation in the lower-right corner of the Page Footer section to the left so that it is to the left of the 9" mark on the horizontal ruler.

   c. Drag the right edge of the entire report to the left as far as possible.

   d. Preview the report and make sure there are no blank pages between printed pages. You may need to move or narrow more controls and narrow the report again in order to accomplish this.

4. **Apply group and sort orders.**

   a. Open the Group, Sort, and Total pane.

   b. Add the Type field as a grouping field between the RealtorNo grouping field and Asking sort field. Make sure the sort order on the Asking field is in descending order (from largest to smallest). (*Hint*: Use the Move up button to move the Type field between the RealtorNo and Asking fields in the Group, Sort, and Total pane.)

   c. Cut and paste the Type combo box from its current position in the Detail section to the Type Header section.

   d. Move the Type combo box in the Type Header section so its left edge is at about the 1" mark on the horizontal ruler.

   e. Delete the Type label in the Page Header section.

   f. Switch to Layout View, and resize the Asking, Square Ft, Bedrooms, and Baths columns as needed so they are more evenly spaced across the page.

5. **Add subtotals and counts.**

   a. Switch to Report Design View, then open the RealtorNo Footer section. (*Hint*: Use the More button on the RealtorNo field in the Group, Sort, and Total pane.)

   b. Add a text box control to the RealtorNo Footer section, just below the Asking text box in the Detail section. Change the label to read **Subtotal:**, and enter the expression **=Sum([Asking])** in the text box.

   c. Drag the bottom edge of the Report Footer section down about 0.25" to add space to the Report Footer.

   d. Copy and paste the new expression in the RealtorNo Footer section to the Report Footer section. Position the new controls in the Report Footer section directly below the controls in the RealtorNo Footer section.

   e. Modify the Subtotal: label in the Report Footer section to read **Grand Total:**.

   f. Preview the last page of the report to view the new subtotals in the RealtorNo Footer and Report Footer sections.

6. **Resize and align controls.**

   a. Switch to Design View, then click the Group & Sort button on the Design tab to close the Group, Sort, and Total pane if it is open.

   b. Click the Asking text box in the Detail section, press and hold [Shift], and then click the expression in the RealtorNo Footer as well as the Report Footer sections to select the three text boxes at the same time. Click the Arrange tab on the Ribbon, click the Align button, then click Right to right-align the edges of the three text boxes.

   c. With all three text boxes still selected, click the Format tab on the Ribbon, click the Apply Comma Number Format button, and click the Decrease Decimals button twice so that the values appear as whole dollar amounts without cents.

   d. Preview the report to view the alignment and format on the Asking data and subtotals.

7. **Format a report.**

   a. In Report Design View, change the Alternate Row Color of the Detail section to No Color.

   b. Change the Alternate Row Color of the Type Header, the RealtorNo Header, and the RealtorNo Footer sections to No Color.

   c. Change the Shape Fill color of the RealtorNo Header section to Green 2. (*Hint*: The Shape Fill button will change the Back Color property in the Property Sheet.)

Skills Review (continued)

d. Select the RLast and RPhone text boxes in the RealtorNo Header section, and change the Shape Fill color to Green 2 to match the RealtorNo Header section.

e. Bold the title of the report, which is the **Listings by Realtor** label in the Report Header, and resize it to make it a little wider to accommodate the bold text.

f. Change the font color of each label in the Page Header section to Automatic (black).

g. Save and preview the report in Print Preview. It should look like FIGURE 4-21. The report should fit on three pages, and the grand total for all Asking values should be 7,957,993. If there are blank pages between printed pages, return to Report Design View and drag the right edge of the report to the left.

FIGURE 4-21

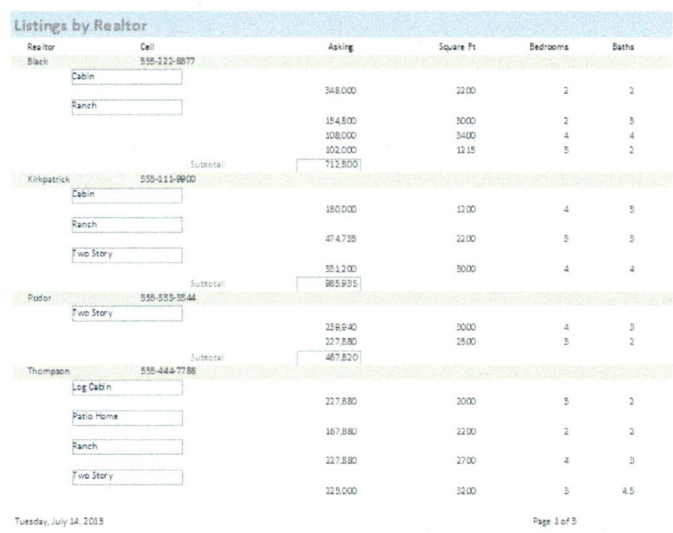

h. In Report Design View, add a label to the left side of the Report Footer section with your name. Be sure to add a label and not a text box control. Make sure that your name is displayed clearly on the last page only in Print Preview.

i. Print the report if requested by your instructor, then save and close the Listings by Realtor report.

8. Create mailing labels.

a. Click the Agencies table in the Navigation Pane, then start the Label Wizard.

b. Choose Avery 5160 labels and the default text appearance choices.

c. Build a prototype label with the AgencyName on the first line, Street on the second line, and City, State, and Zip on the third line with a comma and space between City and State, and a space between State and Zip.

d. Sort by AgencyName, and name the report **Labels Agencies**.

e. Preview then save and close the report. Click OK if a warning dialog box appears regarding horizontal space. The data in your label report does not exceed the dimensions of the labels.

f. Open the Agencies table and change the name of Big Cedar Realtors to *Your Last Name* **Realtors**. Close the Agencies table, reopen the Labels Agencies report, then print it if requested by your instructor.

g. Close the Labels Agencies report, close the LakeHomes-4.accdb database, then exit Access 2016.

Independent Challenge 1

As the office manager of an international convention planning company, you have created a database to track convention, enrollment, and company data. Your goal is to create a report of up-to-date attendee enrollments.

a. Start Access, then open the Conventions-4.accdb database from the location where you store your Data Files. Enable content if prompted.

b. Use the Report Wizard to create a report with the AttendeeLast and AttendeeFirst fields from the Attendees table, the CompanyName field from the Companies table, and the ConventionName and CountryName from the Conventions table. Add the fields in the order listed.

c. View your data by Conventions, add the CompanyName as a second grouping field, then sort in ascending order by AttendeeLast.

d. Use the Block layout and Portrait orientation, then name the report **Convention Attendees**.

e. In Layout View, change the labels in the Page Header section from ConventionName to **Convention** and CompanyName to **Company**. Delete the CountryName, AttendeeLast, and AttendeeFirst labels in the Page Header section.

f. In Report Design View, open the Group, Sort, and Total pane, then open the ConventionNo Footer section.

g. In Report Design View, add a text box to the ConventionNo Footer section just below the AttendeeLast text box in the Detail section. The purpose of the text box is to count the number of people enrolled for each convention. The label should read **Count of Attendees:**, and the expression in the text box should be **=Count([AttendeeLast])**.

h. Resize the new label and text box as needed to make their contents clearly visible.

i. Copy and paste the new label and expression to the Report Footer section. Move and align the controls so they are at the same horizontal position on the page.

j. Change the text color of all labels to Automatic (black). (*Hint*: There are labels in the Report Header, Page Header, ConventionNo Footer, and Report Footer sections.)

k. Preview the report and make sure there are no blank pages between pages. Resize controls in Layout View and narrow the report in Report Design view as needed to remove blank pages.

l. Preview the last page of the report to make sure the subtotal count for each convention and grand total count for the report are aligned as shown in FIGURE 4-22.

m. Add a label with your name to the left side of the Report Footer section, change the text color to Automatic (black), and then print the last page if required by your instructor.

n. Save and close the Convention Attendees report, close the Conventions-4.accdb database, then exit Access 2016.

FIGURE 4-22

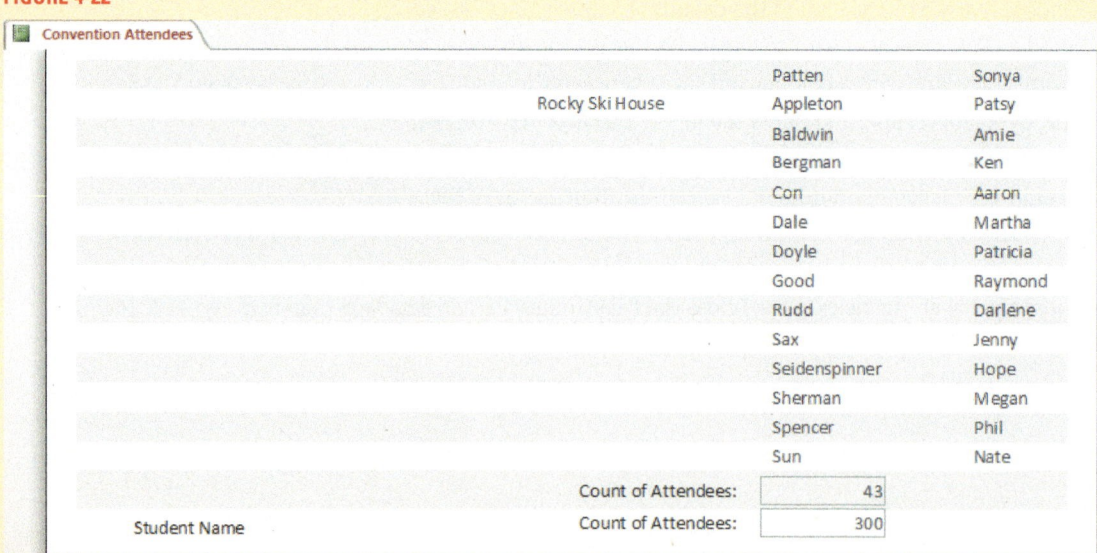

Independent Challenge 2

You have built an Access database to track membership in a community service club. The database tracks member names and addresses as well as their status and rank in the club and their hours of service to the community.

a. Start Access and open the Service-4.accdb database from the location where you store your Data Files. Enable content if prompted.

b. Open the Members table, find and change the name of Micah Ati to *your* name, then close the Members table.

c. Use the Report Wizard to create a report using the FirstName, LastName, and Dues fields from the Members table and the ActivityDate and HoursWorked fields from the Activities table, all in that order.

d. View the data by Members. Do not add any more grouping fields, and sort the records in ascending order by ActivityDate.

e. Use a Stepped layout and Portrait orientation, title the report **Activity Log**, then preview the report.

f. Use Report Layout View to resize the controls to fit the available space and display all data clearly.

g. Change the FirstName label to **First Name**. Change the LastName label to **Last Name**. Change the ActivityDate label to **Date**. Change the HoursWorked label to **Hours**.

h. Switch to Report Design View, then use the Group, Sort, and Total pane to open the MemberNo Footer section.

i. Add a text box to the MemberNo Footer section, just below the HoursWorked text box in the Detail section. Change the label to **Total:** and the expression in the text box to **=Sum([HoursWorked])**.

j. Open the Report Footer section, then copy and paste the **=Sum([HoursWorked])** text box to the Report Footer section. Change the label in the Report Footer section to read **Grand Total:**.

k. Align the HoursWorked text box in the Detail section and the two expressions in the MemberNo Footer and Report Footer sections so that the numbers are perfectly aligned. Be sure to preview the last page of the report to make sure all three controls are aligned as shown in FIGURE 4-23.

l. Add a label to the left edge of the Report Footer section with your name.

m. Preview each page of the report to make sure there are no blank pages. If there are, narrow the controls and the right edge of the report in Report Design View to fix this problem.

n. Print the last page of the report if requested to do so by your instructor.

o. Close the Activity Log report, close the Service-4.accdb database, then exit Access.

FIGURE 4-23

Total:	13
Grand Total:	476

Independent Challenge 3

You have built an Access database to organize the deposits at a salvage center. Various clubs regularly deposit material, which is measured in pounds when the deposits are made.

a. Start Access and open the Salvage-4.accdb database from the location where you store your Data Files. Enable content if prompted.

b. Open the Centers table, change **A1 Salvage Center** to **Your Last Name Salvage**, then close the table.

c. Use the Report Wizard to create a report with the CenterName field from the Centers table, the DepositDate and Weight fields from the Deposits table, and the ClubName field from the Clubs table.

d. View the data by Centers, do not add any more grouping levels, and sort the records in ascending order by DepositDate.

e. Use a Stepped layout and a Portrait orientation, then title the report **Deposit Log**.

f. In Layout View, resize the Weight label and Weight data to better position the data across the report. Rename the DepositDate label to **Date**.

g. Add spaces to the labels so that CenterName becomes **Center Name**, and ClubName becomes **Club Name**.

h. In Report Design View, open the Group, Sort, and Total pane and then open the CenterNumber Footer section.

i. Add a text box to the CenterNumber Footer section just below the Weight text box with the expression **=Sum([Weight])**.

j. Rename the new label to be **Subtotal:**.

k. Copy the new text box and paste it back to the CenterNumber Footer section. Change the new label to **Count:** and the expression to **=Count([Weight])**. Align the new controls directly below the Subtotal and =Sum([Weight]) expression.

l. Paste the controls a second time to the CenterNumber Footer section, and change the new label to **Average:** and the expression to **=Avg([Weight])**.

m. Change the Format property of the =Avg([Weight]) expression to **Standard**, and change the Decimal Places property to **0**. (*Hint*: Open the Property Sheet for the text box and click the Format tab to find the Format and Decimal Places properties.)

n. Expand the Report Footer section, then copy and paste the three text boxes from the CenterNumber Footer section to the Report Footer section.

o. Move and align the text boxes in the CenterNumber Footer and Report Footer sections to be positioned directly under the Weight text box in the Detail section. (*Hint*: You may need to both right-align the text boxes as well as align the right edges of the text boxes.)

p. Change the Subtotal label in the Report Footer section to **Total Sum:**. Change the Count label in the Report Footer section to **Total Count:** and also left-align the labels in the CenterNumber Footer and Report Footer sections.

q. Add a label to the left edge of the Report Footer section with your name and preview the last page of the report, a portion of which is shown in FIGURE 4-24. Your numbers should match.

r. Continue to improve the report as needed to align all numbers and labels and to remove any extra blank space in the report by making your sections as vertically short as possible in Report Design View.

s. Save and close the Deposit Log report, close the Salvage-4.accdb database, then exit Access.

FIGURE 4-24

	1/16/2017	85	Access Users Group
	1/21/2017	150	Boy Scout Troop 324
	Subtotal:	3315	
	Count:	36	
	Average:	92	
	Total Sum:	11360	
Student Name	Total Count:	118	
	Average:	96	

Independent Challenge 4: Explore

One way you can use an Access database on your own is to record and track your job search efforts. In this exercise, you create a report to help read and analyze data in your job-tracking database.

a. Start Access and open the JobSearch-4.accdb database from the location where you store your Data Files. Enable content if prompted.

b. Open the Employers table, and enter five more records to identify five more potential employers.

c. Use subdatasheets in the Employers table to enter five more potential jobs. You may enter all five jobs for one employer, one job for five different employers, or any combination thereof. Be sure to check the spelling of all data entered. For the Desirability field, enter a value from **1** to **5**, 1 being the least desirable and 5 being the most desirable. Close the Employers table.

d. Use the Report Wizard to create a report that lists the CompanyName, EmpCity, and EmpState fields from the Employers table, and the Title, AnnualSalary, and Desirability fields from the Positions table.

e. View the data by Employers, do not add any more grouping levels, and sort the records in descending order by Desirability.

f. Use an Outline layout and a Portrait orientation, then title the report **Jobs**.

g. In Design View, revise the labels in the EmployerID Header section from CompanyName to **Company**, EmpCity to **City**, EmpState to **State**, and AnnualSalary to **Salary**.

h. Right-align the text within the Company, City, and State labels so they are closer to the text boxes they describe.

i. In Report Layout View, resize the Desirability, Title, and Salary labels and text boxes to space the controls evenly across the report.

j. Preview the report, then switch to Report Design View to remove any extra space in the report sections. This will involve moving the controls in the EmployerID Header section as far to the top of that section as possible, then dragging the top edge of the Detail section up.

k. Preview the report, making sure all controls fit within the width of portrait orientation. If not, switch to Report Design View and fix this problem.

l. Print the first page if requested by your instructor.

m. Close the Jobs report, close the JobSearch-4.accdb database, then exit Access 2016.

Visual Workshop

Open the Basketball-4.accdb database from the location where you store your Data Files and enable content if prompted. Open the Players table, change the name of Matthew Douglas to *your* name, then close the table. Your goal is to create the report shown in FIGURE 4-25. Use the Report Wizard, and select the PFirst, PLast, HomeTown, and HomeState fields from the Players table. Select the FieldGoals, 3Pointers, and FreeThrows fields from the Stats table. View the data by Players, do not add any more grouping levels, and do not add any more sorting levels. Use a Block layout and a Portrait orientation, then title the report **Scoring Report**. In Layout View, resize all of the columns so that they fit on a single piece of portrait paper, and change the labels in the Page Header section as shown. In Design View, open the PlayerNo Footer section and add text boxes with expressions to sum the FieldGoals, 3Pointers, and FreeThrows fields and bold those controls. Drag the top edge of the Page Footer section down a little to add a little space between the subtotals in the PlayerNo Footer section and the next set of records for the next player. Move, modify, align, and resize all controls as needed to match FIGURE 4-25. (*Hint*: Change the Shape Outline of the text boxes in the PlayerNo Footer section to Transparent to remove the outline.) Be sure to print preview the report to make sure that it fits within the width of one sheet of paper. Modify the report to narrow it in Report Design View if needed.

FIGURE 4-25

Scoring Report						
Player Name		Home Town	State	Field Goals	3 Pointers	Free Throws
Student First	Student Last	Linden	IA	4	1	3
				5	2	2
				5	3	3
				6	3	5
				4	1	1
				4	2	2
				3	2	1
				4	2	3
				4	2	3
				3	2	1
				42	20	24
Deonte	Cook	Osseo	MN	6	0	4
				4	1	3
				4	0	4

Glossary

Active The currently available document, program, or object; on the taskbar, when more than one program is open, the button for the active program appears slightly lighter.

Add-in Software that works with an installed app to extend its features.

Alignment command A command used in Layout or Design View for a form or report to left-, center-, or right-align a value within its control using the Align Left, Center, or Align Right buttons on the Home tab. In Design View, you can also align the top, bottom, right, or left edge of selected controls using the Align button.

Alternate Back Color property A property that determines the alternating background color of the selected section in a form or report.

Anchoring A layout positioning option that allows you to tie controls together so you can work with them as a group.

AND criteria Criteria placed in the same row of the query design grid. All criteria on the same row must be true for a record to appear on the resulting datasheet.

Animation emphasis effect In Sway, a special effect you can apply to an object to animate it.

Application developer The person responsible for building and maintaining tables, queries, forms, and reports for all of the database users.

Argument Information that a function uses to create the final answer. Multiple arguments are separated by commas. All of the arguments for a function are surrounded by a single set of parentheses.

AutoNumber A field data type in which Access enters a sequential integer for each record added into the datasheet. Numbers cannot be reused even if the record is deleted.

Avg function A built-in Access function used to calculate the average of the values in a given field.

Background image An image that fills an entire form or report, appearing "behind" the other controls; also sometimes called a watermark.

Backstage view Appears when the File tab is clicked. The navigation bar on the left side contains commands to perform actions common to most Office programs, such as opening a file, saving a file, and closing the file.

Backward-compatible Software feature that enables documents saved in an older version of a program to be opened in a newer version of the program.

Bound control A control used in either a form or report to display data from the underlying field; used to edit and enter new data in a form.

Calculation A new value that is created by an expression in a text box on a form or report.

Calendar Picker A pop-up calendar from which you can choose dates for a date field.

Card A section for a particular type of content in a Sway presentation.

Clip A short segment of audio, such as music, or video.

Clipboard A temporary Windows storage area that holds the selections you copy or cut.

Cloud computing Using an Internet resource to complete your work such as saving a database to Microsoft OneDrive or maintaining Microsoft Office 365.

Column separator The thin line that separates field names to the left or right in a datasheet or the query design grid.

Combo box A bound control used to display a drop-down list of possible entries for a field. You can also type an entry from the keyboard into the control so it is a "combination" of the list box and text box controls.

Compatibility The ability of different programs to work together and exchange data.

Contextual tab A tab that appears only when a specific task can be performed; contextual tabs appear in an accent color and close when no longer needed.

Control Any element on a form or report such as a label, text box, line, or combo box. Controls can be bound, unbound, or calculated.

Control Source property A property of a bound control in a form or report that determines the field to which the control is connected.

Cortana The Microsoft Windows virtual assistant that integrates with Microsoft Edge to find and provide information.

Creative Commons license A public copyright license that allows the free distribution of an otherwise copyrighted work.

Criteria Entries (rules and limiting conditions) that determine which records are displayed when finding or filtering records in a datasheet or form, or when building a query.

Criteria syntax Rules by which criteria need to be entered. For example, text criteria syntax requires that the criteria are surrounded by quotation marks (" "). Date criteria are surrounded by pound signs (#).

Current record The record that has the focus or is being edited.

Data type A required property for each field that defines the type of data that can be entered in each field. Valid data types include AutoNumber, Short Text, Long Text, Number, Currency, Yes/No, Date/Time, and Hyperlink.

Database designer The person responsible for building and maintaining tables, queries, forms, and reports.

Database user The person primarily interested in entering, editing, and analyzing the data in the database.

Datasheet A spreadsheet-like grid that displays fields as columns and records as rows.

Datasheet View A view that lists the records of an object in a datasheet. Tables, queries, and most form objects have a Datasheet View.

Date function A built-in Access function used to display the current date on a form or report; enter the Date function as Date().

Design View A view in which the structure of an object can be manipulated. Every Access object (table, query, form, report, macro, and module) has a Design View.

Dialog box launcher An icon you can click to open a dialog box or task pane from which to choose related commands.

Docs.com A Microsoft website designed for sharing Sway sites.

Document window Most of the screen in Word, PowerPoint, and Excel, where you create a document, slide, or worksheet.

Drawing canvas In OneNote, a container for shapes and lines.

Edit mode The mode in which Access assumes you are trying to edit a particular field, so keystrokes such as [Ctrl][End], [Ctrl][Home], [↓], and [↑] move the insertion point within the field.

Edit record symbol A pencil-like symbol that appears in the record selector box to the left of the record that is currently being edited in either a datasheet or a form.

Error indicator An icon that automatically appears in Design View to indicate some type of error. For example, a green error indicator appears in the upper-left corner of a text box in Form Design View if the text box Control Source property is set to a field name that doesn't exist.

Expression A combination of values, functions, and operators that calculates to a single value. Access expressions start with an equal sign and are placed in a text box in either Form Design View or Report Design View.

Field In a table, a field corresponds to a column of data, a specific piece or category of data such as a first name, last name, city, state, or phone number.

Field list A list of the available fields in the table or query that the field list represents. Also, a pane that opens in Access and lists the database tables and the fields they contain.

Field name The name given to each field in a table.

Field selector The button to the left of a field in Table Design View that indicates the currently selected field. Also the thin gray bar above each field in the query grid.

File A stored collection of data; in Access, the entire database and all of its objects are in one file.

Filter A way to temporarily display only those records that match given criteria.

Filter By Form A way to filter data that allows two or more criteria to be specified at the same time.

Filter By Selection A way to filter records for an exact match.

Focus The property that indicates which field would be edited if you were to start typing.

Foreign key field In a one-to-many relationship between two tables, the foreign key field is the field in the "many" table that links the table to the primary key field in the "one" table.

Form An Access object that provides an easy-to-use data entry screen that generally shows only one record at a time.

Form section A location in a form that contains controls. The section in which a control is placed determines where and how often the control prints.

Form View View of a form object that displays data from the underlying recordset and allows you to enter and update data.

Form Wizard An Access wizard that helps you create a form.

Formatting Enhancing the appearance of information through font, size, and color changes.

Free response quiz A type of Office Mix quiz containing questions that require short answers.

Function A special, predefined formula that provides a shortcut for a commonly used calculation, for example, SUM or COUNT.

Gallery A visual collection of choices you can browse through to make a selection. Often available with Live Preview.

Graphic image *See* Image.

Grouping A way to sort records in a particular order, as well as provide a section before and after each group of records.

Groups Each tab on the Ribbon is arranged into groups to make features easy to find.

Hub A pane in Microsoft Edge that provides access to favorite websites, a reading list, browsing history, and downloaded files.

Image A nontextual piece of information such as a picture, piece of clip art, drawn object, or graph. Because images are graphical (and not numbers or letters), they are sometimes referred to as graphical images.

Infinity symbol The symbol that indicates the "many" side of a one-to-many relationship.

Inked handwriting In OneNote, writing produced when using a pen tool to enter text.

Ink to Math tool The OneNote tool that converts handwritten mathematical formulas to formatted equations or expressions.

Ink to Text tool The OneNote tool that converts inked handwriting to typed text.

Inking toolbar In Microsoft Edge, a collection of tools for annotating a webpage.

Insertion point A blinking vertical line that appears when you click in a text box; indicates where new text will be inserted.

Integrate To incorporate a document and parts of a document created in one program into another program; for example, to incorporate an Excel chart into a PowerPoint slide, or an Access report into a Word document.

Interface The look and feel of a program; for example, the appearance of commands and the way they are organized in the program window.

Is Not Null A criterion that finds all records in which any entry has been made in the field.

Is Null A criterion that finds all records in which no entry has been made in the field.

Join line The line identifying which fields establish the relationship between two related tables. Also called a link line.

Key symbol The symbol that identifies the primary key field in each table.

Label control An unbound control that displays text to describe and clarify other information on a form or report.

Label Wizard A report wizard that precisely positions and sizes information to print on a vast number of standard business label specifications.

Landscape orientation A printout that is 11 inches wide by 8.5 inches tall.

Launch To open or start a program on your computer.

Layout A way to group several controls together on a form or report to more quickly add, delete, rearrange, resize, or align controls.

Layout View An Access view that lets you make some design changes to a form or report while you are browsing the data.

Left function An Access function that returns a specified number of characters, starting with the left side of a value in a Text field.

Like operator An operator used in a query to find values in a field that match the pattern you specify.

Link line The line identifying which fields establish the relationship between two related tables.

Live Preview A feature that lets you point to a choice in a gallery or palette and see the results in the document or object without actually clicking the choice.

Logical view The datasheet of a query is sometimes called a logical view of the data because it is not a copy of the data, but rather, a selected view of data from the underlying tables.

Macro An Access object that stores a collection of keystrokes or commands such as those for printing several reports in a row or providing a toolbar when a form opens.

Margin The space between the outer edge of the control and the data displayed inside the control.

Microsoft OneNote Mobile app The lightweight version of Microsoft OneNote designed for phones, tablets, and other mobile devices.

Module An Access object that stores Visual Basic programming code that extends the functions of automated Access processes.

Multiuser A characteristic that means more than one person can enter and edit data in the same Access database at the same time.

Name property A property that uniquely identifies each object and control on a form or report.

Navigation buttons Buttons in the lower-left corner of a datasheet or form that allow you to quickly navigate between the records in the underlying object as well as add a new record.

Navigation mode A mode in which Access assumes that you are trying to move between the fields and records of the datasheet (rather than edit a specific field's contents), so keystrokes such as [Ctrl][Home] and [Ctrl][End] move you to the first and last field of the datasheet.

Navigation Pane A pane in the Access program window that provides a way to move between objects (tables, queries, forms, reports, macros, and modules) in the database.

Note In OneNote, a small window that contains text or other types of information.

Notebook In OneNote, the container for notes, drawings, and other content.

Object A table, query, form, report, macro, or module in an Access database.

OneDrive Microsoft storage system that lets you easily save, share, and access your files from any device with Internet access.

One-to-many line The line that appears in the Relationships window and shows which field is duplicated between two tables to serve as the linking field. The one-to-many line displays a "1" next to the field that serves as the "one" side of the relationship and displays an infinity symbol next to the field that serves as the "many" side of the relationship when referential integrity is specified for the relationship. Also called the one-to-many join line.

One-to-many relationship The relationship between two tables in an Access database in which a common field links the tables together. The linking field is called the primary key field in the "one" table of the relationship and the foreign key field in the "many" table of the relationship.

Online collaboration The ability to incorporate feedback or share information across the Internet or a company network or intranet.

OR criteria Criteria placed on different rows of the query design grid. A record will be selected for the resulting datasheet if it is true for any single row.

Orphan record A record in the "many" table of a one-to-many relationship that doesn't have a matching entry in the linking field of the "one" table. Orphan records cannot be created if referential integrity is enforced on a relationship.

Padding The space between controls.

Page In OneNote, a workspace for inserting notes and other content, similar to a page in a physical notebook.

Pixel (picture element) One pixel is the measurement of one picture element on the screen.

Portrait orientation A printout that is 8.5 inches wide by 11 inches tall.

Previewing Prior to printing, seeing onscreen exactly how the printout will look.

Primary key field A field that contains unique information for each record. A primary key field cannot contain a null entry.

Print Preview An Access view that shows you how a report or other object will print on a sheet of paper.

Property A characteristic that further defines a field (if field properties), control (if control properties), section (if section properties), or object (if object properties).

Property Sheet A window that displays an exhaustive list of properties for the chosen control, section, or object on a form or report.

Query An Access object that provides a spreadsheet-like view of the data, similar to that in tables. It may provide the user with a subset of fields and/or records from one or more tables. Queries are created when the user has a "question" about the data in the database.

Query design grid The bottom pane of the Query Design View window in which you specify the fields, sort order, and limiting criteria for the query.

Query Design View The window in which you develop queries by specifying the fields, sort order, and limiting criteria that determine which fields and records are displayed in the resulting datasheet.

Quick Access toolbar A small toolbar on the left side of a Microsoft application window's title bar, containing icons that you click to quickly perform common actions, such as saving a file.

Read-only An object property that indicates whether the object can read and display data, but cannot be used to change (write to) data.

Reading view In Microsoft Edge, the display of a webpage that removes ads and most graphics and uses a simple format for the text.

Record A row of data in a table.

Record source The table or query that defines the field and records displayed in a form or report.

Referential integrity A set of Access rules that govern data entry and help ensure data accuracy. Setting referential integrity on a relationship prevents the creation of orphan records.

Relational database software Software such as Access that is used to manage data organized in a relational database.

Report An Access object that creates a professional printout of data that may contain such enhancements as headers, footers, and calculations on groups of records.

Report Wizard An Access wizard that helps you create a report.

Responsive design A way to provide content so that it adapts appropriately to the size of the display on any device.

Ribbon Appears below the title bar in every Office program window, and displays commands you're likely to need for the current task.

Ruler A vertical or horizontal guide that appears in Form and Report Design View to help you position controls.

Save As command A command on the File tab that saves the entire database (and all objects it contains) or only the current object with a new name.

Sandbox A computer security mechanism that helps to prevent attackers from gaining control of a computer.

Screen capture An electronic snapshot of your screen, as if you took a picture of it with a camera, which you can paste into a document.

Screen clipping In OneNote, an image copied from any part of a computer screen.

Screen recording In Office Mix, a video you create by capturing your desktop and any actions performed on it.

Section A location of a form or report that contains controls. The section in which a control is placed determines where and how often the control prints.

Section tab In OneNote, a divider for organizing a notebook.

Simple Query Wizard An Access wizard that prompts you for information it needs to create a new query.

Sizing handles Small squares at each corner of a selected control in Access. Dragging a handle resizes the control. Also known as handles.

Slide Notes In Office Mix, the written and displayed version of notes typically used to recite narration while creating a slide recording.

Slide recording In Office Mix, a video you create by recording action with a webcam, a camera attached or built into a computer.

Split form A form split into two panes; the upper pane allows you to display the fields of one record in any arrangement, and the lower pane maintains a datasheet view of the first few records.

SQL (Structured Query Language) A language that provides a standardized way to request information from a relational database system.

Storyline In Sway, the workspace for assembling a presentation.

Subdatasheet A datasheet that is nested within another datasheet to show related records. The subdatasheet shows the records on the "many" side of a one-to-many relationship.

Suite A group of programs that are bundled together and share a similar interface, making it easy to transfer skills and program content among them.

Sum function A mathematical function that totals values in a field.

Sway site A website Sway creates to share and display a Sway presentation.

Sync In OneNote, to save a new or updated notebook so that all versions of the notebook, such as a notebook on OneDrive and a copy on a hard drive, have the same contents.

Syntax Rules for entering information such as query criteria or property values.

Tab Index property A form property that indicates the numeric tab order for all controls on the form that have the Tab Stop property set to Yes.

Tab order property A form property that determines the sequence in which the controls on the form receive the focus when the user presses [Tab] or [Enter] in Form view.

Tab Stop property A form property that determines whether a field accepts focus.

Table A collection of records for a single subject, such as all of the customer records; the fundamental building block of a relational database because it stores all of the data.

Table Design View A view of a table that provides the most options for defining fields.

Tabs Organizational unit used for commands on the Ribbon. The tab names appear at the top of the Ribbon and the active tab appears in front.

Template A sample file, such as a database provided within the Microsoft Access program. In OneNote, a page design you can apply to new pages to provide an appealing background, a consistent layout, or elements suitable for certain types of notes, such as meeting notes or to-do lists.

Text Align property A control property that determines the alignment of text within the control.

Text box The most common type of control used to display field values.

Theme A predefined set of colors, fonts, line and fill effects, and other formats that can be applied to an Access database and give it a consistent, professional look.

Title bar Appears at the top of every Office program window; it displays the document or database name and program name.

To Do tag In OneNote, an icon that helps you keep track of your assignments and other tasks.

Unbound control A control that does not change from record to record and exists only to clarify or enhance the appearance of the form, using elements such as labels, lines, and clip art.

User interface A collective term for all the ways you interact with a software program.

View Each Access object has different views for different purposes. For example, you work with data in Datasheet View. You modify the design of the object in Layout and Design Views. You preview a printout in Print Preview. Common views include Datasheet View for a table or query, or Design View for any Access object.

Wildcard A special character used in criteria to find, filter, and query data. The asterisk (*) stands for any group of characters. For example, the criteria I* in a State field criterion cell would find all records where the state entry was IA, ID, IL, IN, or Iowa. The question mark (?) wildcard stands for only one character.

Web Note In Microsoft Edge, an annotation on a webpage.

Zooming in A feature that makes a printout appear larger but shows less of it on screen at once; does not affect the actual size of the printout.

Zooming out A feature that shows more of a printout on screen at once but at a reduced size; does not affect the actual size of the printout.

Index